NHL PRO HOCKEY
'82 – '83

ABOUT THE AUTHOR

Jim Proudfoot, who has been preparing the *Pro Hockey* yearbooks since their beginning in 1968, is a sports columnist with the *Toronto Star*, Canada's largest newspaper. He joined the *Star* in 1954, direct from the University of Toronto, and became a regular columnist in 1959. He was sports editor from 1970 to 1977.

Proudfoot has travelled extensively on the international sports beat and has covered more than a quarter-century of professional and amateur hockey.

He is a Torontonian, and lives across the street from Maple Leaf Gardens, home of the Maple Leafs.

NHL PRO HOCKEY
'82 – '83

by

Jim Proudfoot

PaperJacks

Markham, Ontario, Canada

AN ORIGINAL CANADIAN

PaperJacks

One of a series of Canadian books
published by PaperJacks Ltd.

NHL PRO HOCKEY '82 − '83

PaperJacks edition published October, 1982

Cover photograph of Mike Bossy by Ron Bull, *Toronto Star*. Used by
permission.
Cover Design/William C. Reid

The author and publisher cannot assume responsibility for player and
personnel changes made after this book went to press.

ISBN 0-7701-0229-8

CONTENTS

PART ONE

THE ISLANDERS HAVE ARRIVED — AT LAST

It is difficult to pinpoint precisely, but at some point during the National Hockey League season of 1981-82, the New York Islanders finally were accorded what they had been wanting so desperately, and had thereto been denied: Acceptance as one of the truly great teams in the entire history of the sport.

In the month beginning January 20, the Islanders won 15 games in succession and thereby set a record that even the mighty Montreal Canadiens failed to approach when they were dominating the NHL. At that time, even the skeptics and the nitpickers were compelled to admit there was something extra special about this Long Island club, which had already captured back-to-back Stanley Cup titles.

Later, the Isles slipped clear of the pack in the race among 21 NHL entrants and finished up with a substantial margin over the upstart Edmonton Oilers. With wondrous Wayne Gretzky in the forefront, the Oilers wrote many of the hockey year's most dramatic stories but, as far as any head-to-head confrontations were concerned, the champions again asserted their supremacy.

And then came the playoffs, the platform for the Islanders' most impressive routine.

They got better as they went along, sweeping the Prince of Wales Conference final in the minimum four games and then winning the title round with similar authority. They were 15-and-4 in the tournament and, over their three consecutive playoff victories, have won 45 of 59. In fact, with the NHL's most important prize at stake, nobody has been able to seriously threaten these Islanders.

What's more, the Long Island roster includes a generous helping of this era's foremost talent. Goalie Bill Smith, defenceman Denis Potvin, and forwards Bryan Trottier, Clark Gillies, John Tonelli and Mike Bossy make regular appearances on the NHL's all-star squad and are in contention for any individual prize worth having.

Until recently, though, the Islanders suspected they weren't getting the respect due to them.

"We always had an idea we weren't receiving the kind of recognition we felt we'd earned," says general manager Bill Torrey. "For purposes of motivation, coming from within, that turned out to be quite useful. But it created a touch of bitterness, too.

"However, I don't think there's the slightest question about it now. Nobody can possibly quarrel with our record, or belittle it in any way. It's there in black and white and compares favorably with all the famous teams in history.

"There are sure to be tremendous obstacles barring our way to number four but we'd have to be the favorites going in, wouldn't you say?"

Indeed. As a matter of fact, the Islanders are getting a break they don't really need, increasing the likelihood they'll retain their grip on NHL leadership, at least through the 1982-83 campaign.

The NHL map has been revamped again, to the titlists' distinct advantage. The Colorado Rockies, shifted to the Meadowlands arena in New Jersey, have been placed in the Lester Patrick Division with the Islanders, Philadelphia Flyers, Pittsburgh Penguins, Washington Capitals and New York Rangers.

What that means is an expanded number of easy evenings on the Isles' 1982-83 calendar.

The Winnipeg Jets, meanwhile, replace the old Denver outfit in the Conn Smythe Division.

As before, the NHL is split into the Prince of Wales and Clarence Campbell Conferences. This author predicts the teams will finish the 1982-83 regular season in the order set out below:

WALES CONFERENCE

Norris Division
Minnesota
St. Louis
Chicago
Toronto
Detroit

Smythe Division
Edmonton
Winnipeg
Calgary
Vancouver
Los Angeles

CAMPBELL CONFERENCE

Adams Division
Boston
Buffalo
Quebec City
Montreal
Hartford

Patrick Division
N.Y. Islanders
Pittsburgh
N.Y. Rangers
Washington
Philadelphia
New Jersey

Each of the 21 teams plays an 80-game schedule with those in the Adams, Smythe, and Norris groups having eight games (four home, four away) against each of its four divisional mates, plus three against each of the other 16 clubs in the league.

In the case of those three dates with the outside 16, teams play once at home and twice on the road, or vice-versa, alternating the extra trip each year.

The six members of the Patrick Division play each other seven times (35 games within their own division) plus three apiece against each of the remaining 15. Again, extra home matches will be alternated each season.

So it works out to 40 here and 40 there for everybody in the circuit, with all points earned to count in the standings. Sixteen teams enter the Stanley Cup tournament, the top four from each section.

The preliminary Cup series features divisional competition that pits the first-place finisher against fourth, and second against third, in best-of-five sets. The winners remain in their divisions and play best-of-seven final rounds, with the team standing higher during the regular schedule getting the extra date on home ice.

Group champions then meet for the conference championships, again best-of-seven.

And finally the conference winners compete for the Stanley Cup.

''There's no question we've saved a lot of money in transportation costs with this arrangement,'' says NHL president John Zeigler. ''But we also feel the rivalries which have sprung up, and will continue to develop, will be extremely good for our game.

"I give you Calgary-Edmonton-Vancouver as an illustration, with Winnipeg now joining in. One of those pairs could hook up 15 times in a season if they met, say, for their divisional title.

"What about the two New York clubs? Or New Jersey and Philly, let's say? And, of course, the Montreal-Quebec thing looks as though it'll become one of the classic match-ups in all of professional sport."

The installation of a franchise in New Jersey and aggressive new ownership in Detroit promise to improve the NHL's health by patching up two of its sorest wounds. But it's Wayne Gretzky who's really enhancing those vital signs.

To find a parallel in the sports world, you have to go all the way back to Babe Ruth saving baseball in the 1920s. The game was dying then because the revelation that the 1919 World Series had been rigged by gamblers had undermined public confidence in the sport. Along came The Babe, hitting home runs in a way that changed the very face of baseball, and in numbers never even dreamt of. His heroic exploits, totally without precedent, ushered in a new era of popularity and profit for baseball.

Gretzky is doing much the same thing at a time when hockey, too, needs some sort of transfusion. There's never been a player like him and fans are reacting to his appeal even in territories where hockey normally creates no stir. He drew sellout crowds wherever he went last season, and got the NHL unbelievable media coverage.

So as the Islanders are at last conceded their rightful place in hockey history, Superkid has opened a whole new chapter, of dimensions we can only guess at. To watch that drama unfold will be one of the joys hockey in the 1980s is going to provide.

PART TWO

THE NATIONAL HOCKEY LEAGUE 1982-83

NEW YORK ISLANDERS

Never Stand Still

1981-82 Finish: First in Patrick, NHL, won Stanley Cup.
Strengths: Balance, deep, strong everywhere.
Weaknesses: None to be found.
Probable 1982-83 Finish: More of the same.

Here's something you can wager upon with the utmost confidence: At some point during the 1982-83 National Hockey League season, New York Islanders will make a major personnel move — a surprise trade, the elevation of a promising youngster, maybe the demotion of a name player. General manager Bill Torrey and coach Al Arbour aren't about to deviate from the formula which has paid off in three successive Stanley Cup championships.

"The temptation, of course, is to stick with a winning combination," Torrey says, "but the name of the game is change and progress. If you stand still, you're actually losing ground — especially in our situation, where we've got 20 clubs taking dead aim at us."

In 1980, Torrey dealt a couple of veterans to Los Angeles Kings for centre Butch Goring, who was the key to the first title in the history of the Long Island franchise.

A year later, Torrey returned to the NHL marketplace and acquired defenceman Mike McEwen in exchange for some more surplus manpower.

The Islander GM chose a different route last season to obtain the annual infusion of fresh blood he now deems essential. At midterm, he brought in 19-year-old Brent Sutter from the Lethbridge, Alta., juniors. Catching on as a regular centre and awakening the entire roster, the youngster generated 21 goals and 22 assists in his first 43 NHL matches.

"But his value to us went a lot further than the statistics indicate," Arbour noted. "He was eager and anxious to prove himself and that gave the entire team a lift, just at a time when we needed it."

Gathering momentum as they proceeded, Islanders went on to win the Patrick Division by a wide margin and pulled ahead of Edmonton in the overall standings, amassing 118 of a possible 160 points for a creditable .737 average.

In the playoff tournament, Islanders encountered no undue difficulty once they had disposed of the pesky Pittsburgh Penguins in round one. So now they're seeking to extend their NHL domination to a fourth campaign and there's really not much reason to think they won't succeed.

"You've got to be impressed with our nucleus," Torrey concedes, "but there are so many variables to take care of. You build up reserves but injuries can kill you anyway. That's why you put new people in, so they'll be ready when they're really needed. It also makes your lineup more dynamic, a little bit hungrier, when everybody knows there's a replacement around.

"So we'll look to do a little fine tuning here and there. Kelly Hrudey, who's 20, was the top goalie in the Central League. We had Greg Gilbert up from the juniors a couple of times and he looked good. We like Paul Boutilier, our first choice in the 1981 draft. He was an all-star junior defenceman in Quebec. And we own Dave Simpson, the junior player of the year in Ontario.

"On the other hand, you'd have to think twice before tinkering much with the roster we had in the playoffs last spring. It was pretty clearly the best."

John Tonelli

It was breakthrough time for husky John Tonelli. He counted 93 points during the 1981-82 season, 37 above his previous high, and was acclaimed second-best left wing in the NHL.

"What it means to me is that hard work does pay off," says Tonelli, who is a typical Islander wingman — big and industrious. "I don't believe there was much difference in my play but

I got more time in offensive situations, so my statistics were better than usual.''

Now 25, Tonelli came to Long Island in 1978 after spending four years in the World Hockey Association. So he has won the Stanley Cup three times in four attempts.

''More than any other guy, probably, John symbolizes what this club is all about,'' says coach Al Arbour. ''He's not the least bit interested in personal achievements as long as the team succeeds. There isn't a better man in the NHL when it comes to going into the corner and getting possession of the puck.''

Bill Smith

History will record that Bill Smith was 31 and had a decade of NHL combat under his belt before he won acceptance as the finest netminder in the business. He was a clear-cut first in the 1981-82 all-star voting and also received the Vezina Trophy as the NHL's most outstanding goalie.

''It's nice for Smitty, of course, but he'd always been the best with money on the line, and what else counts?'' said Islander GM Bill Torrey. ''He always comes up big in the playoffs or when we need a victory, or just one big stop.''

''I always said I preferred my Stanley Cup rings to any individual award I could possibly get, and I still feel the same,'' Smith insists. ''But I'm happy to be appreciated this way, too. It's icing on the cake.''

Smith led the NHL last season by posting 32 victories. Roland Melanson, his 21-year-old understudy, won another 22 but got even less work in Stanley Cup competition where Smith bore almost the entire burden. He had 15 wins against three defeats for a combined 44-and-10 slate in Islanders' three Cup captures. That is known as delivering in the clutch.

Mike Bossy

Last season was a highly productive one for 25-year-old Mike Bossy, quite apart from the fact he helped Islanders bag their third Stanley Cup title in succession. He signed a rich new contract and won two new cars as MVP awards — in the midterm all-star show and, more importantly, in the playoff tournament during April and May.

Then, on the overall all-star ballot, Bossy actually received more support at right wing than Wayne Gretzky did at centre. He was accorded 309 of a possible 315 points when the returns were all in.

Scoring goals at the fastest clip in NHL (pre-Gretzky) history, Bossy recorded 64 goals over the regular schedule for a total of 305 in just five NHL campaigns.

"But the best thing about Bossy is the way he has improved himself," says coach Al Arbour. "He came to us strictly as a scorer but now he's so good defensively that I don't hesitate to use him killing penalties."

Denis Potvin

On the face of it, 1981-82 was a disastrous winter for Denis Potvin. An all-star defenceman the year before, he was nowhere in last spring's honors evaluation. And his scoring production was down to a skimpy 61 points.

But the situation calls for more detailed analysis.

Potvin suffered a groin injury near the end of the 1981 playoffs which had not healed by the time he reported to the Team Canada training camp early in August. He was in distress throughout the Canada Cup and managed to aggravate the situation. He didn't make his first NHL start until well on in November and ended up playing in only 60 matches all year.

"It wasn't all bad," said Potvin. "The way things worked out, I was at my peak and totally fresh when the season got down to the nitty-gritty in February and March. And fatigue was never a factor, as it often is at Stanley Cup time. I wouldn't care to go through a summer and fall like that again, but it wasn't without its benefits."

Bryan Trottier

Wayne Gretzky is now the centre supreme in hockey, but there are those who prefer Bryan Trottier. Islander coach Al Arbour is among them.

"Gretzky is an offensive genius for sure, but at this stage, Trots gives you more things," Arbour claims. "Defensively, he's outstanding. And he's physically tough. He comes up with his 100 points a year, automatically, along with everything else."

"What you don't realize," says Montreal defenceman Larry Robinson, "is that Trottier weighs over 200 pounds. You can't budge the guy or knock the puck off his stick. And he hands out a lot of punishment at close quarters.''

With 129 points last season, Trottier lifted his output to a five-year total of 593. He was second only to Gretzky in the all-star vote among centres and led all Stanley Cup attackers. In the Islanders' three back-to-back playoff triumphs, Trottier has scored or contributed to 58 goals in 56 games.

Stefan Persson

One of the Islanders' most precious assets is their pipeline into Swedish hockey. This connection has furnished them with three first-stringers, defencemen Stefan Persson and Tomas Jonsson, and right wing Anders Kallur.

Jonsson, 22, moved in last season. Persson had been a regular since 1977, and it was Kallur's third term.

''Their skills level is very high. They came to us as finished products, ready to go,'' said Torrey. ''Both Persson and Jonsson are good with the puck, which is vital for a defenceman today, and Kallur is an excellent checker, and has good offensive talents.''

Bob Bourne

From a career high of 76 points, left winger Bob Bourne descended to only 53 last season in the first year of his new contract with the Islanders.

''The thing is, though, Bob never really has a slump. He's too versatile for that,'' says Arbour. ''He skates well and checks so that the fellow opposite him never accomplishes much. So if his scoring tails off a bit, he's still doing you a lot of good.

''And for a real tipoff on Bourne, take a look at his playoff record. That'll tell you a lot.''

It has taken Islanders 54 post-season games to win the last three Stanley Cup championships. During those matches, Bourne has produced 23 goals and 23 assists while taking excellent care of all of his defensive duties.

Ken Morrow

Success seems to come naturally to Ken Morrow. He'd been an All-American defenceman at Ohio's Bowling Green

University in 1978 and '79 when he joined the 1980 U.S. Olympic team.

Three months after helping win the gold medals at Lake Placid, Morrow was celebrating a Stanley Cup victory with the Islanders. That triumph was to be repeated in 1981 and again last May.

''Morrow excels defensively and signing him enabled us to make perhaps the most important trade in the history of this franchise,'' says GM Bill Torrey.

After Morrow arrived, Torrey dealt rearguard Dave Lewis — a defensive specialist hitherto considered indispensable — and Bill Harris, to L.A. for Butch Goring, a centre who gave the Islanders a championship blend on their forward lines.

Billy Smith, Vezina Trophy winner

Mike Bossy, winner of the Conn Smythe Trophy

ISLANDERS' 1982-83 ROSTER

1981-82 RECORD

Forwards	Ht.	Wt.	Place of Birth	Date	1981-82 Club	G	A	Pts.
Mike Bossy	6-0	185	Montreal, Que.	Jan. 22, 1957	Islanders	64	83	147
Bob Bourne	6-2	202	Kindersley, Sask.	June 21, 1954	Islanders	27	26	53
Bill Carroll	5-10	191	Toronto, Ont.	Jan. 19, 1959	Islanders	9	20	29
Greg Gilbert	6-1	194	Mississauga, Ont.	Jan. 22, 1962	Toronto (OMJHL)	41	67	108
Clark Gillies	6-3	218	Moose Jaw, Sask.	April 7, 1954	Islanders	38	39	77
Butch Goring	5-9	166	St. Boniface, Man.	Oct. 22, 1949	Islanders	15	17	32
Anders Kallur	5-10	175	Ludvika, Sweden	July 6, 1952	Islanders	18	22	40
Hector Marini	6-1	204	Timmins, Ont.	Jan. 27, 1957	Islanders	4	9	13
Wayne Merrick	6-1	198	Sarnia, Ont.	April 23, 1952	Islanders	12	27	39
Bob Nystrom	6-1	200	Stockholm, Sweden	Oct. 10, 1952	Islanders	22	25	47
Brent Sutter	5-11	175	Viking, Alta.	June 11, 1962	Islanders	21	22	43
Duane Sutter	6-1	181	Viking, Alta.	March 16, 1960	Islanders	18	35	53
John Tonelli	6-1	195	Hamilton, Ont.	March 23, 1957	Islanders	35	58	93
Bryan Trottier	5-10	205	Val Marie, Sask.	July 17, 1956	Islanders	50	79	129

Defencemen

Tomas Jonsson	5-10	177	Falun, Sweden	April 12, 1960	Islanders	9	25	34
Gordie Lane	6-1	185	Brandon, Man.	March 31, 1953	Islanders	0	13	13
Dave Langevin	6-2	215	St. Paul, Minn.	May 15, 1954	Islanders	1	20	21
Mike McEwen	6-1	185	Hornepayne, Ont.	Aug. 10, 1956	Islanders	10	39	49
Ken Morrow	6-4	205	Flint, Mich.	Oct. 17, 1956	Islanders	1	18	19
Stefan Persson	6-1	189	Umea, Sweden	Dec. 22, 1954	Islanders	6	37	43
Denis Potvin	6-0	205	Ottawa, Ont.	Oct. 29, 1953	Islanders	24	37	61

Goalies

						GPI	GA	Avg.
Kelly Hrudey	5-10	182	Edmonton, Alta.	Jan. 13, 1961	Indianapolis (CHL)	49	143	2.95
Roland Melanson	5-10	178	Moncton, N.B.	June 28, 1960	Islanders	36	114	3.23
Bill Smith	5-10	185	Perth, Ont.	Dec. 12, 1950	Islanders	46	133	2.97

EDMONTON OILERS

A Supporting Cast

1981-82 Finish: First in Smythe, second overall.
Strengths: Gretzky, Gretzky, Gretzky.
Weaknesses: Need balance, depth, experience.
Probable 1982-83 Finish: A repetition.

What Edmonton Oilers will be out to prove, as they head into
their fourth year as members of the National Hockey League,
is that they are something more than merely a one-man team.

Until they can put that idea across and make it stick, they
appear doomed to varying encores of their 1981-82 pattern —
encouraging accomplishments, stopping just short of ultimate
success. Put it another way: once they can provide Wayne
Gretzky with an adequate supporting cast, they should become
well nigh invincible.

Gretzky, of course, is a fearsome weapon, the most dynamic
individual performer in all of professional sport. He scored, or
helped to score, 212 goals last season, and that alone is almost
enough to make a whole club successful. Yet the Oilers concluded their schedule seven points behind New York Islanders.

And Gretzky contributed 12 points in five playoff matches
— his customary average — yet the Oilers were bounced out
of Stanley Cup competition.

An improved Gretzky is difficult to visualize, but keep in
mind he's only 21. However, even his most fervent admirers
don't suggest he alone will ever be able to get Edmonton an
NHL title.

"It's dangerous to depend on a single individual, even when
it's Wayne. You're just too vulnerable," says Glen Sather,
coach and general manager of the Edmonton organization. "I
don't apologize for the way we've used Gretzky, the amount of
ice time we've given him. A person would be insane not to do
that. You can't stand in the way of history.

"But nobody can deny that we're making tremendous

headway in other parts of our lineup. Our scouts and our organization have produced, and will continue to produce, the kind of people who complement Gretzky and give us the kind of blend it takes to win.''

Gretzky wasn't Edmonton's only all-star; for example, Mark Messier made it at left wing, as well, and the second team included two more Oilers, goalie Grant Fuhr and defenceman Paul Coffey.

''We've got all kinds of promising kids,'' Sather claims, ''and we made deals last year for guys like Laurie Boschman, Randy Gregg, Lance Nethery, and Jaroslav Pouzar from Czechoslovakia.

''And two of the best juniors in the country, Marc Habscheid and Todd Strueby, belong to us, too.''

In a recent trade involving Philadelphia and Hartford, the Oilers acquired Flyers' top point-getter, Ken Linseman, who notched 24 goals and 68 assists for 92 points in '81-'82. From Hartford the Oilers received center-left wing Don Nachbauer in exchange for Risto Siltanen and third-round draft pick Brent Loney. The Flyers obtained Mark Howe from the Whalers in return for Greg Adams and a first-round draft pick.

Said Sather, ''It is never easy to trade a player, especially when he is as popular as Risto, but I have to think only of improving the Edmonton Oilers to the point where we can seriously challenge for the Stanley Cup.''

Jari Kurri

Wayne Gretzky made one very significant prediction last spring. He said right winger Jari Kurri, from Finland, would become an NHL all-star in 1983.

''We're just beginning to see what he can do,'' said Gretzky, who sometimes plays centre for the 22-year-old Finn. ''You've got to remember there's quite an adjustment for a fellow like him. It takes time just to get feeling comfortable in a strange country.''

Kurri, representing a master stroke by Edmonton chief scout Barry Fraser, scored 32 goals in each of his first two NHL campaigns. Several clubs interested in Kurri backed away at a time when Fraser's research uncovered the player's unexpected availability.

Grant Fuhr

The Oilers seemed well-fixed in goal when they ended the 1980-81 season but, two months afterwards, they drafted netminder Grant Fuhr from Victoria, B.C., juniors.

"You'll see why," promised Barry Fraser, the chief scout.

Fuhr, the first black goalie in NHL history, won a regular job at 19 and was so impressive only Islanders' Bill Smith received more all-star votes than he did. He was beaten only five times all year while posting 28 victories and 14 ties.

"In Fuhr, we saw an opportunity to improve ourselves," Fraser explained, "so we took him, even though most people insisted we didn't need a goalie. In a way we didn't, but you've got to keep moving forward."

Among NHL rookies, the taciturn Fuhr was rated behind only Dale Hawerchuk and Barry Pederson.

Wayne Gretzky

Of all the accolades heaped upon Wayne Gretzky last season, surely his Hart Trophy was the most meaningful. All 63 panelists felt he was the NHL's most valuable performer; he was the first unanimous Hart Trophy winner.

Or try this: Playing for Canada, he was the leading scorer at the Canada Cup in September and the world championships in April.

His statistics, of course, were staggering, and without NHL precedent — 92 goals, 120 assists, 212 points, 513 for his first three years.

At one stage, it had appeared certain he'd surpass 100 goals, as against the former record of 76.

"People ask me about those things and it's hard to answer," says Gretzky. "I mean I'm only 21. I've got plenty to learn. So I suppose I ought to improve.

"My idea is team success has to come first. If your team does well, the individual achievements will just naturally fall in place. My objective is the Stanley Cup. That's what you play the game for. When we get it, I can tell you, I won't be worrying about any other stats."

Gretzky negotiated a new contract early in 1982, through agent Gus Badali. The numbers speculated upon are gigantic but seem like a bargain when stacked up beside the publicity, excitement and attendance increases he generates wherever he goes.

Glenn Anderson

The Edmonton players call Glenn Anderson ''Mork'' because he bears a certain resemblance to that television character.

His hockey skills are somewhat superhuman, too, as it turns out.

''We felt he was the best all-round player on Canada's 1980 Olympic team,'' said Sather, who had drafted the Vancouver youngster one year before. ''We believed he could step right into the NHL and be a star. And he did.''

That assessment was indeed correct. Anderson had 30 goals as a rookie, and last season scored 38 while assisting on 67, and was fifth right winger on the all-star ballot, ahead of players like Rick Vaive, Guy Lafleur and Ron Duguay.

Mark Messier

Wayne Gretzky can be a help, even when you're not skating on his line.

''Because of him, you feel a responsibility to do well,'' says Mark Messier, who is eight days older than Edmonton's illustrious centre.

Messier's dedication to duty had been in question during the early part of his NHL career but he became very serious in 1981 because, he says, of Gretzky's example.

With the new outlook, Messier quickly became a dominant force on left wing, scoring 50 goals and earning an all-star nomination over John Tonelli and Bill Barber.

He had totalled only 35 goals over his first two campaigns, so you get some idea of how dramatic a forward stride these latest achievements display.

Paul Coffey

The 1981-82 season was a marvelous experience for defenceman Paul Coffey until the very end. With 89 points, he led NHL rearguards in scoring and he was named to the second all-star team after playing consistently well over the entire schedule.

But Coffey struggled badly during Oilers' Stanley Cup loss to Los Angeles Kings, and eventually was benched.

"I've really got something to make up for now, something to prove," says Coffey, a 21-year-old who joined the Edmonton roster out of junior competition in 1980. "Going into my third year in the NHL, I've got something very special in the way of incentive."

Dave Semenko

Minnesota North Stars drafted Dave Semenko in 1977, but he elected to sign with Edmonton's World Hockey Association club instead. Stars reclaimed him in 1979 when the Oilers were entering the NHL, and that's when Semenko found out what his employers thought of him. They gave the Minnesota outfit two high draft picks to get Semenko back.

"Every NHL club has got to have a little muscle somewhere in its lineup and Semenko has more than his share," said coach Sather.

"He's a good player anyway, but he knows how to use his size and is willing to do so. Anybody who decides to push some of our people around will have to deal with Semenko. And that makes a lot of guys have second thoughts, believe me."

Kevin Lowe

When Team ·Canada was assembling its defence for the world championships last spring, the coaches made sure they invited Wayne Gretzky's roommate, Kevin Lowe, along.

"The assets that make him so effective in the NHL will be doubly valuable on the bigger European rinks," said coach Dave King. "He is mobile and he's superb with the puck. And he is not preoccupied with scoring a lot of points, so you never have to worry about him being trapped up ice. He's content to stick around his own zone and keep it clear of things like pucks and opposition players."

Many analysts, of course, contend that Lowe is actually Edmonton's best defenceman. A few all-star voters thought so in May. They had him seventh on the 1981-82 ballot.

Wayne Gretzky, all-star centre

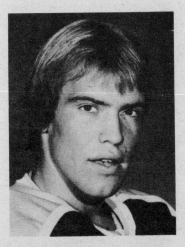

Mark Messier, all-star left wing

OILERS' 1982-83 ROSTER

Forwards	Ht.	Wt.	Place of Birth	Date	1981-82 Club	1981-82 RECORD		
						G	A	Pts.
Glenn Anderson	5-11	175	Vancouver, B.C.	Oct. 2, 1960	Edmonton	38	67	105
Laurie Boschman	6-0	185	Major, Sask.	June 4, 1960	Tor.-Edm.	11	22	33
Curt Brackenbury	5-10	197	Kapuskasing, Ont.	Jan. 31, 1952	Edmonton	0	2	2
Wayne Gretzky	5-11	165	Brantford, Ont.	Jan. 26, 1961	Edmonton	92	120	212
Matti Hagman	6-1	184	Helsinki, Finland	Sept. 21, 1955	Edmonton	21	38	59
Pat Hughes	6-1	180	Calgary, Alta.	March 25, 1955	Edmonton	24	22	46
Dave Hunter	5-11	195	Petrolia, Ont.	Jan. 1, 1958	Edmonton	16	22	38
Jari Kurri	6-1	185	Helsinki, Finland	May 18, 1960	Edmonton	32	54	86
Ken Linseman	5-11	175	Kingston, Ont.	Aug. 11, 1958	Philadelphia	24	68	92
Dave Lumley	6-0	185	Toronto, Ont.	Sept. 1, 1954	Edmonton	32	42	74
Mark Messier	6-1	190	Edmonton, Alta.	Jan. 18, 1961	Edmonton	50	38	88
Don Nauchbauer	6-2	200	Kitimat, B.C.	Jan. 30, 1959	Hartford	5	21	26
Lance Nethery	6-1	185	Toronto, Ont.	June 28, 1957	NYR-Edm.	0	2	2
Tom Roulston	6-1	184	Winnipeg, Man.	Nov. 20, 1957	Edmonton	11	3	14
Dave Semenko	6-3	215	Winnipeg, Man.	July 12, 1957	Edmonton	12	12	24
Gary Unger	6-0	185	Edmonton, Alta.	Dec. 7, 1947	Edmonton	7	13	20

Defencemen

Paul Coffey	6-1	185	Weston, Ont.	June 1, 1961	Edmonton	29	60	89
Lee Fogolin	6-0	204	Chicago, Ill.	Feb 15, 1955	Edmonton	4	25	29
Randy Gregg	6-4	215	Edmonton, Alta.	Feb. 19, 1956	Japan	—	NA	—
Charlie Huddy	6-0	200	Toronto, Ont.	June 2, 1959	Edmonton	4	11	15
Garry Lariviere	6-0	190	St. Catharines, Ont.	Dec. 6, 1954	Edmonton	1	21	22
Kevin Lowe	6-2	197	Hawkesbury, Ont.	April 15, 1959	Edmonton	9	31	40

Goalies

						GPI	GA	Avg.
Grant Fuhr	5-10	181	Edmonton, Alta.	Sept. 21, 1962	Edmonton	48	157	3.31
Ron Low	6-1	205	Birtle, Man.	June 23, 1950	Edmonton	29	100	3.86
Andy Moog	5-9	165	Penticton, B.C.	Feb. 18, 1960	Edmonton	8	32	4.81

MONTREAL CANADIENS

It's a Time for Change

1981-82 Finish: First in Adams, third overall.
Strengths: Good coach, decent nucleus.
Weaknesses: Key parts wearing, replacements uncertain.
Probable 1982-83 Finish: Drop to fourth.

Times are a-changing around the Montreal Forum — and then some. It is almost impossible to believe but the 1981-82 Canadiens didn't have a man among the National Hockey League's leading 20 scorers. For the second year in succession, there wasn't a Montreal player on the all-star team. Guy Lafleur was no longer a commanding figure on right wing. The prominent figures were people like Keith Acton, Rick Walmsley and Brian Engblom.

A disaster? Well, not quite that.

Only two clubs in the entire circuit had records superior to Canadiens and, under the supervision of their new coach, Bob Berry, the Montrealers iced the NHL's most efficient overall defence.

It's just that the ending was so bad.

Canadiens were again eliminated from the opening round of the Stanley Cup tournament. Edmonton Oilers had done it to them in 1981. This time, Quebec Nordiques were responsible. And that was especially painful because these St. Lawrence River neighbours have begun what promises to be a lively rivalry for supremacy within their division.

Until that April comeuppance, everybody had been profoundly impressed by Berry, a Montreal native whose first coaching position had been with Los Angeles Kings.

''We were extremely disappointed about what happened in the playoffs but it certainly didn't cancel out all the good things we achieved during the season,'' managing director Irving Grundman observed.

Berry arranged to work several excellent newcomers into his

lineup: rookies Walmsley, Mark Hunter, Craig Laughlin and Gilbert Delorme, plus veteran defenceman Robert Picard. And he established his authority by passing all tests, which included fining superstar Lafleur and getting rid of Pierre Larouche.

The way would seem to have been cleared for a new era in the Canadiens' history. Make no mistake about this, either: it's a time of reconstruction and change.

Some of the best-known Montreal standbys will continue to appear in prominent roles, to be sure. But the turnover Berry and Grundman inaugurated so auspiciously is bound to continue. That's just the way it is in the NHL of 1982.

Rick Walmsley

The search for Ken Dryden's successor appears over at last, three years after the Canadiens' great goaltender called it quits.

Rick Walmsley, a junior when Dryden retired in 1979, was awarded the job last season when he won 23 and tied seven of 37 decisions and yielded an average of only 2.75 enemy goals per game. He and second-stringer Denis Herron were the first winners of the Jennings Trophy, saluting the NHL's top defensive statistics.

"The Canadiens didn't rush me after I was drafted," says Walmsley, 22. "I had two seasons in the American League before they decided I was ready and I'm grateful to have been given that opportunity."

Walmsley was third in the all-star poll, behind only Billy Smith and Grant Fuhr.

Bob Gainey

Montreal Canadiens have had only 18 captains since they were established in 1917, so Bob Gainey, who wears the "C" on his jersey now, carries on a noble tradition. He was appointed last season after Serge Savard retired.

"With Bob, it's leadership by example. He's probably our most consistent player," says Grundman. "He rarely plays anything but a great game. And while he's not a big talker, he makes a lot of sense when he does speak."

Now 28, Gainey had won the Selke Trophy as the NHL's best defensive forward each of the first four times it was awarded. Last year, he was runner-up to Boston's Steve Kasper.

Another sign of the esteem in which he's held: He was chosen for two Team Canada rosters, in the 1981 Canada Cup and at the '82 world championships.

Keith Acton

The 103rd junior selected at the NHL's 1978 amateur draft, and the eighth by Canadiens, was Keith Acton. And there was little in his first two pro seasons, with the Nova Scotia farmhands, to indicate he was anything more than an efficient, unspectacular journeyman forward.

But the 24-year-old centre broke through as Montreal's top producer last term with 88 points, 49 more than he'd contributed as a rookie the year before.

"Having Guy Lafleur as your right winger helps a lot," Acton understated. "It improves your play, as well as your point total. And it does a lot for your confidence."

Mark Hunter

The Hunters of Petrolia, Ont., have sent three sons to the NHL. They're not exactly threatening Alberta's Sutter family, with six boys under pro contracts, but it's still remarkable productivity.

Dave Hunter plays for Edmonton Oilers. Dale is with Quebec Nordiques. And 18-year-old Mark caught on with Canadiens last season after being claimed in the 1981 junior draft.

Scrappily competitive, like his brothers, Hunter scored 18 times as a freshman right wing and worked with Doug Jarvis and Bob Gainey on Montreal's (and one of the NHL's) best checking lines.

He was Canadiens' most successful number one pick since Mark Napier in 1977.

Guy Lafleur

Has the Flower begun to wilt? Is the bloom disappearing already?

These things seemed entirely possible last season. On the

other hand, it says a lot about Lafleur's stature in hockey when 37 goals and 57 assists constitute a mediocre performance and a cause for concern.

Lafleur, who'd been an all-star in six of the previous 10 campaigns, didn't get so much as a single third-place vote.

"I'm only 31 so I don't think the fire's quite out yet," said Lafleur, "but it may not burn as brightly as it once did."

Nevertheless, take a look at the man's numbers, for his 11 NHL seasons: 469 goals and 1,095 points altogether.

Brian Engblom

Canadiens' best man last season, according to the all-star voters, was rearguard Brian Engblom. He placed fourth in the defence contest and therefore earned a spot on the second team.

"I think coming up to the Canadiens when I did was excellent preparation," says Engblom, a University of Wisconsin product out of Winnipeg. "That was in 1978 and they had guys who were terrific at carrying the puck. I learned to stay at home and protect our zone and that was tremendous discipline, which is paying off now."

Just 26, Engblom was selected for Team Canada's defence in the 1981 Canada Cup tournament.

Steve Shutt

Can it really be true — Steve Shutt an oldtimer?

"Well, I'm only 30 but all the kids coming into the NHL today certainly make me feel elderly," says left winger Shutt. He noted that Mark Messier, last season's all-star at his position, was barely 21.

However, Shutt shows no sign of losing his deft scoring touch. His 1981-82 output, 31 goals, was his lowest since 1975, but injuries had limited him to 57 games and he missed the playoffs.

"That's another thing about hitting 30," he notes. "You don't recover as fast and little things bother you more."

Over an NHL decade, Shutt's accuracy and quick releases have accumulated 357 goals.

Larry Robinson

Canadiens' defensive statistics, tops in the NHL, won goalies Rick Walmsley and Denis Herron the Jennings Trophy last season, but it's also clear their rearguards must have been just about the best in the business.

Brian Engblom, fourth in all-star voting, was one key workman. Larry Robinson, who stood sixth, was the other.

That marked a sort of slump for the Big Bird, because he'd been a first or second pick in each of the six previous campaigns and had won the Norris Trophy on two occasions.

"It wasn't vintage Robinson, perhaps, but being sixth in the NHL isn't bad, eh?" said Grundman. "And with a 31-year-old guy, you don't expect any downward trend to be permanent — just the opposite, in fact."

Keith Acton

CANADIENS' 1982-83 ROSTER

| Forwards | Ht. | Wt. | Place of Birth | Date | 1981-82 Club | 1981-82 RECORD |
						G	A	Pts.
Keith Acton	5-8	167	Peterborough, Ont.	April 15, 1958	Montreal	36	52	88
Bob Gainey	6-2	195	Peterborough, Ont.	Dec. 13, 1953	Montreal	21	24	45
Rejean Houle	5-11	167	Rouyn, Que.	Oct. 25, 1949	Montreal	11	32	43
Mark Hunter	6-0	194	Petrolia, Ont.	Nov. 12, 1962	Montreal	18	11	29
Doug Jarvis	5-9	165	Brantford, Ont.	March 24, 1955	Montreal	20	28	48
Guy Lafleur	6-0	180	Thurso, Que.	Sept. 20, 1951	Montreal	27	57	84
Craig Laughlin	5-11	198	Toronto, Ont.	Sept. 19, 1957	Montreal	12	11	23
Pierre Mondou	5-11	178	Sorel, Que.	Nov. 17, 1955	Montreal	35	33	68
Mark Napier	5-10	185	Toronto, Ont.	Jan. 28, 1957	Montreal	40	41	81
Chris Nilan	6-0	200	Boston, Mass.	Feb. 9, 1958	Montreal	7	4	11
Dough Risebrough	5-11	183	Kitchener, Ont.	Jan. 29, 1954	Montreal	15	18	33
Steve Shutt	5-11	184	Toronto, Ont.	July 1, 1952	Montreal	31	24	55
Mario Tremblay	6-0	185	Alma, Que.	Sept. 2, 1956	Montreal	33	40	73
Doug Wickenheiser	6-0	197	Regina, Sask.	March 30, 1961	Montreal	12	23	35

Defencemen

Gilbert Delorme	6-1	205	Longueuil, Que.	Nov. 25, 1962	Montreal	3	8	11
Brain Engblom	6-2	200	Winnipeg, Man.	Jan. 27, 1955	Montreal	4	29	33
Gaston Gingras	6-1	195	Temiskaming, Que.	Feb. 13, 1959	Montreal	6	18	24
Rod Langway	6-3	215	Maag, Taiwan	May 3, 1957	Montreal	5	34	39
Robert Picard	6-2	210	Montreal, Que.	May 25, 1957	Montreal	2	26	28
Larry Robinson	6-3	215	Winchester, Ont.	June 2, 1951	Montreal	12	47	49

Goalies

						GPI	GA	Avg.
Denis Herron	5-11	165	Chambly, Que.	June 18, 1952	Montreal	27	68	2.64
Richard Sevigny	5-8	170	Montreal, Que.	April 11, 1957	Montreal	19	53	3.10
Rick Walmsley	5-10	178	Simcoe, Ont.	May 25, 1959	Montreal	38	101	2.75

BOSTON BRUINS

A New Leaf for the Coach

1981-82 Finish: Second, Adams Division.
Strengths: Good kids, scoring.
Weaknesses: Aging in spots, defence thin.
Probable 1982-83 Finish: First.

Looking back at it, in perspective, Gerry Cheevers is now prepared to admit he did a poor job in his first year as a National Hockey League coach. Cheevers had been one of Boston Bruins' goaltenders in the spring of 1980. Four months later, he was the man in charge.

The transition wasn't the simple matter he thought it would be. "I found out, during that initial season, that I'd have to be a lot more intense and stern," he said. "I needed to be a lot more in command and on top of things. I was too passive behind the bench.

"You can be too close to your players and it's a mistake to try. After all, I'd been one of them very recently. But if you're one of the guys, you tend to slough off errors and, as coach, you can't afford to do that.

"It just took me a while to understand what being the boss really means. The old relationships have had to change and that's all there was to it."

The statistics would tend to support the suggestion a changed Cheevers was more effective the second time around. Bruins finished up nine points better and, while still second in the Adams Division, rose to fourth place in the overall NHL standings. That was a significant climb from eighth spot the year before.

And don't forget this advancement was accomplished in the midst of a far-reaching reconstruction project.

That process continued last summer.

Bruins had used 20-year-old Mike Moffat, up from the juniors, as their playoff goalie, and were anything but dissatisfied. But they still bolstered themselves at this key position by acquiring Philadelphia's first-stringer, Pete Peeters, in exchange for defenceman Brad McCrimmon.

That move became feasible when Bruins acquired an excellent young rearguard in the amateur draft.

They had procured Colorado Rockies' first-round priority in a 1981 deal and that became the No. 1 choice when Rockies finished dead last. So the Bruins had the pick of the crop.

The Bruins' original idea had been to claim gifted young Brian Bellows, a right winger, and it was a bit of a surprise when they opted for Gord Kluzak, instead.

"We already have the best right winger in the league, Rick Middleton, and he's only 28. But the time isn't far off when we'll have to replace a couple of veterans on defence," general manager Harry Sinden reasoned. "Under the circumstances, it seemed Kluzak would be more useful to us, even though Bellows is likely to become a big star in the NHL."

There was a bonus, too. Minnesota North Stars, anxious to get Bellows as their No. 2 selection, gave Sinden two players as a reward for passing on him. The names — Dave Donnelly and Brad Palmer.

Rick Middleton

Fellows like Rick Middleton are becoming a rarity in hockey today. He manages to play the game effectively without breaking its rules.

Last season, for example, he incurred only six minor penalties in 75 games and still scored 51 goals and 43 assists. That admirable blend got him the Lady Byng Trophy as the NHL player who best combines skill and sportsmanship.

"The interesting angle is that Middleton is able to check aggressively without committing fouls," says coach Gerry Cheevers. "He's no namby-pamby player."

Middleton's 1981-82 deeds got him an all-star nomination at right wing on the second team, behind only Mike Bossy.

"Where Rick opened a lot of eyes was in the Canada Cup," Cheevers notes. "He was one of Canada's best guys. I thought he was the best, going both ways."

Raymond Bourque

He hasn't exactly erased memories of Bobby Orr, but Ray Bourque has swiftly established himself as Boston's leading defenceman — and one of the very best in the entire NHL.

As a rookie, he earned a berth on the 1979-80 all-star squad and won the Calder Trophy for freshmen. He was a second all-star in his sophomore season. And now he's back on the first list again, second only to Doug Wilson in rearguard ratings.

"Bourque will be 22 years old midway through his fourth campaign and that is remarkable," says Sinden. "In terms of consistency, he has been the NHL's top defenceman over his first three years as a pro."

Bourque expects to begin his 1982-83 campaign slowly after breaking his left arm in a summer softball game.

Barry Pederson

Assistant coach Jean Ratelle gets credit for Barry Pederson's superb NHL debut last season — 44 goals and 38 assists, followed by a handsome 7-and-11 mark in 15 playoff matches.

Pederson hadn't expected to make the varsity at all when he reported to Bruins' 1981 training camp as a 20-year-old draftee out of junior ranks.

"I didn't think I'd be able to play well enough defensively but Ratelle was able to overcome my shortcomings in a very brief time," Pederson says.

"He also helped me with my faceoffs and in little things like knowing when to break for the goal and when to hang back."

And at the end, only Winnipeg's Dale Hawerchuk ranked ahead of Pederson among NHL newcomers.

Steve Kasper

The Frank Selke Trophy goes to the NHL's best defensive forward and its 1981-82 winner was Boston centre Steve Kasper, 21.

Kasper has become somewhat more famous as the only enemy checker able to control Wayne Gretzky. In three games against Kasper last season, Gretzky produced a sub-par one goal and four assists.

"The Gretzky thing gets him a lot of attention," says Cheevers, "but the fact is he does a solid job against anybody he faces. And he's a 20-goal man to boot."

Says Kasper: "The key is to keep yourself between the guy you're trying to cover and the puck and try to force him to the outer edges of the ice surface."

Gretzky adds: "He does a lot more than just shadow me, because he seems to know when to pick me up and when to leave. He's not right on top of me all the time but always seems to show up at the right moment."

Peter McNab

Though born in Canada (Vancouver), Peter McNab played his early hockey in San Diego and at Denver University. So he is the biggest NHL scorer ever developed in the U.S., having reached 276 goals at age 30.

McNab had launched his NHL career with Buffalo Sabres but was dealt to Boston in 1976. His six-year total with Bruins is now 227 goals.

"He's a goal-scoring specialist, sort of like a designated hitter," says Gerry Cheevers. "He's got the same accuracy and quick release as Mike Bossy or Richard Martin. And he has the size to maintain a position in the slot."

McNab is the son of the New Jersey Devils' vice-president, Max McNab.

Terry O'Reilly

It is impossible to condone the misbehaviour which caused Terry O'Reilly to begin the 1982-83 season with a 10-game suspension. Many felt he was lucky to be punished so lightly when he slapped referee Andy van Hellemond at the end of a playoff game last spring.

However, the incident did serve to underline the fierce intensity which 31-year-old O'Reilly brings to his work. A more customary outlet for his unmatched competitive zeal is the sheer industry with which he plays all the time he is on the ice. The desire to excel, and to win, is written all over him.

"O'Reilly is a self-made player," coach Cheevers says.

"He came into the league with a minimum of skills and succeeded by outworking everybody else."

That dedication was doubled last season because O'Reilly's 1980-81 production had fallen off to only seven goals. He got that figure back up to a respectable 22.

Pete Peeters

Something had to be done about Boston's netminding. It had been an uncertain quantity since Gerry Cheevers retired to become coach and, last season, the situation grew desperate. Bruins were reduced to going with minor leaguer Marco Baron and, in the Stanley Cup tournament, were trying to get by with a 20-year-old junior, Mike Moffat.

"We're very high on the kid," Cheevers noted, "but it's just not fair to dump the entire burden on his shoulders at this stage. Therefore, getting an NHL goalie was a priority item in the off-season."

Philadelphia Flyers furnished the solution. They had a logjam at the goalkeeping position and, to get defenceman Brad McCrimmon from Bruins, were prepared to give up Pete Peeters, ostensibly their first-stringer.

Peeters, 25, became a Philly regular in 1979 and has made at least 40 starts in each of his three NHL seasons. He posted a 3.71 average last term behind a mediocre defence and had 23 wins, 18 losses and three ties.

Brad Park

The knees of Brad Park represent almost a complete course of study for a medical student hoping to become an orthopedic specialist. It is nothing short of amazing that they can continue to carry Park to the highest levels among NHL defencemen.

"Park is not the dominant figure he once was," admits Cheevers. "But he's no charity case. He continues to be one of our best. He plays because he belongs on the ice. And he's doing it on one wheel, with severely restricted manoeuvrability."

Park, who's now 34, had been an NHL all-star four times before moving from Rangers to Bruins in the historic Phil Esposito trade of 1975. There was to be one more all-star nomination before Park's underpinnings began to give him trouble.

Even so, he managed to work 75 games last season and was in on 56 Boston goals.

Peter McNab

BRUINS' 1982-83 ROSTER

1981-82 RECORD

Forwards	Ht.	Wt.	Place of Birth	Date	1981-82 Club	G	A	Pts.
Wayne Cashman	6-1	208	Kingston, Ont.	June 24, 1945	Boston	12	31	43
Bruce Crowder	6-0	180	Essex, Ont.	March 25, 1957	Boston	16	11	27
Keith Crowder	6-0	190	Windsor, Ont.	Jan. 6, 1959	Boston	23	21	44
Tom Fergus	6-0	179	Chicago, Ill.	June 16, 1962	Boston	15	24	39
Mike Gillis	6-1	195	Sudbury, Ont.	Dec. 1, 1958	Boston	9	8	17
Stan Jonathan	5-8	175	Oshweken, Ont.	Sept. 5, 1955	Boston	6	17	23
Steve Kasper	5-8	159	Montreal, Que.	Sept. 28, 1961	Boston	22	30	52
Mike Krushelnyski	6-2	200	Montreal, Que.	April 27, 1960	Erie (AHL)	31	52	83
Norm Leveille	5-10	175	Montreal, Que.	Jan. 10, 1963	Boston	14	19	33
Don Marcotte	5-10	186	Asbestos, Que.	April 15, 1947	Boston	13	22	35
Peter McNab	6-3	203	Vancouver, B.C.	May 8, 1952	Boston	36	40	76
Rick Middleton	5-11	170	Toronto, Ont.	Dec. 4, 1953	Boston	51	43	94
Terry O'Reilly	6-1	199	Niagara Falls, Ont.	June 7, 1951	Boston	22	30	52
Brad Palmer	6-0	185	Duncan, B.C.	Sept. 14, 1961	Minnesota	22	23	45
Barry Pederson	5-11	171	Big River, Sask.	March 13, 1961	Boston	44	48	92

Defencemen

Ray Bourque	5-11	197	Montreal, Que.	Dec. 28, 1960	Boston	17	49	66
Randy Hillier	6-1	178	Toronto, Ont.	March 30, 1960	Boston	0	8	8
Gord Kluzak	6-3	200	Climax, Sask.	April 3, 1964	Billings (WHL)	9	24	33
Larry Melnyk	6-0	181	New Westminster, B.C.	Feb. 21, 1960	Boston	0	8	8
Mike Milbury	6-1	202	Brighton, Mass.	June 17, 1952	Boston	2	10	12
Mike O'Connell	5-9	180	Chicago, Ill.	Nov. 25, 1955	Boston	5	34	39
Brad Park	6-0	200	Toronto, Ont.	July 6, 1948	Boston	14	42	56
Dick Redmond	5-11	178	Kirkland Lake, Ont.	Aug. 14, 1949	Boston	0	0	0

Goalies

						GPI	GA	Avg.
Marco Baron	5-11	179	Montreal, Que.	April 8, 1959	Boston	44	144	3.44
Mike Moffat	5-10	165	Galt, Ont.	Feb. 14, 1962	Kingston (OMJHL)	46	184	4.15
Pete Peeters	6-0	180	Edmonton, Alta.	Aug. 15, 1957	Philadelphia	44	160	3.71
Rogie Vachon	5-7	165	Palmarolle, Que.	Sept. 8, 1945	Boston	38	132	3.66

MINNESOTA NORTH STARS

Lou Got His Man

1981-82 Finish: First, Norris Division.
Strengths: Excellent team, improving.
Weaknesses: Lacks muscle, fire.
Probable 1982-83 Finish: More of the same.

There are two things you need to know if you're to comprehend just how special a young hockey player Brian Bellows is, and what he can mean to the Minnesota North Stars.

First of all, the universal view was that Bellows was the exceptional junior of his time, on the same exalted level as people like Bobby Orr, Guy Lafleur, Wayne Gretzky and Dale Hawerchuk at the same stage.

Secondly, general manager Lou Nanne moved heaven and earth to make certain Bellows would be part of the North Stars' future. Bellows was to turn 18 in 1982, becoming eligible for employment in the National Hockey League, and there was a frenzied scramble among clubs seeking high draft priorities — in hopes of being first in line.

Nanne gave up two players for Detroit Red Wings' first-round place, figuring it might be No. 1. Boston Bruins obtained Colorado Rockies' pick with the same idea in mind. Philadelphia Flyers struck a similar bargain with the Hartford Whalers.

As it happened, Rockies were last in the league so, using their top spot, Bruins would be first to choose on drafting day in June. They were thinking about claiming a defenceman, however, and Nanne offered extra encouragement in the form of two more bodies.

So Gord Kluzak went to Boston and Nanne got his man.

"Everybody agrees this is the kind of athlete who can turn a franchise around," Nanne says. "We've been just on the fringe so it's sensible to think Bellows can move us into the championship class."

A shoulder separation limited Bellows to 47 games with

Kitchener juniors last season, but he still accumulated 45 goals and 52 assists. Significantly, on the final day of the Memorial Cup tournament, with the national championship at stake, Bellows produced three goals and two assists in a 7-4 victory.

"And the tip-off on the kid is the fact I had him run the team when I was suspended," said Kitchener coach Joe Crozier.

Mind you, the Minnesota club was in genuine need of help. A Stanley Cup finalist in 1981, it lurched through a mediocre 1981-82 campaign and, while first in the Norris Division, was an undistinguished fifth overall. And the Stars endured the humiliation of being dumped in their very first playoff series.

"So Bellows became even more of a need," Nanne said. "We had to have strong leadership and he's that type of a player.

"We also needed some strength among our forwards, which is why I got Willi Plett from Calgary."

Stars dealt Steve Christoff and Bill Nyrop to the Flames for Plett, a 6-foot-3, 210-pound winger who served 288 penalty minutes last season, compared to the Stars' worst individual total of 138. You can see the point. Plett is a hitter and a scrapper, and an excellent scorer to boot.

Craig Hartsburg

A seven-year contract, the longest in Stars' history, was granted to Craig Hartsburg after a season in which he assisted on 60 goals, placed fourth in Norris Trophy voting, and made the second all-star team at the world championships in Finland.

Coach Glen Sonmor was delighted with his 23-year-old defenceman.

"Not only has he been an offensive threat and a kingpin defensively," said Sonmor, "he has grown into an important leadership role with this team, notably through the period when Tim Young, our captain, was hurt. It was something that just evolved naturally."

Hartsburg was chosen for both Team Canada rosters last year — at the Canada Cup tournament and then for the '82 global tournament overseas.

Neal Broten

Herb Brooks said Neal Broten was the best player he ever coached at the University of Minnesota. The youngster won the 1981 Hobey Baker Award as the outstanding performer in U.S. college hockey. And then he joined the Stars for the Stanley Cup playoffs that same spring.

Good in his debut, Broten was absolutely superb in his first full pro campaign. No Minnesota player was named star of the game as often. His 97 points were second among all NHL freshmen and he placed fourth in Calder Trophy voting.

"And that's just the beginning," says Nanne, who claimed Broten's rights in the 1979 NHL draft before he played for the victorious U.S. Olympic entry.

Dino Ciccarelli

Of the 55 goals popular Dino Ciccarelli popped in last season, 15 were the first of the game (equalling an NHL record) and 20 came on Minnesota power plays. Almost all of them resulted from Ciccarelli's special attributes.

"He's always in the right place around the nets. It looks like he's lucky but that's not it. It's skill and know-how," says Sonmor.

"Another thing — he perseveres. You knock him down and he'll get right back up into scoring position. He's prepared to take a beating any time to score a goal. Nothing discourages him."

Ciccarelli's exploits were recognized by enough all-star voters to place him third among the candidates at right wing.

And here's the remarkable part: It was his first complete NHL season. He'd played in 32 games the year before, just enough to disqualify him from Calder Trophy contention.

Gilles Meloche

Several Minnesota players compiled impressive statistics last season but when it came time to select the individual who had contributed the most, veteran goalie Gilles Meloche got the nod. He was named Stars' most valuable member.

Meloche, 32, won 26 and tied nine of 50 netminding decisions. After the campaign was over, Meloche got some overdue recognition on an international scale when he was selected to compete for Team Canada at the world championships in Finland. He excelled, too, against the Russians, Czechs, and the rest.

Meloche's 20-year-old understudy, Don Beaupre — he of the magical catching hand — made 29 appearances.

Steve Payne

North Stars were playoff flops last April, but you couldn't apply that description to left wing Steve Payne, who had six points in four Stanley Cup games.

Coach Sonmor wasn't surprised to see Payne, 24, acquire consistency, and a mastery of tough situations. ''He's a big kid, over six feet and 200 pounds, and has just discovered how to utilize that size,'' the coach said.

''He and his linemates get a lot of scoring opportunities when he physically eliminates people in the offensive zone, which is easy for him. And that stuff is even more effective in the playoffs.''

Payne shows 128 goals for his first four NHL campaigns.

Fred Barrett

Vancouver general manager Harry Neale described Fred Barrett of the Minnesota rearguard as one of the most under-rated NHL players. ''You hate to play against him because he must get 10 hits a night,'' Neale said. ''He defends in the classic way, by taking people right out of the play and, as often as not, it hurts.''

Barrett, 32, has now completed 12 years in the NHL.

''I used to get injured a lot myself, probably as a result of playing the body the way I did,'' Barrett says. ''But that trend seems to be past. Maybe I'm protecting myself a little better. Now I'd like to win a Stanley Cup before I pack it in. So it's got to be pretty soon.''

Gordie Roberts

Detroit's Roberts family named a son after Gordie Howe of the Red Wings, but he turned out to be a defenceman instead of a high-scoring right wing.

But Roberts is a first-rate rearguard. Indeed, he was named Minnesota's most improved man last season, a year after he'd been obtained in a trade with the Hartford Whalers.

Mike Fidler, the other man in the exchange, played two games for Hartford and assisted on a single goal.

Tom McCarthy

Any assessment of Stars' 1981-82 performance must be tempered by the knowledge Tom McCarthy missed half the schedule.

The skillful young winger fractured an ankle, his second major accident in two seasons. He had needed surgery to fix a damaged wrist the year before.

"We know McCarthy has tremendous potential," says Sonmor, "and it's certainly through no fault of his that he hasn't been able to deliver it so far."

Curt Giles

Stocky Curt Giles has failed to make a great deal of impact publicly in two years as a North Star defenceman, but all that changed when he was invited to become a member of Canada's entry at the world championships in Finland.

"Giles is extremely mobile and handles the puck extremely well," said Dave King, one of the Canadian coaches. "Those are assets in the NHL, but much greater ones on the large European ice surfaces."

A Canadian, Giles received his hockey training at Minnesota University at Duluth.

Curt Giles

NORTH STARS' 1982-83 ROSTER

1981-82 RECORD

Forwards	Ht.	Wt.	Place of Birth	Date	1981-82 Club	G	A	Pts.
Kent-Erik Andersson	6-2	190	Orebro, Sweden	May 24, 1951	Minnesota	9	12	21
Brian Bellows	6-0	195	St. Catharines, Ont.	Aug. 1, 1964	Kitchener (OMJHL)	45	52	97
Neal Broten	5-9	160	Roseau, Minn.	Nov. 29, 1959	Minnesota	38	59	97
Jack Carlson	6-3	210	Virginia, Minn.	Aug. 23, 1954	Minnesota	8	4	12
Dino Ciccarelli	5-11	185	Sarnia, Ont.	Aug. 8, 1960	Minnesota	55	52	107
Mike Eaves	5-10	178	Denver, Colo.	June 10, 1956	Minnesota	11	10	21
Andres Hakansson	6-2	191	Munkfors, Sweden	April 27, 1956	Minnesota	12	4	16
Mark Johnson	5-9	160	Madison, Wisc.	Sept. 22, 1957	Pitt.-Minn.	12	13	25
Al MacAdam	6-0	180	Charlottetown, P.E.I.	March 16, 1952	Minnesota	18	43	61
Tom McCarthy	6-2	200	Toronto, Ont.	July 31, 1960	Minnesota	12	30	42
Steve Payne	6-2	205	Toronto, Ont.	Aug. 16, 1958	Minnesota	33	44	77
Willi Plett	6-3	205	Paraguay	June 7, 1955	Calgary	21	36	57
Bobby Smith	6-4	210	North Sydney, N.S.	Feb. 12, 1958	Minnesota	43	71	114
Ken Solheim	6-3	210	Hythe, Alta.	March 27, 1961	Minnesota	4	5	9
Tim Young	6-2	192	Scarborough, Ont.	Feb. 22, 1955	Minnesota	10	31	41

Defencemen

Fred Barrett	5-11	194	Ottawa, Ont.	Jan. 26, 1950	Minnesota	1	15	16
Curt Giles	5-8	180	The Pas, Man.	Nov. 30, 1958	Minnesota	3	12	15
Craig Hartsburg	6-1	200	Stratford, Ont.	June 29, 1959	Minnesota	17	60	77
Brad Maxwell	6-2	197	Brandon, Man.	July 8, 1957	Minnesota	10	21	31
Ron Meighan	6-3	194	Montreal, Que.	May 26, 1963	Niagara Falls (OMJHL)	27	41	68
Gordie Roberts	6-0	195	Detroit, Mich.	Oct. 2, 1957	Minnesota	4	30	34
Gary Sargent	5-10	210	Red Lake, Minn.	Feb. 8, 1954	Minnesota	0	5	5

Goalies

						GPI	GA	Avg.
Don Beaupre	5-8	155	Kitchener, Ont.	Sept. 19, 1961	Minnesota	29	101	3.71
Gilles Meloche	5-9	180	Montreal, Que.	July 12, 1950	Minnesota	51	175	3.47

BUFFALO SABRES

The Scotty Bowman Clean-up

1981-82 Finish: Third, Adams Division.
Strengths: Good forwards, good kids.
Weaknesses: On defence, team in transition.
Probable 1982-83 Finish: Second.

The uniforms remain the same, but otherwise the Buffalo Sabres of today bear only a slight resemblance to the National Hockey League team Scotty Bowman inherited when he became its general manager in 1979.

Inside a two-year span, Bowman weeded out such Buffalo fixtures as Danny Gare, Richard Martin, Rene Robert, Don Luce, Jim Schoenfeld, Don Edwards and Jerry Korab.

"I checked and discovered that group hadn't won the Stanley Cup too often," says Bowman, explaining the upheaval he caused. "Besides, this is a time for change and youth in the NHL and teams that don't follow suit are going to be left far behind."

In keeping with this philosophy, Bowman had three choices on the opening round of last summer's NHL amateur draft: his own, that of Los Angeles (the Korab trade of 1980), and Calgary's (payment for Edwards).

His first claim was Phil Housley, a Minnesota high school player who is described as the next Bobby Orr. Then he took left winger Paul Cyr, a 108-point man last season with Victoria, B.C. juniors. And his final selection was centre Dave Andreychuk from the Oshawa Generals. He had accumulated 101 points.

Bowman also mentions the exploits of other juniors Sabres already owned: Mike Moller and Sean McKenna, 1981-82 all-stars in their respective leagues, and Jeff Eatough, who had 90 points in 67 matches.

"You try for numbers," Bowman elaborated, "because that improves your chances, on account of the law of averages, and also puts you in position to make trades. It's the thinking Sammy Pollock used to put Canadiens on top and keep them there.''

Clearly, Sabres' 1982-83 fate hinges on how rapidly some of Bowman's youngsters can develop.

That's a big part of it. The other question to be answered concerns the mass trade he swung with Detroit Red Wings last winter. He gave up his captain, Gare, plus Schoenfeld and centre Derek Smith, to get Dale McCourt, Mike Foligno and Brent Peterson.

''I'll admit I was dealing known commodities for potential and the verdict isn't in yet,'' Bowman concedes. ''But if we're right about these new people, this franchise has a very bright future.''

Bob Sauve

It took 41 nights with the lowly Detroit Red Wings to give goalie Bob Sauve a new appreciation of the Buffalo defence. He had averaged 2.51 goals a game in seven appearances with Sabres before being sent to Detroit, where his mark soared to 4.19.

As it turned out, the transfer was only temporary. Sauve wasn't under contract when the Sabres traded him. Wings subsequently decided not to sign him, so he reverted to Buffalo. And when Bowman traded Edwards, he immediately concluded a five-year agreement with Sauve.

''The experience showed me how nice it is to work behind a strong club,'' says Sauve, 27. ''I mean, it gets discouraging with a club like Detroit because so many shots are going by. You can play a terrific game and let in eight goals.''

Sauve will carry a heavier workload, on the basis of his 48 starts last season, but understudy Jacques Cloutier will handle his share after a campaign interrupted by injury.

Jean Francois Sauve

You guessed it. Sabre centre J. F. Sauve is the younger brother of goalie Bob, from Ste. Genevieve in Quebec. J. F. is also the smallest player in the NHL at 5-foot-6.

Sauve was passed over in the NHL's junior draft of 1979

because of his size, so Scotty Bowman signed him for Buffalo as a free agent. He was Quebec junior scoring champion the following season and then, as a rookie pro, a second team all-star selection in the American League.

Sauve gave Sabres a very creditable 19 goals and 36 assists in his initial NHL campaign.

Mike Foligno

Six players were involved in last season's Detroit-Buffalo swap but right winger Mike Foligno was the one Sabres' Scotty Bowman was after in particular.

"Dale McCourt has a lot of unrealized potential but I took him because Detroit wouldn't make the deal unless I did," Bowman revealed." We think Foligno is going to become one of the dominant figures in the NHL."

You couldn't support that claim with Foligno's 1981-82 statistics. In 56 Buffalo appearances, the big 23-year-old counted only 20 goals — although six of them were game-winners.

Centre McCourt, once the key person in the entire Detroit organization, played 52 games for his new employers and totalled 42 points.

"He was supposed to be the next superstar but all he's done is create a lot of skeptics," Bowman noted. "He's got a great deal to prove to a lot of people."

Craig Ramsay

Each season, one Buffalo player is given the Tim Horton Trophy as the fellow whose contributions have exceeded the recognition he has received. That seems an apt description of Craig Ramsay's life in hockey and he won the award for the second time last season.

A good indication of Ramsay's importance may be the fact he has survived the Scotty Bowman purge despite being an old Buffalo standby.

"Hey," says Bowman, "anybody would be happy to have a guy who does as thorough a checking job as Ramsay does, makes no mistakes, and gets you more than 20 goals a year for nine consecutive seasons."

Ramsay, 31, has played in 721 successive Sabre games. He was third in last season's voting for the Selke Trophy, which honors the NHL's most proficient defensive forward.

Yvon Lambert

It cost the Sabres $2,500 to draft veteran left winger Yvon Lambert when Montreal Canadiens dropped him just before the 1981-82 schedule opened. Scotty Bowman, of course, had coached Lambert in Montreal.

"What a bargain that was," said Scotty. "Lambert is one of the best corner men in the NHL, and also strong in the goalmouth. And he's only 32."

Lambert put in 25 goals for Buffalo and assisted on 39 others.

"I thought I'd end up with one of the lower teams," Lambert said. "It was lucky for me Buffalo picked me up. This is one of the good outfits in the league."

John van Boxmeer

Until he fractured a finger early in 1982, defenceman John van Boxmeer had been Sabres' leading attacker.

The injury kept van Boxmeer out of the mid-season all-star game, for which he had been elected, and he eventually missed 11 matches in all. But he still wound up fourth among all Buffalo scorers with 68 points.

"That's why I got him. These days, an NHL team has to have some offence from its defencemen," notes Bowman, who obtained van Boxmeer from the Colorado Rockies before his first year with the Sabres even began. "He can move the puck and pass and he has an excellent shot from the point."

Ric Seiling

"I'm a fortunate guy," Ric Seiling said, when he rejoined Sabres for their Stanley Cup playoff series in April.

Seiling, 24, had been struck in the eye during a game in February and, for weeks, the possibility existed that his sight would be affected. If it had been, of course, his hockey career would have been over.

But he was up to his old tricks at Stanley Cup time, doing

a thorough defensive job and producing more than his share of offence.

"That's the way I was taught," Seiling said, "that hockey is a two-way game."

Mike Ramsey

Immediately after the U.S. Olympic victory in 1980, defenceman Mike Ramsey launched his NHL career with Buffalo. Since then, he has gone from the heights to the depths, and back up again.

"I was benched in 1981 and that really shattered my confidence," says Ramsey, 21.

"But I took on some responsibility last season, after Jim Schoenfeld was traded. I think I became a better defenceman because of it. I began to pick spots for carrying the puck. I was more conscious of protecting our zone and being content just to throw the puck ahead to our forwards."

There will be increased opportunities, of course, for that type of leadership from now on.

Gilbert Perreault

Nobody had seen Gil Perreault play better hockey than he did in the first four games of the 1981 Canada Cup tournament. He seemed to have discovered new stores of resourcefulness. Skating with dazzling speed, he had nine points at the time he fractured an ankle.

So his NHL start was delayed. He finally joined Buffalo in the 19th match of their 1981-82 schedule — and took up just where he had left off in September.

Before the campaign was over, Perreault had become the 16th man to surpass 1,000 points in an NHL career. It was his 13th year with the Sabres and his 73-point output left him at 1,001. He added seven assists in Buffalo's four Stanley Cup games.

Gilbert Perrault

SABRES' 1982-83 ROSTER

Forwards	Ht.	Wt.	Place of Birth	Date	1981-82 Club	1981-82 RECORD		
						G	A	Pts.
Mike Foligno	6-2	192	Sudbury, Ont.	Jan. 29, 1959	Det.-Buff.	33	44	77
Yvon Lambert	6-0	195	Drummondville, Que.	May 20, 1950	Buffalo	25	39	64
Dale McCourt	5-10	180	Falconbridge, Ont.	Jan. 26, 1957	Det.-Buff.	33	36	69
Tony McKegney	6-1	198	Montreal, Que.	Feb. 15, 1958	Buffalo	23	29	52
Sean McKenna	6-0	186	Asbestos, Que.	March 7, 1962	Sherbrooke (QJHL)	57	33	90
Bob Mongrain	5-10	176	LaSarre, Que.	Aug. 31, 1959	Rochester (AHL)	37	37	74
Steve Patrick	6-4	206	Winnipeg, Man.	Feb. 4, 1961	Buffalo	8	8	16
Gilbert Perreault	6-0	202	Victoriaville, Que.	Nov. 13, 1950	Buffalo	31	42	73
Brent Peterson	6-0	190	Calgary, Alta.	Feb. 15, 1958	Det.-Buff.	10	5	15
Craig Ramsay	5-10	176	Weston, Ont.	March 17, 1951	Buffalo	16	35	51
Lindy Ruff	6-2	190	Warburg, Sask.	Feb. 17, 1960	Buffalo	16	32	48
Jean-Francois Sauve	5-6	175	Ste. Genevieve, Que.	Jan. 23, 1960	Buffalo	19	36	55
Andre Savard	6-1	185	Temiscamingue, Que.	Sept. 2, 1953	Buffalo	18	20	38
Ric Seiling	6-1	178	Elmira, Ont.	Dec. 15, 1957	Buffalo	22	25	47

Defencemen

Bill Hajt	6-3	204	Borden, Sask.	Nov. 18, 1951	Buffalo	2	9	11
Larry Playfair	6-4	201	Fort St. James, B.C.	June 23, 1958	Buffalo	6	10	16
Mike Ramsey	6-3	190	Minneapolis, Minn.	Dec. 3, 1960	Buffalo	7	23	30
John van Boxmeer	6-0	192	Petrolia, Ont.	Nov. 20, 1952	Buffalo	14	54	68
Hannu Virta	6-0	176	Turku, Finland	March 22, 1963	Buffalo	0	1	1

Goalies

						GPI	GA	Avg.
Jacques Cloutier	5-7	154	Noranda, Que.	Jan. 3, 1960	Buffalo	7	13	2.51
Paul Harrison	6-1	196	Timmins, Ont.	Feb. 11, 1955	Pitt.-Buff.	19	78	4.50
Bob Sauve	5-8	165	Ste. Genevieve, Que.	June 17, 1955	Buff.-Det.	55	200	3.10

NEW YORK RANGERS

The Herb Brooks Magic at Work

1981-82 Finish: Second, Patrick Division.
Strengths: Fine coach, superb youth, speed.
Weaknesses: Problems in goal, on defence.
Probable 1982-83 Finish: Third.

It's difficult to believe now but there actually were pessimists who predicted Herb Brooks would fail as a coach in the National Hockey League.

Winning the 1980 Olympics with a band of U.S. college boys was one thing, they sniffed, but handling professionals in the majors would be an entirely different proposition.

"I understood this was a totally new situation and that some adjustments would be necessary. I prepared myself," said Brooks, who spent part of a winter in Swiss hockey before accepting the post with the Rangers.

"Mostly, though, it's a selling job. If you can show people your system can be successful, they'll buy it. And once that happens, the problems disappear."

The results were entirely convincing: Brooks was a great success.

Rangers added 18 points to their mediocre 1980-81 total and climbed six notches in the overall NHL standings to seventh position, while placing second in their own section. What's more, as they got the hang of Brooks' flowing offensive patterns, they became a treat to watch, and had an obvious capacity for improvement.

"I think you have to give Craig Patrick a lot of credit for the player moves he made as the season progressed," Brooks noted. "After all, a coach can't do much unless he has the right material."

Patrick, Rangers' general manager, had been Brooks's assistant in the Olympic program so they operate on the same wavelength. Patrick knew the sort of athletes Brooks preferred to work with and brought in a few, while also scrambling to offset a catastrophic series of injuries.

Only centre Mike Rogers suited up for all 80 scheduled games and several key players were sidelined for extended stretches. Indeed, there was no guarantee Ulf Nilsson, Anders Hedberg, John Davidson and Ron Greschner would be able to resume their careers at all.

The highly productive Rogers, of course, had been one of Patrick's most important acquisitions. He was obtained just before the 1981-82 schedule opened. Goaltender Eddie Mio and centre Robbie Ftorek were other valuable additions, as a result of Patrick's manoeuvring.

"When you look at the guys who played better than ever before and who came through under difficult circumstances," says Patrick, "I think you'll begin to realize what superb coaching Herb gave us. Our injuries were horrendous. He never had a full lineup to work with. So given just normal luck in that department, plus reasonable improvement, I think we'll now be able to build on a very satisfying start."

Mike Rogers

Rangers faced an emergency at centre as their 1981 training camp was concluding. Walt Tkaczuk had joined Phil Esposito in retirement and now Ulf Nilsson was badly hurt. So general manager Patrick packaged three players (Doug Sulliman, Chris Kotsopoulos and Gerry McDonald) and traded them to Hartford for Mike Rogers, 27.

Rogers had counted 105 points in each of his two NHL campaigns after moving up from the World Hockey Association. And he didn't disappoint his new bosses, either, producing 103 in New York.

The little centre is optimistic about the future.

"We're just beginning to adapt to Herb Brooks's offensive ideas, which have tremendous potential," he says, "so I think you'll see us continue our improvement."

Robbie Ftorek

Counting his World Hockey Association deeds, 30-year-old Robbie Ftorek is the greatest scorer ever developed in U.S. hockey circles. He had four 100-point WHA campaigns before hitting the NHL as captain of Quebec Nordiques in 1979.

"I've tended to emphasize defence more in the NHL," says Ftorek. "That aspect of the game has never been difficult for me but, in the WHA, it was less important. With both Quebec and now the Rangers, it was what I was asked to do."

Still, Ftorek got the Rangers 33 points in 30 games and then another 11 in 10 playoff outings. To acquire him, the Madison Square Garden outfit sent Quebec Dean Talafous and Jere Gillis, and later Pat Hickey when Talafous retired rather than accept the transfer.

Eddie Mio

Edmonton Oilers had more goalies than they could use last season so Eddie Mio, their first-stringer the year before, was placed on the market in December. Rangers, whose need was urgent, gave the Oilers centre Lance Nethery to get him.

The combative Mio, 28, won 13 and tied five of his 24 starts for New York and was 4-and-3 in the playoffs.

But that's only part of Rangers' netminding story. The rest of it concerns Steve Weeks, who'd been apprenticing in the minors when injuries hit Rangers' backstopping corps.

Without relief, Weeks carried them through that difficult stretch and he ended up working 49 matches over the entire campaign, with 26 victories and nine draws.

"It was a great performance by a first-year guy, when we were just about desperate," says GM Patrick. "Weeks is part of the reason our goaltending picture has gone from cloudy to bright."

Reijo Ruotsalainen

Coach Herb Brooks says Reijo Ruotsalainen, the Finnish rookie on his Ranger rearguard, is the best skater in the NHL.

"That means mobility and balance, as well as speed," Brooks notes.

A gifted playmaker, Ruotsalainen runs the New York attack from his rearguard post and makes the power play function.

He was recommended by Lars-Erik Sjoberg, Rangers' scout in the Scandinavian countries. On his say-so, they took Ruotsalainen in the 1980 junior draft and later signed centre Mikko Leinonen.

It took Leinonen a while to earn a regular spot in the lineup but once he did, he made some history. It was a Stanley Cup record when he amassed seven points (one goal, six assists) in a single playoff game — a victory over Philadelphia.

Ron Duguay

Manhattan's gossip columnists mention Ron Duguay's name almost as often as the sports writers do. He is a regular in chic night spots, usually accompanied by glamorous celebrities.

"Doogie might be a little hard to take if it weren't for one thing," a teammate says. "On the ice, he delivers the goods. Nobody works harder. He's no fancy dan. He gets down there and sweats."

It was that characteristic, his unswerving dedication, that got Duguay on Team Canada's roster in the 1981 Canada Cup tournament, and the 1981-82 campaign was merely an extension of that admirable effort. Right winger Duguay enjoyed his most productive year ever with 76 points, 13 above his previous high.

Mark Pavelich

After helping Team U.S. win an Olympic gold medal in 1980, centre Mark Pavelich spent a winter in Switzerland, playing second division hockey for Lugano.

But Herb Brooks, his 1980 coach, hadn't forgotten him and invited him to Rangers' training camp, where he caught on as a free agent.

It was a fortunate turn of events for both the club and athlete. Only four NHL rookies rated ahead of Pavelich in Calder Trophy voting. He counted 33 goals and 43 assists.

Rangers also dealt for Rob McClanahan partway through the schedule. He and sophomore pro Dave Silk, plus Pavelich, gave Brooks three of his ex-Olympians on his first NHL squad.

Nick Fotiu

Rangers' most popular player is mammoth Nick Fotiu. Part of the reason is the fact he comes from Staten Island. He's also unfailingly friendly with the fans and plays the game with entertaining enthusiasm.

Now a strange development is in prospect. Under the tutelage of coach Brooks, Fotiu is learning skills to go with his thumping. He can lay down or accept a pass. He shoots well. He's controlling his temper and reducing foolish penalties.

Fotiu had started out in the NHL with Rangers and returned to them in 1980 after spending two lonesome years with Hartford. He missed his people almost as much as they missed him.

Barry Beck

Bubba Beck was only 22 when Rangers got him from the Colorado Rockies in 1979, giving up five bodies as barter. But even at that tender age, he was prepared for the demanding role he'd be given.

He was to become the individual to whom his teammates would turn for leadership. He was to be Rangers' most skillful player, the one who'd come through with heroics when that was required, and their steadiest hand in times of emergency.

Towering at 6-foot-3, huge at 220 pounds, Beck has carried out that challenging assignment with distinction and, as the Rangers rise in years to come, his prominence is sure to grow. Already he's just on the fringe of the NHL's inner circle of outstanding defencemen.

"You always think of Beck when you're enumerating the top NHL players," says Brooks. "And what has deprived him of even more recognition is the fact we haven't yet emerged as one of the dominant clubs. When we do, Beck will become No. 1, too."

Nick Fotiu

RANGERS' 1982-83 ROSTER

Forwards	Ht.	Wt.	Place of Birth	Date	1981-82 Club	G	A	Pts.
Mike Allison	6-0	200	Fort Frances, Ont.	March 28, 1961	Rangers	7	15	22
Ron Duguay	6-2	210	Sudbury, Ont.	July 6, 1957	Rangers	40	36	76
Nick Fotiu	6-2	210	Staten Island, N.Y.	May 25, 1952	Rangers	8	10	18
Robbie Ftorek	5-10	155	Needham, Mass.	Jan. 2, 1952	Que.-NYR	9	33	42
Eddie Johnstone	5-9	175	Brandon, Man.	March 2, 1954	Rangers	30	28	58
Mikko Leinonen	6-0	175	Tampere, Finland	July 15, 1955	Rangers	11	19	30
Don Maloney	6-1	190	Lindsay, Ont.	Sept. 5, 1958	Rangers	22	36	58
Rob McClanahan	5-10	180	St. Paul, Minn.	Jan. 9, 1958	Hart.-NYR	5	12	17
Mark Pavelich	5-8	170	Eveleth, Minn.	Feb. 28, 1958	Rangers	33	43	76
Mike Rogers	5-9	170	Calgary, Alta.	Oct. 24, 1954	Rangers	38	65	103
Dave Silk	5-11	190	Situate, Mass.	Jan. 1, 1958	Rangers	15	20	35
Steve Vickers	6-0	185	Toronto, Ont.	April 21, 1951	Rangers	9	11	20
Peter Wallin	5-10	175	Stockholm, Sweden	April 30, 1957	Rangers	2	9	11
Tom Younghans	5-11	175	St. Paul, Minn.	Jan. 22, 1953	Minn.-NYR	4	5	9

Defencemen

Name	Ht	Wt	Birthplace	Birthdate	Team	G	A	Pts
Barry Beck	6-3	215	Vancouver, B.C.	June 3, 1957	Rangers	9	29	38
Tim Bothwell	6-3	190	Vancouver, B.C.	May 6, 1955	Rangers	0	3	3
Andre Dore	6-2	200	Montreal, Que.	Feb. 2, 1958	Rangers	4	16	20
Ron Greschner	6-2	205	Goodsoil, Sask.	Dec. 22, 1954	Rangers	5	11	16
Ed Hospodar	6-2	210	Bowling Green, Ohio	Feb. 9, 1959	Rangers	3	8	11
Tom Laidlaw	6-2	215	Brampton, Ont.	April 15, 1958	Rangers	3	18	21
Dave Maloney	6-1	195	Kitchener, Ont.	July 31, 1956	Rangers	13	36	49
Reijo Ruotsalainen	5-8	170	Oulu, Finland	April 1, 1960	Rangers	18	38	56
Carol Vadnais	6-1	210	Montreal, Que.	Sept. 25, 1945	Rangers	5	6	11

Goalies

Name	Ht	Wt	Birthplace	Birthdate	Team	GPI	GA	Avg.
Steve Baker	5-11	165	Boston, Mass.	May 6, 1957	Rangers	6	33	6.04
John Davidson	6-3	205	Ottawa, Ont.	Feb. 27, 1953	Rangers	1	1	1.00
Eddie Mio	5-10	180	Windsor, Ont.	Jan. 31, 1954	Ed.-NYR	25	89	3.56
Steve Weeks	5-11	165	Scarborough, Ont.	June 30, 1958	Rangers	49	179	3.72

PHILADELPHIA FLYERS

Taking Off in a New Direction

1981-82 Finish: Third, Patrick Division.
Strengths: Sound forwards, solid management.
Weaknesses: Weak defence, aging in spots.
Probable 1982-83 Finish: Fifth.

Philadelphia's Broad St. Bullies were the first of the National Hockey League's expansion franchises to succeed in a big way. They won the Stanley Cup in 1974 and '75 and reached the final as recently as 1980 after finishing atop the combined NHL standings.

But they have been declining steadily since then and dropped to 87 points over last season's 80-game schedule for their worst showing since 1973. There was no redemption in the playoffs, either; Flyers were quickly exterminated in the first round.

Seeking to get his outfit moving in a new, productive direction, general manager Keith Allen changed coaches near the end of the schedule. Pat Quinn, who'd been given a contract extension only the year before, was replaced by Bob McCammon.

"Bob was with our American League farm club in Maine and doing such a good job we'd have lost him from the organization if we hadn't promoted him immediately," Allen said. McCammon also was named Allen's assistant.

"We're not saying that coaching was our entire problem," Allen said. "It's just that it looked as though a fresh approach might help.

"It was also obvious, though, that our personnel needed to be upgraded. Specifically, we have to improve on defence."

Injuries had clouded the defensive picture somewhat. After getting a chronic shoulder problem corrected, Bob Dailey shattered an ankle, missed 68 matches, and faced an uncertain future after two operations. Behn Wilson was hurt, too, and the Flyers eventually were forced to trade rugged Mel Bridgman to get giant Brad Marsh from the Calgary Flames.

The Flyers then failed to land the standout junior rearguard they'd been hoping to acquire in the amateur draft. But Steve Smith, a defender they had claimed in 1981, was an all-star in Ontario's junior league and Allen got talented Brad McCrimmon from Boston Bruins in a swap for goalie Pete Peeters.

That transaction partially clarified the netminding situation, which had been muddled ever since Bernie Parent's retirement. Peeters's departure leaves the job to Rick St. Croix and Sweden's Pelle Lindbergh, with a nudge from Bob Froese after a brilliant year in the American League.

The three-way trade with Hartford and Edmonton netted the Flyers Mark Howe who'll certainly bolster the blue line. However, they gave up their top scorer, Ken Linseman, to the Oilers.

Darryl Sittler

Back on left wing, where he started out in hockey, Darryl Sittler looks forward to a second career in Philly. He'd been a centre through almost all of his 11 seasons in Toronto but his new employers want him on the flank.

"I'm very comfortable there," says Sittler, 32, the Toronto captain until he asked for a trade last winter. "I was a winger when Leafs drafted me in 1970 and I played that spot in the world championships last April. I was on left wing, too, when I scored the winning goal in the 1976 Canada Cup final."

Disputes with management led to Sittler's departure from a city where he had been the most popular sports figure in town.

"That's behind me now," he says. "I'm just happy to be with a progressive organization that is prepared to do what's necessary to win."

Sittler had 32 points in his first 35 Flyer matches and ran his total, for 12 NHL seasons, to 948 — 403 goals, 545 assists.

Jim Watson

It was nothing short of miraculous that Jimmy Watson was able to work 76 games on the Philadelphia defence last season. Just a year before, there seemed almost no chance he'd ever play hockey again.

Damaged spinal discs were disabling him, but in an operation in January of 1981 bone was grafted from his hip in such a way that pressure from the injury was relieved. He wore a cast throughout four months but by September, was ready for training camp.

"Bob Dailey and Behn Wilson got hurt, you know, so I'd hate to think what our defence would have been like if Jimmy hadn't bounced back so well," said GM Keith Allen.

Bill Barber

A damaged knee kept Bill Barber out of the 1981 Canada Cup tournament but he got another international opportunity at the '82 world championships in Finland last April. And he made the most of it, scoring eight goals in 10 games and being chosen all-star left wing.

"We saw here what an outstanding all-around player Barber really is," said New Jersey's Marshall Johnston, who coached the Canadian entry.

Barber, 30, enjoyed his customary excellent season with Philadelphia, trailing only Mark Messier and John Tonelli in NHL all-star voting. He scored 45 goals and assisted on 44 others. And he provided all enemy right wingers with thorough defensive coverage.

"If you were describing the ideal hockey player," Johnston said, "you'd list many of Barber's qualities."

Ron Flockhart

In a lot of NHL seasons, Ron Flockhart's 1981-82 achievements would have earned him recognition as an exceptional rookie. But the crop of NHL newcomers was so outstanding that Flockhart placed only seventh on the Calder Trophy ballot.

Following an introductory professional campaign in the American League, Flockhart caught on as a centreman in Philly for Brian Propp (who scored 44 goals) and Ray Allison. His own output consisted of 33 goals and 39 assists.

A glowing tribute came from L.A. defenceman Dave Lewis.

"He reminds me of Gil Perreault because he comes down the middle at the same speed," said Lewis. "And he's just as unpredictable."

Paul Holmgren

There are risks involved in the way hard-hitting Paul Holmgren plays hockey: a fellow can hurt himself and he can get in trouble.

Both things befell Holmgren last season. In hurling his muscular body at the opposition, he separated a shoulder. And, as a particularly fiery competitor, he drew a six-game suspension for scuffling with a referee.

In the final accounting, Holmgren had only 41 matches and nine goals on his tab. He's normally a 25-goal shooter.

Holmgren, a University of Minnesota product, is the roughest customer ever to come out of U.S. college competition.

Bobby Clarke

Rumors of Bobby Clarke's collapse have been exaggerated. He played some of the finest hockey in his entire career during the world championships last April, after the conclusion of a long NHL campaign.

"I don't have the pep I once did. I have to pace myself a bit more carefully," said Clarke, a 32-year-old diabetic. "But on a given shift, I'm as good as ever. I don't recover at the same rate and the little injuries I used to shrug off are more of a problem now."

Clarke missed 18 of Flyers' 80 scheduled games last season because of a foot injury but still managed 63 points for a 13-year aggregate of 1,065.

"As it happened, I was out when we got Darryl Sittler, so the set-up Flyers had in mind didn't materialize," Clarke explained. "But we'll get around to it eventually, Sittler and I together."

Ilkka Sinisalo

There were times, during Ilkka Sinisalo's first year in North American hockey, when he thought seriously of retreating to his home in Finland.

But the picture brightened near the end of the 1981-82 schedule when Bob McCammon took over as Philly coach. He liberated Sinisalo from a seat on the bench and put him to work, which was all the Finn wanted.

"He has the kind of speed you've got to take advantage of in the NHL today," McCammon said. "He's one of the fastest guys around."

Flyers signed Sinisalo in Helsinki several months before personnel boss Marcel Pelletier gave final approval at the 1981 world championships. The Finnish youngster would report to training camp that fall.

As a 24-year-old rookie, with limited ice time, Sinisalo managed 15 goals and gave indications there'd be plenty more to come, once he got fully acclimatized.

Mark Howe

Midway through the 1980-81 schedule, there were many who felt Mark Howe had become the NHL's best defenceman. He outpointed Larry Robinson, Randy Carlyle and Borje Salming in all-star voting at that time.

Then came a grave injury which almost ended Howe's career. He was impaled on the sharp point of a goal's frame and, as a matter of fact, almost lost his life.

"It's pretty clear Mark has never fully recovered from that critical situation," said Howe's former coach, Larry Kish. "I mean he's healthy again and everything but for whatever reason, hasn't returned to his former level as a defenceman."

The Flyers are obviously banking on a healthy Mark Howe to improve their defence. The Flyers gave up Ken Linseman to the Oilers in a three-way deal to get Howe.

Bill Barber

Brad McCrimmon

FLYERS' 1982-83 ROSTER

1981-82 RECORD

Forwards	Ht.	Wt.	Place of Birth	Date	1981-82 Club	G	A	Pts.
Ray Allison	5-10	190	Cranbrook, B.C.	March 4, 1959	Philadelphia	17	37	54
Bill Barber	6-0	190	Callander, Ont.	July 11, 1952	Philadelphia	45	44	89
Bobby Clarke	5-10	185	Flin Flon, Man.	Aug. 13, 1949	Philadelphia	17	46	63
Ron Flockhart	5-11	174	Smithers, B.C.	Oct. 10, 1960	Philadelphia	33	39	72
Tom Gorence	6-0	180	St. Paul, Minn.	March 11, 1957	Philadelphia	5	8	13
Al Hill	6-1	175	Nanaimo, B.C.	April 22, 1955	Philadelphia	6	13	19
Paul Holmgren	6-3	210	St. Paul, Minn.	Dec. 2, 1955	Philadelphia	9	22	31
Tim Kerr	6-3	215	Windsor, Ont.	Jan. 5, 1960	Philadelphia	21	30	51
Brian Propp	5-9	185	Lanigan, Sask.	Feb. 15, 1959	Philadelphia	44	47	91
Ilkka Sinisalo	6-1	190	Valeakoski, Finland	July 10, 1958	Philadelphia	15	22	37
Darryl Sittler	6-0	195	Kitchener, Ont.	Sept. 18, 1950	Tor.-Phil.	32	38	70

75

Defencemen

Name								
Fred Arthur	6-5	190	Toronto, Ont.	March 6, 1961	Philadelphia	1	7	8
Frank Bathe	6-1	190	Oshawa, Ont.	Sept. 27, 1954	Philadelphia	1	3	4
Glen Cochrane	6-2	184	Cranbrook, B.C.	Jan. 29, 1958	Philadelphia	6	12	18
Bob Dailey	6-5	220	Kingston, Ont.	May 3, 1953	Philadelphia	1	5	6
Bob Hoffmeyer	6-0	180	Dodsland, Sask.	July 27, 1955	Philadelphia	7	20	27
Mark Howe	5-11	180	Detroit, Mich.	May 28, 1955	Hartford	8	45	53
Brad Marsh	6-2	210	London, Ont.	March 31, 1958	Cal.-Phil.	2	23	25
Brad McCrimmon	5-11	193	Dodsland, Sask.	March 29, 1959	Boston	1	8	9
Jim Watson	6-0	195	Smithers, B.C.	Aug. 19, 1952	Philadelphia	3	9	12
Behn Wilson	6-3	210	Kingston, Ont.	Dec. 19, 1958	Philadelphia	13	23	36

Goalies

Name						GPI	GA	Avg.
Bob Froese	5-11	178	St. Catharines, Ont.	June 30, 1958	Maine (AHL)	31	96	3.20
Pelle Lindbergh	5-9	160	Stockholm, Sweden	May 24, 1959	Philadelphia	8	35	4.38
Rick St. Croix	5-10	175	Kenora, Ont.	Jan. 3, 1955	Philadelphia	29	112	3.89

QUEBEC NORDIQUES

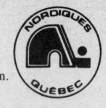

It Was Only A Beginning

1981-82 Finish: Fourth in Adams Division.
Strengths: Superb offence, good goalies.
Weaknesses: Defenders still learning.
Probable 1982-83 Finish: Third.

The astounding Quebec Nordiques furnished one of 1982's more remarkable success stories in the National Hockey League.

Occasionally brilliant, but mostly inconsistent, Nordiques stumbled their way through the regular calendar to an undistinguished fourth-place finish in the Adams standings, but suddenly rose up boldly in the Stanley Cup tournament and, as not-so-humble underdogs, despatched Montreal Canadiens and Boston Bruins to the sidelines. Canadiens had been 27 points ahead of them after the 1981-82 schedule, and the Bruins 14.

It took the title-bound New York Islanders to get the Quebecois halted in the Wales Conference final, one step from the actual Cup round.

"This was, of course, a great success and I am sure it gave our players confidence which will help them in the future," said Michel Bergeron, who coaches the Nordiques with the scholarly assistance of Charles Thiffault.

"But we must not lose sight of the fact we are still building. In particular, we are attempting to develop a defence that is capable of winning championships, and that is going to take time."

Nordiques have pursued this objective by giving on-the-job training to three immensely promising youngsters. Pierre Lacroix is 23, Dave Pichette 22, and Normand Rochefort 21. They are progressing by leaps and bounds.

"In addition, we drafted Randy Moller in 1981 but permitted him to spend one season more with his junior club in Lethbridge," Bergeron said. "Perhaps he will be ready to help us soon."

That would seem to be a genuine possibility. Moller was a second team all-star in Canada's western junior league, close behind three youngsters who are expected to be in the NHL this winter — Garth Butcher, Gary Nylund and Gord Kluzak.

Marian Stastny

All the time they were dazzling NHL defences as 1980-81 newcomers, Anton and Peter Stastny kept saying: "Just wait until our brother gets here and then you'll really see something."

Right winger Marian, eldest of the Slovak siblings, finally did arrive in the summer of 1981 and completed the magical threesome. He'd been suspended at home the season before in reprisal for the earlier Stastny defections, but despite the layoff, managed to make a huge impression. As promised, he was a polished flanker who combined neatly with the other two, and he stood fourth among rookie scorers with 35 goals and 54 assists.

Despite those figures, he received only scanty support from the Calder Trophy selectors. Peter Stastny had won that award in 1981 and the decision was criticized because of his vast experience in Czech and international competition. That controversy seemed to hurt Marian's chances, even though he was officially eligible at 29.

Anton Stastny

Left winger Tony is the youngest of the Stastny boys from Bratislava in the Slovakian section of Czechoslovakia. He and Peter, the centre, escaped in August, 1980, and signed with the Nordiques. Marian joined them for the 1981-82 campaign.

Only 23 today, the baby of the clan didn't join Czechoslovakia's national side until 1979 although the three of them were already operating as a forward line back home. They were a unit at the 1980 Olympics in Lake Placid and, in six games, counted 16 goals and 17 assists. Gilles Leger, Nordiques' director of player development, was on the trail even then.

Nobody has been the least bit disappointed in the Stastnys since they immigrated but Tony came the closest last season.

He duplicated the 46 assists he recorded as a freshman but his goal production was down from 30 to 26.

"The Stastnys are most effective when they work together," a rival coach notes, "but I can appreciate what a temptation it is to spread their talent around. It sometimes hurts them individually, though."

Peter Stastny

It has taken only two years for Peter Stastny to earn acceptance as one of hockey's premier centres. As a sophomore pro last season, he was third in scoring with 136 points and third at the all-star polls, behind only Wayne Gretzky and Bryan Trottier.

"European players have something to prove in the NHL," said coach Bergeron, "and I think Peter passed the test in the Stanley Cup playoffs."

The middle Stastny missed four of the April matches because of a kidney injury but, in the 11 he did play in, recorded seven goals and 11 assists and contributed importantly to the Nordiques' surprise victories over Montreal and Boston.

"Everybody knows the checking is closer and tougher at Stanley Cup time, but it didn't even slow Peter down," Bergeron explained. "He was setting up plays as neatly as he did in the easiest game we had all season."

Wilf Paiement

After false starts in Kansas City, Denver and Toronto, 26-year-old Wilf Paiement may have discovered a congenial hockey home in Quebec City. Paiement is French-speaking, and hails from northern Ontario.

"I had no problems to speak of anywhere I played, but I do get a good feeling here," said Paiement, who had 13 points in eight games after Nordiques obtained him from Toronto in exchange for Miroslav Frycer. It was a trade of right wingers.

As an 18-year-old, Paiement had been drafted by Kansas City Scouts in 1974 and went to Denver with them when they became Colorado Rockies. He was dealt to Leafs midway through the 1979-80 campaign.

Paiement's eight-year tab shows 238 goals.

Michel Goulet

In the beginning, Michel Goulet was one of the Baby Bulls. That was in 1978, when Birmingham Bulls of the World Hockey Association signed a group of juniors who, under the existing rules, were too young for the NHL.

Goulet, 18, counted 28 goals in that initial pro campaign.

"It was good experience. Because of it, I was able to play in the NHL the following year," says right winger Goulet.

The WHA folded in 1979 and Goulet joined Quebec's new NHL entry.

"Without that season in the WHA, I probably wouldn't have made it," he says.

Goulet had 22 goals as an NHL rookie, 32 in his second term, and 42 last season. Naturally, he's looking for 52 now.

Dan Bouchard

Nordiques were about to face the 1981-82 NHL schedule with 20-year-old Clint Malarchuk in goal when Danny Bouchard ended a long, bitter holdout and signed a new contract.

That occurred just eight months after Bouchard had moved to Quebec in the deal which made Nordiques serious NHL contenders. Up until then, they had been struggling along without a quality netminder, but all that changed when Bouchard was obtained from the Calgary Flames. He lost only five of his 29 starts that winter and, last season, had 27 victories and 11 draws against only 22 defeats.

"We had to improve our goalkeeping somehow," said general manager Maurice Filion, "but we were very lucky to get one of the best there was."

Bouchard was given a capable assistant last spring when veteran John Garrett was acquired from Hartford.

Marc Tardif

Life wouldn't seem normal in Quebec City if there weren't some squabble swirling around the hugely talented Marc Tardif.

He started out last season by popping 20 goals in Nordiques' first 28 matches, but had tailed off so badly by April that he didn't participate at all in the final playoff series against the Islanders.

So his future with the Quebec organization is uncertain, as usual, even though his rich contract has two years more to run.

Tardif, 33, has amassed 359 goals in eight years since leaving Montreal Canadiens to join Quebec's old World Hockey Association entry.

It is that undeniable skill which makes his up-and-down fortunes such a worry for both management and fans.

Real Cloutier

Buddy Cloutier was one of the World Hockey Association's most prominent athletes, but the skeptics said he'd be far less effective against the NHL's tougher defences.

That was demonstrated to be a falsehood. Cloutier got 42 goals in his NHL debut.

A broken ankle ruined his sophomore statistics but he bounced back last season with 37 goals and 60 assists.

"There never should have been any question Cloutier would succeed," said Filion, "because a player who works as hard as he does will always do well."

Dale Hunter

Nordiques own some of hockey's foremost offensive stars, but that alone wouldn't be enough to account for their recent successes. They also can send out some of the best checkers in the business to offset enemy attacks.

Michel Goulet is one. He had six goals against opposition power plays last season. Alain Cote is another. But the best is centre Dale Hunter, who specializes in defensive assignments.

While always covering his man thoroughly, Hunter managed to improve his statistics as a second-year player, rising from 63 to 72 points. He is Nordiques' toughest competitor, with 298 penalty minutes on his sheet, and was at his fiery best in those two playoff triumphs last April.

Michel Goulet

NORDIQUES' 1982-83 ROSTER

					1981-82 RECORD		
Forwards	Ht.	Wt.	Place of Birth	Date	1981-82 Club	G	A	Pts.
Pierre Aubry	5-10	170	Cap de la Madeleine, Que.	April 15, 1960	Quebec	10	13	23
Real Cloutier	5-10	185	St. Emile, Que.	July 30, 1956	Quebec	37	60	97
Alain Cote	5-10	203	Matane, Que.	May 3, 1957	Quebec	15	16	31
Richard David	6-0	194	Notre Dame, Que.	April 8, 1958	Fredericton (AHL)	51	32	83
Jere Gillis	6-0	190	Bend, Ore.	Jan. 18, 1957	NYR-Que.	5	10	15
Michel Goulet	6-1	195	Peribonqua, Que.	April 21, 1960	Quebec	42	42	84
Dale Hunter,	5-9	190	Petrolia, Ont.	July 31, 1960	Quebec	22	50	72
Wilf Paiement	6-1	205	Earlton, Ont.	Oct. 16, 1955	Tor.-Que.	25	46	71
Jacques Richard	5-11	170	Quebec City, Que.	Oct. 7, 1952	Quebec	15	26	41
Anton Stastny	6-0	185	Bratislava, CSSR	Aug. 5, 1959	Quebec	26	46	72
Marian Stastny	5-10	192	Bratislava, CSSR	Jan. 8, 1953	Quebec	35	54	89
Peter Stastny	6-1	200	Bratislava, CSSR	Sept. 18, 1956	Quebec	46	93	139
Marc Tardif	6-0	180	Granby, Que.	June 12, 1949	Quebec	39	31	70

Page 83

Defencemen

Name	Ht	Wt	Birthplace	Birthdate	Team			
Andre Dupont	6-0	202	Trois-Rivieres, Que.	July 27, 1949	Quebec	4	12	16
Jean Hamel	5-11	195	Asbestos, Que.	June 6, 1952	Quebec	1	6	7
Dale Hoganson	5-10	190	North Battleford, Sask.	July 8, 1949	Quebec	0	6	6
Pierre Lacroix	5-11	185	Ste. Foy, Que.	April 11, 1959	Quebec	4	23	27
Rick LaPointe	6-2	200	Victoria, B.C.	Aug. 2, 1955	St. Louis	2	20	22
Mario Marois	5-11	180	Ancienne Lorette, Que.	Dec. 15, 1957	Quebec	11	32	43
Randy Moller	6-2	205	Red Deer, Alta.	Aug. 23, 1963	Lethbridge Juniors		NA	
Dave Pichette	6-3	200	Grand Falls, Nfld.	Feb. 4, 1960	Quebec	7	30	37
Normand Rochefort	6-1	200	Trois-Rivieres, Que.	Jan. 28, 1961	Quebec	4	14	18
Gaston Therrien	5-10	186	Montreal, Que.	May 27, 1960	Quebec	0	7	7
Wally Weir	6-2	200	Verdun, Que.	June 3, 1954	Quebec	3	5	8

Goalies

Name	Ht	Wt	Birthplace	Birthdate	Team	GPI	GA	Avg.
Dan Bouchard	6-0	190	Val D'Or, Que.	Dec. 12, 1950	Quebec	60	230	3.86
John Garrett	5-8	175	Trenton, Ont.	June 17, 1951	Hart.-Que.	28	125	4.89
Clint Malarchuk	5-10	172	Grande, Alta.	May 1, 1961	Fredericton (AHL)	50	333	6.88

WINNIPEG JETS

Now It Becomes Difficult

1981-82 Finish: Second, Norris Division.
Strengths: Well-run, progressive young club.
Weaknesses: Ahead of schedule?
Probable 1982-83 Finish: Second, Smythe Division.

''We came a long, long way,'' Tom Watt said, ''but it could get tougher from here on. In fact, it probably will.''

Winnipeg Jets, the team Watt directs, made the greatest leap forward in National Hockey League annals last season by advancing a staggering 48 points to a mix of 33 victories, 33 losses, and 14 ties. The resulting 80 points gave Jets second position in the Norris Division and 10th among all 21 of the NHL's members — and the feat got Watt the Jack Adams Award as the year's best coach.

''Building on that showing won't be easy because we're moving up into an area where the competition is considerably stronger,'' Watt noted.

''What I mean is, going from 10th to ninth is a lot more difficult than 21st to 20th. But there's certinly no reason why we shouldn't be every bit as eager. Getting eliminated in the first round of the playoffs, as we were, was a sobering experience. And there's the additional challenge of switching divisions, besides.''

Jets are shifting into the Smythe section in place of the Colorado Rockies, now stationed in New Jersey. That'll mean longer road trips, but four of the Jets' new divisional rivals had worse 1981-82 records than they did. Only the Edmonton Oilers were better.

''Our objectives will be fairly easy to define,'' Watt said. ''I mean that Stanley Cup loss underlined a lot of shortcomings. I think every individual on our roster can be expected to improve and, if that happens, our total performance ought to be better. Obviously, we'll be aiming to participate in more than four playoff matches.''

Watt, of course, represents the new breed of NHL coaches, having come from a background of college sport like Herb Brooks of the New York Rangers and the new man with Calgary Flames, Bob Johnson. The difference, in Watt's case, is that he's a Canadian, from the University of Toronto.

Watt's acquisition in the summer of 1981 was just one of many masterful moves made by general manager John Ferguson, others being deals for defenceman Serge Savard and goalies Ed Staniowski and Doug Soetart.

"Things broke awfully well for us all year," Ferguson cautions. "The only serious setback we had was the loss, due to a chronic hand injury, of captain Barry Long."

Serge Savard

Jets got their leader when John Ferguson finally persuaded defence great Serge Savard to give up retirement before the midway point in the 1981-82 schedule. He'd been working on the project since Savard left Montreal Canadiens the previous September.

"I knew he'd play tremendous hockey for us. He was only 36, after all," Ferguson said. "I knew he'd teach our guys a lot. And off the ice, he'd show the kids what it means to be a big leaguer and a winner."

And sure enough, it didn't take Savard long to become just as efficient as his old teammate predicted he'd be.

"It's unbelievable, the difference Serge made," said 20-year-old David Babych, one of Savard's eager pupils. "I learn just by watching him. Like, I previously thought of playing the man first and then the puck. He showed me how you've got to do both things at once."

Thomas Steen

Statistics reveal that, in terms of two-way effectiveness, rookie Thomas Steen from Sweden was Winnipeg's best player last season. That is to say he displayed the finest blend of defensive work, combined with offensive output.

Steen was only 21 when general manager John Ferguson signed him, but he already had three years' experience in the major Swedish league.

"Steen's got the high skill level you find among Swedes," said Ferguson, "and he has the extra dimension of being pretty tough. He can't be intimidated."

Coach Watt placed Steen at centre on a forward line with countrymen Bengt Lundholm and Willy Lindstrom. Steen had 44 points, Lundholm the same, and the veteran Lindstrom potted 32 goals and had 27 assists.

Dale Hawerchuk

It was strictly on merit that 18-year-old Dale Hawerchuk became the youngest person ever to take part in a NHL all-star game. He was on the 1982 Campbell Conference squad because he really was one of the best centres in that section.

In post-season voting, covering the entire loop, Hawerchuk was sixth in the all-star poll and received the Calder Trophy as the season's most outstanding rookie.

"He was also fifth for the most valuable player award, the Hart Trophy, and I think that's the most accurate of all," said Ferguson, "because he really was important in our scheme of things.

"We tried various schemes to ease the pressure on him, because he was carrying us. But he took it all in stride and handled it beautifully. He got us 104 points and if that's not a dynamite debut, tell me about one."

David Babych

"Suddenly, things began to click for me," says David Babych, speaking of his second season on the Winnipeg defence.

The first had been a nightmare. As Jets' No. 1 draft choice of 1980, Babych had to play regularly and he was up among the leaders in errors — naturally, because of his inexperience. He and his blueline colleagues threatened the NHL record for futility by giving up 400 opposition goals in 80 games.

"I learned because I don't think there was a costly mistake I didn't make," Babych admits. "It wasn't an enjoyable experience but it's paying off now. I'm glad I went through it."

Wearing No. 44, Babych has learned how to employ his

huge body to control Winnipeg territory and punish the enemy. And he exhibited impressive offensive skill last season, scoring or arranging 68 goals.

"I don't see how he can help being one of the very best in the business," says GM John Ferguson. "And I mean real soon."

Ed Staniowski

John Ferguson is blunt about it now: "We were going nowhere, spinning our wheels, until we could get reliable NHL goaltending."

Fergie took care of that little problem with a pair of 1981 deals.

First he sent defenceman Scott Campbell to St. Louis in exchange for Ed Staniowski, who had been the Blues' big netminding hope until Mike Liut checked in. Also in the package were Paul MacLean, a 36-goal winger for the 1981-82 Jets, and regular rearguard Bryan Maxwell.

Staniowski played 45 games last season, winning 20 and tying six.

A 13-14-8 mark belonged to Doug Soetart, who was obtained from the New York Rangers. He had been with the New York club when Ferguson was Ranger GM.

"They considered Soetart surplus. I knew he could play," says Ferguson. "These two guys are only 27, too, so we're in good shape for a while."

Morris Lukowich

The highest rating given any Winnipeg player by the NHL's 1981-82 all-star panel went to Morris Lukowich. Only Mark Messier, John Tonelli and Bill Barber received more votes among the left wingers.

"You define what you'd like a hockey player to do and you've pretty well described Luke," says coach Tom Watt. "He defends his position well. He covers his man, being one of the best skaters in the league. And he got us 43 goals, as well."

That total constituted a new high for Lukowich since he entered the NHL in 1979. He had played three years in the

World Hockey Association before that and had gone as high as 65 goals.

"Yet, with all that experience," Watt adds, "he's only 26."

Dave Christian

John Ferguson, the Winnipeg GM, is a student of thoroughbred racing and therefore a firm believer in bloodlines.

That's part of the reason he claimed centre Dave Christian in the 1979 amateur draft. The kid had great genes. A father and an uncle had played for the U.S. team that won the 1960 Olympic championship.

Two decades later, the younger Christian helped another American squad bag another set of gold medals.

Then he turned to professional competition with the Jets, and in his next 175 games, accounted for 165 points — 75 of them last season.

"Christian is only 23, so with him, Dale Hawerchuk, and Thomas Steen at centre, we're in a very favorable position there," says Ferguson. "Christian is the oldest and may be the fastest, but not by much."

Lucien DeBlois

The Jets didn't want Ivan Hlinka, but knew Vancouver Canucks did, so they claimed him in a special 1981 draft of Czechoslovakian players. In the shuffle that ensued, they wound up getting winger Lucien DeBlois as payment for giving up Hlinka.

"And we did want him," said Ferguson, who'd claimed DeBlois when working for the New York Rangers in 1977. "He's the kind of hard-working two-way guy you need to stock your team with. He's fast and he's got size, which is a must on the wings."

Rangers had traded DeBlois to Colorado Rockies, who had grabbed another of Vancouver's Czechs, Jiri Bubla.

The outcome was that the Rockies got Brent Ashton off the Canucks' roster, the Jets were given DeBlois, and Hlinka and Bubla wound up as Vancouver property.

"I believe," Ferguson said, "that everybody was happy when it was all settled."

**Tom Watt, Coach, Winnipeg Jets. Jack Adams
Award winner.**

JETS' 1982-83 ROSTER

1981-82 RECORD

Forwards	Ht.	Wt.	Place of Birth	Date	1981-82 Club	G	A	Pts.
Scott Arniel	6-1	170	Kingston, Ont.	Sept. 17, 1960	Winnipeg	1	8	9
Dave Christian	5-11	170	Warroad, Minn.	May 12, 1959	Winnipeg	25	51	76
Lucien DeBlois	5-11	200	Joliette, Que.	June 21, 1957	Winnipeg	25	27	52
Norm Dupont	5-10	185	Montreal, Que.	Feb. 5, 1957	Winnipeg	13	25	38
Dale Hawerchuk	5-11	170	Toronto, Ont.	April 4, 1963	Winnipeg	45	58	103
Larry Hopkins	6-1	214	Oshawa, Ont.	March 17, 1954	Winnipeg	10	15	25
Willy Lindstrom	6-1	172	Grunns, Sweden	May 5, 1951	Winnipeg	32	27	59
Morris Lukowich	5-9	167	Speers, Sask.	June 1, 1956	Winnipeg	43	49	92
Bengt Lundholm	6-0	165	Falun, Sweden	Aug. 4, 1955	Winnipeg	14	30	44
Paul MacLean	6-0	190	Grostenquin, France	March 9, 1958	Winnipeg	36	25	61
Jimmy Mann	6-0	202	Montreal, Que.	April 17, 1959	Winnipeg	3	2	5
Doug Smail	5-9	175	Moose Jaw, Sask.	Sept. 2, 1957	Winnipeg	17	18	35
Thomas Steen	5-10	195	Tockmark, Sweden	June 8, 1960	Winnipeg	15	29	44
Tim Trimper	5-9	185	Windsor, Ont.	Sept. 28, 1959	Winnipeg	8	8	16
Ron Wilson	5-9	168	Toronto, Ont.	May 13, 1956	Winnipeg	3	13	16

Defencemen								
David Babych	6-1	205	Edmonton, Alta.	May 23, 1961	Winnipeg	19	49	68
Craig Levie	5-10	192	Calgary, Alta.	Aug. 17, 1959	Winnipeg	4	9	13
Moe Mantha	6-2	197	Lakewood, Ohio	Jan. 21, 1961	Winnipeg	0	12	12
Bryan Maxwell	6-3	210	Lethbridge, Alta.	Sept. 7, 1955	Winnipeg	1	9	10
Serge Savard	6-2	210	Montreal, Que.	Jan. 22, 1946	Winnipeg	2	5	7
Don Spring	5-11	195	Maracaibo, Venezuela	June 15, 1959	Winnipeg	0	16	16
Tim Walters	5-11	180	Kamloops, B.C.	July 25, 1959	Winnipeg	2	22	24
Goalies						GPI	GA	Avg.
Doug Soetart	6-0	170	Edmonton, Alta.	April 21, 1955	Winnipeg	39	155	4.31
Ed Staniowski	5-9	170	Moose Jaw, Sask.	July 7, 1955	Winnipeg	45	174	3.95

Wayne Babych, St. Louis Blues

Dale Hawerchuk, Winnipeg Jets

Bob Sauve, Buffalo Sabres

John Anderson, Toronto Maple Leafs

Steve Kasper, Boston Bruins, Selke Trophy winner

Ron Duguay, New York Rangers

Gilles Meloche, Minnesota North Stars

Mike Bossy, New York Islanders

VANCOUVER CANUCKS

Roaring with Roger

1981-82 Finish: Second in Smythe, Stanley Cup final.
Strengths: Sound leadership, good team defence.
Weaknesses: Lack punch, balance, power play.
Probable 1982-83 Finish: Fourth.

Vancouver Canucks had an elaborate plan all worked out, ready to set in motion during the summer of 1982.

General manager Jake Milford would ascend to a loftier postion in the front office, to be replaced by head coach Harry Neale. Roger Neilson, Neale's assistant, would succeed him.

That timetable was advanced dramatically last April during the most successful and thrilling two-month period in the history of Vancouver's National Hockey League franchise.

It began, strangely enough, when Neale was suspended for a fracas with some spectators in the Coliseum at Quebec City. While he was serving his sentence, the club caught fire under Neilson — so much so that Neale, when his eligibility was restored, declined to tinker with a successful combination.

A strong finish edged Canucks into second place ahead of Calgary Flames in the Smythe Division standings. But that was only a hint of what lay ahead.

The Vancouver club, which never had won a Stanley Cup series, proceeded to knock off Calgary, Los Angeles Kings, and Chicago Black Hawks before yielding to the mighty New York Islanders in the championship round.

It was a magnificent triumph for the strategies and techniques Neilson had become famous for in previous NHL sojourns at Toronto and Buffalo — tight coverage, positional discipline and avoidance of all risk.

But it was also a vitally important boost for the organization, which had been facing indifference among its customers during yet another fruitless campaign.

"The people really got behind us, and that was something we needed desperately," said Neale. "What we did in the playoffs restored our credibility, I feel. It certified a lot of the moves we'd been making. And I can think of about a dozen players whose confidence was totally renewed.

"All in all, I would have to think it was a major turning point for this club."

Milford couldn't have sung a sweeter swan song. Canucks are very much his handiwork, the result of deals all over the NHL and in Sweden and Czechoslovakia, and of wise scouting and shrewd drafting, and of praiseworthy patience.

"I think we have an excellent future," said Milford, who's now a senior vice-president. "Look at a kid like Neil Belland, coming right out of junior hockey when we ran into injuries on defence. Garth Butcher, who was the top defenceman in the western juniors, didn't look out of place with us late in the season and in the playoffs. Moe Lemay was all-star left wing in Ontario. And Patrik Sundstrom, our newest Swede, is something extra special."

Kevin McCarthy

Canucks' 1982 playoff achievements become even more remarkable when you bear in mind they were playing without the man generally considered their best defenceman — Kevin McCarthy, their captain.

McCarthy broke an ankle in a voluntary workout just before the opening series against Calgary began.

"Looking back, I can't see where we had a weakness," said coach Roger Neilson, "but logic says we'd have been stronger if McCarthy had been able to play."

McCarthy, 25, was obtained during the 1978-79 season in the deal that sent Dennis Ververgaert to Philadelphia.

Thomas Gradin

General manager Harry Neale finds Thomas Gradin amazing in a number of ways, but one he often mentions is the Swedish centre's unselfishness.

Gradin doesn't think it's a remarkable quality. Says he: "It makes no difference who gets the points as long as we win. Look at it this way: if we lose, the points you get mean nothing whatever."

Even so, Gradin accounts for more than his share of goals and assists. He led Canucks all the way last term with 86 points during the regular schedule and 19 more in the playoffs.

Afterwards, Gradin ended speculation that Canada's tough tax laws would drive him back to Europe by signing a new contract with Vancouver. Canucks had first acquired him in a 1978 deal with Chicago Black Hawks.

Dave Williams

Tiger Williams was worrying management in the early stages of the 1981-82 campaign. A 35-goal man the year before, he had just four after his first 22 matches and had gone eight without incurring a penalty.

"It wasn't the lack of goals that was troubling me. He was letting the rest of his work slip," said Harry Neale, then the coach. "He wasn't hitting. And the guys on the other teams weren't screaming at him. He wasn't causing trouble and, when he isn't doing that, he's not effective."

Williams got back in gear before long and, although he ended up with only 17 goals, he was second in the league with 341 penalty minutes — normal, in other words.

He was at his irascible, irritating best in the playoffs. His combative zeal had a lot to do with Canucks' splendid showing and, to keep the fires ablaze, he had to serve 116 minutes more. Of the three goals he had, two were decisive in Vancouver victories.

Stan Smyl

The nickname tells you a great deal about Stan Smyl. He's known as Steamer — "because he chugs straight ahead," says GM Harry Neale.

Smyl believes in the work ethic, that your rewards are in keeping with what you put out and that there's no easy route to success.

"This is why he's so popular with the spectators, because he's got 'try' written all over him," Neale adds.

Smyl was a well-liked junior in neighbouring New Westminster and the Vancouver club drafted him in 1978. His industrious approach was particularly productive in the defensive end of the playoffs last April and May. He produced nine goals and nine assists.

Ivan Hlinka

Vancouverites didn't appreciate it at first but Ivan Hlinka, a newcomer there last season, has been one of the world's most famous hockey players.

He posted a career total of 848 points in Czechoslovakia's main league and collected another 355 in 269 appearances with the national side. He was the all-star centre, ahead of the NHL's best, in the 1976 Canada Cup tournament.

Jake Milford hired Hlinka and defenceman Jiri Bubla in 1981 after Czech authorities agreed to let them compete in North America. Bubla's debut was postponed by a broken ankle but centre Hlinka, after a tentative beginning, got the Canucks 23 goals and 37 assists.

"He has something you don't see too often any more, a great wrist shot," said Milford. "He's big and mobile, and at 31 ought to get better once he learns the ropes about playing in the NHL."

Lars Molin

Canucks scouted Sweden's Lars Molin at the 1981 world championships in Stockholm and Gothenburg, and confirmed their findings during the Canada Cup that autumn. Molin was signed immediately afterwards.

"He's fast. He shoots well. He's clever with the puck. And he can play at any position on the forward line," said Harry Neale.

"And I like his toughness."

Molin was a great success throughout the 1981-82 schedule, but was even more useful in the playoffs when he put in two winning goals and assisted on nine other scores.

Richard Brodeur

Canucks originally acquired Richard Brodeur as netminding insurance, a dependable backup for Glen Hanlon. That was their thinking when they got him from the Islanders just before the start of the 1980-81 schedule.

Injuries continued to plague Hanlon that year and Brodeur was even more important than his new employers had anticipated.

There was another development last season. Canucks decided Brodeur, 29, would be their first-stringer of the future and used Hanlon in a trade with St. Louis.

Brodeur admitted to no surprise concerning this turn of events. "All I ever wanted or needed," he said, "was a chance to play regularly in the NHL."

He started all 17 of Canucks' playoff matches and lost only six of them.

Jim Nill

Scrappy Jim Nill is the ninth member of Canada's 1980 Olympic squad to find steady employment in the NHL.

He had turned professional in the St. Louis organization after the Lake Placid competition and, as a rookie pro, made the Central League's second all-star team at right wing.

That earned him advancement to St. Louis' NHL lineup, but near the end of the 1981-82 schedule, he and Tony Currie were traded to the Canucks for goalie Glen Hanlon.

"It was a stroke of luck because we got to the Stanley Cup playoffs," says Nill, "and I'm not just talking about the extra bonus money I collected. It was great experience."

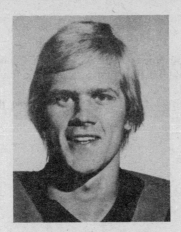

Thomas Gradin

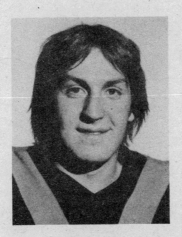

Stan Smyl

CANUCKS' 1982-83 ROSTER

Forwards	Ht.	Wt.	Place of Birth	Date	1981-82 Club	G	A	Pts.
Ivan Boldirev	6-0	190	Zrenjanin, Yugoslavia	Aug. 15, 1949	Vancouver	33	40	.73
Per-Olov Brasar	5-9	175	Falun, Sweden	Sept. 30, 1950	Vancouver	6	12	18
Marc Crawford	5-11	183	Belleville, Ont.	Feb. 13, 1961	Vancouver	4	8	12
Tony Currie	5-11	170	Sydney Mines, N.S.	Nov. 12, 1956	St. L.-Van.	23	25	48
Ron Delorme	6-2	185	North Battleford, Sask.	Sept. 3, 1955	Vancouver	9	8	17
Curt Fraser	6-0	195	Cincinnati, Ohio	Jan. 12, 1958	Vancouver	28	39	67
Thomas Gradin	5-11	175	Solleftea, Sweden	Feb. 18, 1956	Vancouver	37	49	86
Ivan Hlinka	6-2	213	Most, CSSR	Jan. 26, 1950	Vancouver	23	37	60
Moe Lemay	5-11	172	Saskatoon, Sask.	Feb. 18, 1962	Ottawa (OMJHL)	68	70	138
Gary Lupul	5-9	172	Powell River, B.C.	April 4, 1959	Vancouver	10	7	17
Blair MacDonald	5-10	180	Cornwall, Ont.	Nov. 17, 1953	Vancouver	18	15	33
Gerry Minor	5-8	172	Regina, Sask.	Oct. 27, 1958	Vancouver	0	1	1
Lars Molin	6-0	165	Ornskoldsvik, Sweden	May 7, 1956	Vancouver	15	31	46
Jim Nill	6-0	175	Hanna, Alta.	April 11, 1958	St. L.-Van.	10	14	24
Darcy Rota	5-11	190	Vancouver, B.C.	Feb. 16, 1953	Vancouver	20	20	40
Stan Smyl	5-8	190	Glendon, Alta.	Jan. 23, 1958	Vancouver	34	44	78
Dave Williams	5-11	195	Weyburn, Sask.	Feb. 3, 1954	Vancouver	17	21	38

1981-82 RECORD

Defencemen

Name	Ht	Wt	Birthplace	Birthdate	Team			
Neil Belland	5-11	175	Parry Sound, Ont.	April 3, 1961	Vancouver	3	6	9
Garth Butcher	6-0	185	Regina, Sask.	Jan. 8, 1963	Regina — western all-star		NA	8
Colin Campbell	5-9	160	London, Ont.	Jan. 28, 1953	Vancouver	0	8	8
Anders Eldebrink	5-11	187	Kalix, Sweden	Dec. 11, 1960	Vancouver	1	8	9
Doug Halward	6-1	184	Toronto, Ont.	Nov. 1, 1955	Vancouver	4	13	17
Rick Lanz	6-2	195	Karlovy Vary, CSSR	Sept. 16, 1961	Vancouver	3	11	14
Lars Lindgren	6-1	205	Pitea, Sweden	Oct. 12, 1952	Vancouver	5	16	21
Kevin McCarthy	5-11	195	Winnipeg, Man.	July 14, 1957	Vancouver	6	39	45
Harold Snepsts	6-3	215	Edmonton, Alta.	Oct. 24, 1954	Vancouver	3	14	17

Goalies

Name	Ht	Wt	Birthplace	Birthdate	Team	GPI	GA	Avg.
Richard Brodeur	5-7	160	Longueuil, Que.	Sept. 15, 1952	Vancouver	52	168	3.35
Frank Caprice	5-9	147	Hamilton, Ont.	May 2, 1962	London (OMJHL)	45	196	4.50
Wendell Young	5-8	178	Halifax, N.S.	Aug. 1, 1963	Kitchener (OMJHL)	60	195	3.37

PITTSBURGH PENGUINS

A Very Potent Power Play

1981-82 Finish: Fourth, Patrick Division.
Strengths: Power play, kids, coaching.
Weaknesses: Defence, depth.
Probable 1982-83 Finish: Up to second.

It's not a good idea to take a lot of penalties when you're playing against the Pittsburgh Penguins.

This is a lesson several National Hockey League teams learned, at great cost, last season. Penguins' power play established a record by scoring 99 times while the opposition was operating shorthanded.

"Your so-called 'special' units are becoming vital in the NHL now," coach Eddie (E.J.) Johnston said. "Once we get our penalty killing up to the same level as the power play, we'll be in excellent shape.

"The thing is, see, a club will be intimidated in the way it plays if it knows penalties can result in a lot of damage. It's an edge Islanders enjoy. A lot of people try to play cautiously against them because penalties are so harmful. That hurts their chances. And the Islanders themselves operate confidently because they know they can kill penalties so well."

Johnston deploys two specialists when the enemy is under-staffed: Paul Gardner at centre, and defenceman Randy Carlyle on the point.

Gardner led the NHL with 21 power-play goals last season, even though he missed 21 matches because of a broken jaw. And Carlyle's 64 assists was tops for rearguards.

"Actually," E.J. noted, "our plans were upset somewhat. Mario Faubert was supposed to be on the right point but he broke a leg and missed the rest of the schedule."

The 1981-82 Penguins were one point better than they'd been the year before, but moved up to 12th place from 15th in the combined NHL tables.

"That's about where we belong, in the middle," Johnston conceded. "To rise much further, we've got to get some numbers, some depth. That's why we've started up an American League farm team.

"At the same time, we're very happy with the juniors we've been breaking in — Steve Gatzos, Kevin McClelland, Randy Boyd, Doug Shedden and Pat Graham. And I think we struck oil in the 1982 junior draft."

Penguins' claim last June was right winger Rich Sutter of the famous Alberta clan.

Michel Dion

Coach Eddie Johnston is an expert on goalies, having been one himself. And he wasn't a bit concerned when Greg Millen left the Pittsburgh organization in 1981 and signed with Hartford as a free agent.

"I knew the guy we were signing, Michel Dion, would be the best in the league," E.J. said.

He had seen Dion play for Winnipeg and Quebec and, though greatly impressed, had diagnosed that Dion had poor vision.

Specialists in Pittsburgh agreed and fitted the newcomer with contact lenses. Johnston's prophecy was fulfilled. Dion won 25 and tied 12 of 61 netminding decisions and placed third when NHL general managers rated all goalies for the new Vezina Trophy.

Paul Gardner

Winnipeg's Jimmy Mann was suspended for the punch which broke Paul Gardner's jaw last January. Without that mishap, there's no telling what the crafty Pittsburgh centre might have achieved.

He counted 36 goals and 33 assists in the 59 games he did play.

"But I had been unable to eat properly during the time my jaw was wired up," he pointed out, "so I was weak and underweight when I finally did rejoin the club. That injury cost me a lot more than 21 games."

Gardner was a 30-goal man in each of his first three NHL seasons but the Toronto Maple Leafs sent him to the minors because his defensive work didn't satisfy them.

Penguins dealt for him in late 1980 and he has given them 143 points in 121 matches.

Rick Kehoe

From career peaks of 55 goals and 88 points, Rick Kehoe slipped to 33-85 last season but pronounced himself content with his 1981-82 results. He was Pittsburgh's leading producer, and he played well.

"I've never thought a lot about statistics in themselves. They're only numbers. My objective always has been just to play consistently," says Kehoe, a 31-year-old right wing. "I think it's a mistake to put pressure on yourself by shooting for certain totals."

Adds coach Johnston: "He'll always get his share because he's a good scorer by nature. He doesn't need many chances. Give him three in a game and he'll get you a goal for sure."

Paul Baxter

The NHL crowned a new penalty king last season in Pittsburgh — defenceman Paul Baxter. And apart from the 452 minutes Dave Shultz had served seven years before, Baxter's 407 minutes were the most in history.

"I'm not proud of being first in that category, but I happily admit that I play a rough style of hockey," says Baxter, 26.

"I do object to being labelled a goon, however. That is simply not true. My approach to the game is tough and physical but I'm not out there to injure or intimidate anybody."

Baxter had NHL and World Hockey Association background before Penguins signed him in 1980 after his contract with Quebec Nordiques had expired. They gave Nordiques Curt Brackenbury, who's now Edmonton property, as compensation.

Randy Carlyle

"I had a lot to prove last season," says Randy Carlyle.
He was determined to demonstrate it hadn't been a fluke

when he was named the NHL's top defenceman at the end of the 1980-81 season. At the same time, he was anxious to offset the embarrassment of having been released by Team Canada 1981 at its summer training camp.

"Well, I didn't make all-star," Carlyle notes in review, "but I was satisfied that I had accomplished what I set out to do."

Given enormous responsibility by coach Johnston, the 26-year-old ex-Leaf again handled most of the difficult defensive situations and directed Penguins' attack with his very special playmaking skills.

Mike Bullard

There was something strange about the voting for the Calder Trophy last spring. Pittsburgh centre Mike Bullard didn't receive a single nod.

"I don't say he should have won it, but he definitely deserved to be among the leading rookie candidates," said Johnston. "Maybe they didn't realize he was eligible."

Bullard had played 15 games for the 1980-81 Penguins and then was sent back to the Brantford, Ont. juniors for further seasoning.

"It was the best thing that ever happened to me," said Bullard, 21. "It relieved the pressure. I had a chance to build up my strength and acquire some maturity."

The youngster worked the full 1981-82 campaign and had 37 goals.

Pat Boutette

The Penguins were unconcerned in 1981 when goalie Greg Millen left. In some ways, they were even pleased. They knew they were signing an adequate replacement in Michel Dion. And Hartford Whalers, who hired Millen, had to turn over some bodies to make up for the loss.

One was an excellent junior, Kevin McClelland. The other was veteran left winger Pat Boutette.

"A team's got to have a fiery, gung-ho competitor like Boutette," said Johnston. "I'll never know why Toronto traded him to Hartford in the first place. Guys like him make you win."

With Whalers, Boutette also had bloomed as a good scorer, enjoying an 80-point year. On a Pittsburgh line with Paul Gardner and Rick Kehoe last season, he posted 23 goals and 51 assists.

Rick MacLeish

Pittsburgh general manager Baz Bastien thinks he got a bargain last season when he obtained Rick MacLeish from Hartford in exchange for defenceman Russ Anderson.

"Here's a 32-year-old guy who's one of the best scorers in the NHL and who's got a background of winning Stanley Cups," Bastien says. "And for an easy skater like him, 32 is young."

MacLeish had counted 317 goals in nine complete years with Philadelphia, capturing the 1974 and '75 playoff championships. Transferred to Hartford, he failed to produce and Whalers gave up — too quickly, in Bastien's view.

"The pattern of his career shows he bounces back with a big season after being below normal," Bastien notes. "If it happens again, we've got ourselves a real bonus."

Paul Baxter

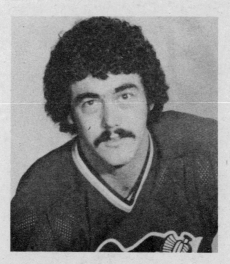

Rick Kehoe

PENGUINS' 1982-83 ROSTER

| | | | | | 1981-82 RECORD | | |
Forwards	Ht.	Wt.	Place of Birth	Date	1981-82 Club	G	A	Pts.
Pat Boutette	5-8	175	Windsor, Ont.	March 1, 1952	Pittsburgh	23	51	74
Mike Bullard	5-10	185	Ottawa, Ont.	March 10, 1961	Pittsburgh	37	27	64
George Ferguson	6-0	195	Trenton, Ont.	Aug. 22, 1952	Pittsburgh	22	31	53
Paul Gardner	5-11	178	Toronto, Ont.	March 5, 1956	Pittsburgh	36	33	69
Steve Gatzos	5-11	182	Toronto, Ont.	June 22, 1961	Pittsburgh	6	8	14
Pat Graham	6-1	190	Toronto, Ont.	May 25, 1961	Pittsburgh	6	8	14
Jim Hamilton	6-0	180	Barrie, Ont.	Jan. 18, 1957	Pittsburgh	5	3	8
Rick Kehoe	5-11	180	Windsor, Ont.	July 15, 1951	Pittsburgh	33	52	85
Peter Lee	5-9	180	Ellesmere, England	Jan. 2, 1956	Pittsburgh	18	16	34
Rick MacLeish	5-11	185	Lindsay, Ont.	Jan. 3, 1950	Hart.-Pitt.	19	28	47
Greg Malone	6-0	190	Fredericton, N.B.	March 8, 1956	Pittsburgh	15	24	39
Keven McClelland	6-0	180	Oshawa, Ont.	July 4, 1962	OMJHL-Pitts.	1	4	5
Rod Schutt	5-10	185	Bancroft, Ont.	Oct. 13, 1956	Pittsburgh	8	12	20
Doug Shedden	6-0	184	Wallaceburg, Ont.	April 26, 1951	Pittsburgh	10	15	25
Gregg Sheppard	5-8	170	North Battleford, Sask.	April 23, 1949	Pittsburgh	11	10	21
Andre St. Laurent	5-10	178	Rouyn-Noranda, Que.	Feb. 16, 1953	L.A.-Pitt.	10	9	19

Defencemen								
Paul Baxter	5-11	200	Winnipeg, Man.	Oct. 25, 1955	Pittsburgh	9	34	43
Randy Boyd	5-11	195	Coniston, Ont.	Jan. 23, 1962	Ottawa (OMJHL)	9	29	38
Randy Carlyle	5-10	200	Sudbury, Ont.	April 19,1956	Pittsburgh	11	64	75
Marc Chorney	6-0	200	Sudbury, Ont.	Nov. 8, 1952	Pittsburgh	1	6	7
Mario Faubert	6-1	175	Valleyfield, Que.	Dec. 2, 1954	Pittsburgh	4	8	12
Greg Hotham	5-11	183	London, Ont.	March 7, 1956	Tor.-Pitt.	4	6	10
Pat Price	6-2	200	Nelson, B.C.	March 24, 1955	Pittsburgh	7	31	38
Ron Stackhouse	6-3	210	Haliburton, Ont.	Aug. 26, 1949	Pittsburgh	2	19	21
Goalies						**GPI**	**GA**	**Avg.**
Michel Dion	5-10	184	Granby, Que.	Feb. 11, 1954	Pittsburgh	62	226	3.79
Gary Edwards	5-9	165	Toronto, Ont.	Oct. 5, 1947	Ed.-St. L.-Pitt.	16	67	4.25
Nick Ricci	5-10	160	Niagara Falls, Ont.	June 3, 1959	Erie (AHL)	39	174	4.65

CALGARY FLAMES

That Was a Fizzle

1981-82 Finish: Third, Smythe Division.
Strengths: Splendid attack, excellent coach.
Weaknesses: Rebuilding, defence a question.
Probable 1982-83 Finish: Third again.

Stung by unsatisfactory 1981-82 results, Calgary Flames sallied forth dramatically to put their house in order.

"Well, the time had come to act," said general manager Cliff Fletcher, pointing to the club's poorest National Hockey League showing since 1974, and a quick exit from the opening round of the Stanley Cup tournament.

"And yet," Fletcher added, "we remain convinced we've got a lot of the right ingredients."

If that really is the case, Fletcher's summertime manoeuvres could very well bear fruit in the campaign ahead. He boldly broke new ground with his selection of a new coach, importing Bob Johnson from U.S. college hockey to replace Al MacNeil, who was made director of personnel.

And then Fletcher improved his goaltending by obtaining talented Don Edwards from the Buffalo Sabres.

Those definitely were the patch-up moves of an executive who's convinced his roster is basically sound.

"You can't excuse what happened in the playoffs," Fletcher noted, "but as far as the regular season is concerned, you've got to remember how badly we were hurt by injuries to Kent Nilsson, Guy Chouinard and Paul Reinhart. Nobody can withstand losses like that."

Johnson's coaching career closely parallels that of Herb Brooks, who accomplished so much with last season's New York Rangers — college success, coupled with international experience.

In 15 years at the University of Wisconsin, Johnson won three U.S. national championships. He handled America's entries at the 1981 world tournament and in the Canada Cup that fall, and produced impressive teams in both instances.

"I think it'll be a great advantage to have worked with professionals in those two competitions last year," says Johnson. "And I've kept in close touch with the NHL scene because my son, Mark, has been playing there."

The pioneering angle to Fletcher's decision, of course, concerned going outside Canada to fill the vacancy created by MacNeil's promotion.

To help make the incoming boss feel at home, Fletcher acquired a couple of the NHL's more accomplished American players, Steve Christoff and Bill Nyrop, sending Willi Plett to the Minnesota North Stars in exchange.

Johnson's appointment is crucial, of course, for a franchise which entered the NHL at the same time the New York Islanders did and suffers badly in any comparison.

But the acquisition of Edwards is almost as important.

"The emphasis in the NHL is on offence these days," Fletcher admitted, "but the guy between the pipes still makes or breaks you. That's the bottom line in hockey."

Lanny McDonald

Flames always had talent, oodles of it, but lacked that intangible something or other called leadership. It's what they were after when they dealt Don Lever and Bob MacMillan to the Colorado Rockies for Lanny McDonald early last season.

"Character is the one word that comes to mind," said Calgary GM Cliff Fletcher, "when you watch the way Lanny plays hockey and conducts himself at all times. It's a quality we needed."

McDonald, who turned pro with Toronto in 1973, played 55 games for the 1981-82 Flames and counted 67 scoring points. He upped his 10-year goals total to 310.

"He's got that great wrist shot, one of the best," Fletcher noted, "and he's also a super checker who gives you a strong physical game. He really knows the art of bodychecking."

Don Edwards

No list of the NHL's best goalies would be complete without the name of Don Edwards, who joins Calgary after six excellent seasons with the Buffalo Sabres. Flames, liberally supplied with youth, gave up a package of draft futures to get him and defenceman Richie Dunn from the Sabres last summer.

"When we were picking the Team Canada roster last year, everybody agreed Edwards would have to be one of the netminders," said Calgary boss Cliff Fletcher. "That was good enough for me."

Actually, Edwards was No. 3 man for the Canadian selection, behind Mike Liut and Bill Smith.

Only 27 now, Edwards was the NHL's second all-star in 1978 and won a share of the 1980 Vezina Trophy. He appeared in 62 games last season, one of the NHL's heaviest workloads.

Kent Nilsson

They call Kent Nilsson "Mr. Magic" because of the things he can do, so easily, with a hockey puck. The Flames rewarded him last spring with the richest contract ever given a Swedish player.

"He's our big guy, our Wayne Gretzky," says Fletcher, "and it's just up to us to give him the right tools to work with."

Nilsson had amassed 131 points during the 1980-81 campaign, but had a severe shoulder separation as Flames commenced their first year in Calgary. Ultimately, he got into only 41 games, too late to salvage much from a very bad term.

Still, his statistics speak eloquently of his offensive skills — 279 points in 201 matches since he was reclaimed from Winnipeg's World Hockey Association roster in 1979.

Guy Chouinard

In 1974, at the time of the World Hockey Association player raids, the NHL permitted each of its members to draft one 18-year-old junior. Flames, then in Atlanta, selected a Quebecker named Guy Chouinard.

Three unproductive years ensued and some members of the organization wanted to get rid of the youngster. Chief scout Don Graham fought the idea and eventually convinced his associates to give Chouinard another chance.

Just look now at what Chouinard has done over the past four seasons — 347 points in 272 games.

A severe groin injury kept Chouinard out of 16 Calgary matches last season and had a lot to do with the club's early failures. But he eventually played 64 times, producing 80 points.

And consider this: Because of that early beginning, Chouinard is still a youngster of 25.

Mel Bridgman

In Kent Nilsson and Guy Chouinard, Flames have two of the NHL's slickest centres, but there was an important element missing.

"You also need muscle through the middle," said GM Cliff Fletcher "and we didn't have it."

Stocky Mel Bridgman was the prototype of what Fletcher wanted. And he eventually did get Bridgman from Philadelphia. But the price was steep — captain Brad Marsh.

"Luckily for us, Philly had to have some help on defence," Fletcher explained.

Bridgman, 27, generated the best attack of his career with 26 goals and 49 assists in 63 Calgary games.

"A lot of that was due to increased ice time," Bridgman said. "In Philly, we had people like Bobby Clarke, Rick MacLeish and Kenny Linseman to play centre in the good offensive situations. Here, Nilsson and Chouinard were out so I got a lot of chances."

Paul Reinhart

Originally, as a junior, Paul Reinhart played centre. The transition to defence was made shortly before he became a 19-year-old rookie with the 1979-80 Flames.

"My defensive work needed a lot of attention," says Reinhart, "but all that background as a forward was useful because today's defenceman handles the puck a lot and is expected to be an integral part of the offence.

"But you have to keep a lid on your attacking instincts and remember what your basic responsibility is."

After playing on the home side in the 1981 Canada Cup, Reinhart missed 18 Calgary games while an ankle injury was mending. Then in April, after the Flames were eliminated from the Stanley Cup playoffs, he went to Finland for the 1981 world championships. He was named one of the three best players on Canada's third-place entry.

Pekka Rautakallio

It could be that Calgary's Kent Nilsson is the best Swedish player in the NHL. And the Flames are utterly convinced defenceman Pekka Rautakallio is the finest Finn.

Rautakallio had returned to his old Finnish club in 1977 after two professional campaigns with the Phoenix Roadrunners in the World Hockey Association. Flames signed him in 1979.

"So he had a pro background. That was a help. There was no adjustment period. He could step right in," noted Fletcher. "Pekka has the playmaking skills and the shot to run our offence from the blue line."

The 1981-82 campaign was Rautakallio's most prolific ever — 17 goals and 51 assists — but at the end, he was contemplating retirement and a return to Finland.

Jim Peplinski

Patience and restraint paid off handsomely for the Flames in the case of centre Jim Peplinski.

They claimed Peplinski in the 1979 junior draft, but left him with Toronto Marlboros for an additional winter of education and preparation.

Peplinski also completed his college studies and, when he finally did enter the NHL in 1980, it was as a finished product. He had 13 goals and 25 assists as a freshman, then went 30-37 last season as injuries to Kent Nilsson and Guy Chouinard caused him to assume extra duties.

An ironic angle is that Peplinski developed under Maple Leaf noses in their Toronto building and didn't go to the Flames until round five of the draft, the 75th player taken.

Pekka Rautakallio

Paul Reinhart

FLAMES' 1982-83 ROSTER

1981-82 RECORD

Forwards	Ht.	Wt.	Place of Birth	Date	1981-82 Club	G	A	Pts.
Mel Bridgman	6-0	190	Trenton, Ont.	April 28, 1955	Phil.-Cal.	33	54	87
Guy Chouinard	5-11	182	Quebec City, Que.	Oct. 20, 1956	Calgary	23	57	80
Steve Christoff	6-1	180	Richfield, Minn.	Jan. 23, 1958	Minnesota	26	30	56
Denis Cyr	5-11	186	Verdun, Que.	Feb. 4, 1961	Calgary	12	10	22
Jamie Hislop	5-10	180	Sarnia, Ont.	Jan. 20, 1954	Calgary	16	25	41
Dan Labraaten	6-0	190	Leksand, Sweden	June 9, 1951	Calgary	10	12	22
Kevin Lavallee	5-8	180	Sudbury, Ont.	Sept. 16, 1951	Calgary	32	29	61
Lanny McDonald	6-0	190	Hanna, Alta.	Feb. 16, 1953	Col.-Cal.	40	42	82
Kent Nilsson	6-1	185	Nynashann, Sweden	Aug. 31, 1956	Calgary	26	29	55
Jim Peplinski	6-2	201	Renfrew, Ont.	Oct. 24, 1960	Calgary	30	37	67

Defencemen

Name			Birthplace	Birthdate	Team			
Charles Bourgeois	6-4	205	Moncton, N.B.	Nov. 11, 1959	Calgary	2	13	15
Richie Dunn	6-0	192	Boston, Mass.	May 13, 1957	Buffalo	7	19	26
Steve Konroyd	6-0	195	Scarborough, Ont.	Feb. 10, 1961	Calgary	3	14	17
Bill Nyrop	6-2	205	Washington, D.C.	July 23, 1952	Minnesota	4	8	12
Pekka Rautakallio	5-11	185	Pari, Finland	July 25, 1953	Calgary	17	51	68
Paul Reinhart	5-11	216	Kitchener, Ont.	Jan. 8, 1960	Calgary	13	48	61
Pat Ribble	6-4	210	Leamington, Ont.	April 26, 1954	Wash.-Cal.	1	2	3
Phil Russell	6-2	200	Edmonton, Alta.	July 6, 1952	Calgary	4	25	29

Goalies

Name			Birthplace	Birthdate	Team	GPI	GA	Avg.
Don Edwards	5-9	160	Hamilton, Ont.	Sept. 28, 1955	Buffalo	62	205	3.51
Rejean Lemelin	5-11	160	Sherbrooke, Que.	Nov. 19, 1954	Calgary	34	135	4.34

ST. LOUIS BLUES

Another Life for the Cat

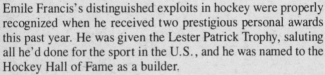

1981-82 Finish: Third, Norris Division.
Strengths: Fine attack, good reinforcements.
Weaknesses: Thin on defence.
Probable 1982-83 Finish: Second.

Emile Francis's distinguished exploits in hockey were properly recognized when he received two prestigious personal awards this past year. He was given the Lester Patrick Trophy, saluting all he'd done for the sport in the U.S., and he was named to the Hockey Hall of Fame as a builder.

The 56-year-old Cat does not propose to rest on those well-deserved laurels. Indeed, if he conquers the latest challenge he has tackled, only a combination of the Victoria Cross and the Congressional Medal of Honor will suffice.

Francis, who's been president and general manager of the St. Louis Blues, is now the coach, too. In other words, he's doing the work of three men, with the Stanley Cup and the National Hockey League championship as his twin objectives.

"I really believe we now have the talent necessary to do precisely that, to be No. 1," Francis stated.

It was Francis's confidence in Blues' personnel that prompted him to replace coach Red Berenson near the end of the 1981-82 schedule. From second spot the year before, Blues had descended to the nether regions of the standings and were playing ineptly.

"I knew we had certain shortcomings," Francis allowed, "but I still felt we should have been better than we were."

Under Francis's supervision, Blues held third spot in the Norris Division and upset the Winnipeg Jets in the opening playoff round.

That was encouraging. And a couple of personnel moves Francis swung occasioned even greater optimism.

He dealt with Vancouver Canucks for Glen Hanlon, one of the brightest young netminding stars in all of hockey. So now, in Hanlon and Mike Liut, Blues are extraordinarily strong at the most important position.

Then, in the summer, Francis obtained defenceman Rob Ramage from the Colorado Rockies. The cost was heavy — Blues' first-round draft choices in 1982 and '83. But Ramage himself had been the premier pick of '79.

"We'd have to finish at or near the bottom of the heap to draft anybody as good as Ramage," Francis reasoned. "And getting a quality defenceman had become an absolute must for us — now. That was the missing ingredient.

"It's no secret defence has been our glaring weakness. But we've improved tremendously there. Besides, getting Ramage, which was the key, we have a great veteran in Guy Lapointe and we've been working in a couple of excellent juniors, Jim Pavese and Ric Wilson."

Mike Liut

A whisper around the NHL last season hinted Mike Liut, No. 1 goalie the year before, had lost his touch. The rumor said he'd been totally demoralized by Canada's loss to Russia in the Canada Cup final.

"That's really crazy," retorted St. Louis boss Emile Francis. "He could even be better than before. Most nights, he's our best man. But he's just not getting the same help from the rest of our team. That's the only difference."

Liut, 26, played in 64 games, more than any other NHL netminder, and of 63 decisions, won 28, lost 28 and tied seven.

He'll be able to get more relief in the future. In a spring transaction, Francis acquired Glen Hanlon, who had starred in Vancouver before running into a series of knee injuries.

Joe Mullen

Here's the first NHL player developed in the Manhattan kids' leagues, a subway ride away from Madison Square Garden. Joe Mullen came along too late to be a candidate for the 1982 Calder Trophy but made an indelible impression, just the same.

He had scored 21 goals in the Central League when Blues

called him in last December 30. From that point on, he played in 45 NHL matches and accumulated 25 goals and 34 assists, tacking on a splendid 7-and-11 playoff mark.

Mullen turned down a bid to join the successful U.S. Olympic team and started out in pro competition instead, becoming the top 1979-80 CHL rookie. The following winter, he was scoring champion on the same circuit.

Rob Ramage

Playing for the hopeless Colorado Rockies got to be discouraging, Rob Ramage now admits, and his work was beginning to deteriorate.

"When you're with a struggling team, you try to take things into your own hands and do it all," he says. "And that just won't work. Then you get deeper in the dumps."

Ramage had been counted upon to rescue the Denver franchise after being signed in 1979, and the burden increased when Barry Beck was traded away. After three years of growing frustration, Ramage asked to be dealt to another team and that wish was granted in the summer when he was transferred to St. Louis.

"In giving up so much to get me, St. Louis demonstrated a lot of confidence in me and now I'll attempt to repay them," Ramage vows.

Wayne Babych

The 1981-82 campaign was simply a nightmare for right winger Wayne Babych.

He had scored 54 goals the previous year and was looking forward to more of the same. But, after bruising a shoulder in an exhibition match, he missed the first month of the schedule. The injury was repeated in January, causing another absence. And he ripped up a knee during the Stanley Cup playoffs.

Altogether, Babych was unavailable for 32 faceoffs. He shot 19 goals during the regular campaign even so, and another three prior to his playoff crash.

"Maybe I had my quota of injury problems all at once," says Babych who, at just 24, can be expected to reclaim his old excellence.

Perry Turnbull

When hockey men discuss the NHL's most respected scrappers, left winger Perry Turnbull is invariably mentioned. Large and tough, he has assembled an impressive string of fisted victories.

He's also a skillful two-way forward, so all in all, Blues' playoff hopes plummeted last spring when his right leg was slashed for 35 stitches. A tendon was severed, too, requiring surgical repairs.

Turnbull, 23, had scored 33 goals during the regular 1981-82 schedule for a three-year NHL total of 83.

Brian Sutter

Back in 1977, when he joined St. Louis, Brian Sutter established a pattern that would be duplicated by each of his five younger brothers. All six of the Alberta farm boys are now employed by NHL clubs and they're much the same: talented, intensely competitive, each a catalyst for his teammates.

The eldest NHL Sutter at 25, Brian is the St. Louis captain. Typically, he led last season's Blues in goals (39) and penalty minutes (239). Also typically, he was at his best in Stanley Cup combat with 14 points in 10 games.

"Let me put it this way," says Emile Francis, "no NHL team should be without a Sutter. It's an essential part of your equipment, like a skate sharpener."

Bernie Federko

It's only a matter of time now until Bernie Federko becomes the leading attacker in the history of the St. Louis franchise.

With 449 career points, he's second only to Garry Unger. And because he's only 26, he should soon move into first place.

"The way offence is emphasized in the NHL now, you have got to have a big gun like Federko," says Francis. "And for a good reading on the guy, you ought to look at his playoff statistics — 18 points in 10 games. That's really the bottom line."

Over his last four regular campaigns, Federko's haul is an even more imposing 385 points.

Guy Lapointe

"This guy knows what it means to win and that's a quality you need," said Francis upon acquiring veteran defenceman Guy Lapointe from the Montreal Canadiens last spring.

Lapointe, 34, was in on six Stanley Cup captures with Canadiens. And he was a first or second all-star on four occasions.

"He has had injury problems in recent years but, with a reduced workload, he should be very important in our operation," Francis notes.

Lapointe assisted on six goals while playing the last eight matches of the Blues' 1981-82 schedule, and notched the winning goal in an important Stanley Cup playoff victory over Winnipeg.

Brian Sutter

Perry Turnbull

BLUES' 1982-83 ROSTER

1981-82 RECORD

Forwards	Ht.	Wt.	Place of Birth	Date	1981-82 Club	G	A	Pts.
Perry Anderson	6-0	194	Barrie, Ont.	Oct. 14, 1961	Salt Lake City (CHL)	32	32	64
Wayne Babych	5-11	191	Edmonton, Alta.	June 6, 1958	St. Louis	19	25	44
Blair Chapman	6-0	190	Lloydminster, Sask.	June 13, 1956	St. Louis	6	11	17
Mike Crombeen	5-11	192	Sarnia, Ont.	April 16, 1957	St. Louis	19	8	27
Blake Dunlop	5-11	175	Hamilton, Ont.	April 4, 1953	St. Louis	25	53	78
Bernie Federko	6-0	190	Foam Lake, Sask.	May 12, 1956	St. Louis	30	62	92
Pat Hickey	6-1	190	Brantford, Ont.	May 15, 1953	Tor.-NYR-Que.-St. L.	15	15	30
Ralph Klassen	5-11	175	Humboldt, Sask.	Sept. 15, 1955	St. Louis	3	7	10
Joe Mullen	5-9	180	New York, N.Y.	Feb. 26, 1957	St. Louis	25	34	59
Larry Patey	6-1	185	Toronto, Ont.	March 19, 1953	St. Louis	14	12	26
Jorgen Pettersson	6-2	185	Gothenburg, Sweden	July 11, 1956	St. Louis	38	31	69
Mark Reeds	5-10	188	Burlington, Ont.	Jan. 24, 1960	St. Louis	1	3	4
Brian Sutter	5-11	173	Viking, Alta.	Oct. 7, 1956	St. Louis	39	36	75
Perry Turnbull	6-2	200	Rimbey, Alta.	March 6, 1959	St. Louis	33	26	59
Mike Zuke	6-0	180	Sault Ste. Marie, Ont.	April 16, 1954	St. Louis	13	40	53

Defence

Bill Baker	6-1	175	Grand Rapids, Minn.	Nov. 29, 1956	Col.-St.L.	3	8	11
Jack Brownschidle	6-1	180	Buffalo, N.Y.	Oct. 2, 1955	St. Louis	5	33	38
Kari Eloranta	6-2	200	Lahti, Finland	Feb. 29, 1956	Cal.-St. L.	1	12	13
Gerry Hart	5-9	198	Flin Flon, Man.	Jan. 1, 1948	St. Louis	0	1	1
Ed Kea	6-3	199	Weesp, Holland	Jan. 19, 1948	St. Louis	2	14	16
Guy Lapointe	6-0	205	Montreal, Que.	March 19, 1948	Mont.-St. L.	1	25	26
Jim Pavese	6-2	204	New York, N.Y.	June 8, 1962	St. Louis	2	9	11
Rob Ramage	6-2	200	Byron, Ont.	Jan. 11, 1959	Colorado	13	29	42
Ric Wilson	6-0	180	Long Beach, Calif.	June 17, 1962	St.Louis	3	18	21

Goalies

						GPI	GA	Avg.
Glen Hanlon	6-0	180	Brandon, Man.	Feb. 20,1957	Van.-St.L.	30	114	4.05
Rick Heinz	5-10	165	Essex, Ont.	May 30, 1955	Van.-St. L.	12	44	3.75
Mike Liut	6-2	195	Weston, Ont.	Jan. 7, 1956	St. Louis	64	250	4.06
Paul Skidmore	6-0	185	Smithstown, N.Y.	July 22, 1956	Salt Lake City (CHL)	50	192	3.85

124

CHICAGO BLACK HAWKS

They're on Their Way

1981-82 Finish: Fourth, Norris Division.
Strengths: Good young defence, improving attack, fine coach.
Weaknesses: Uncertain in nets, lack depth.
Probable 1982-83 Finish: Third.

Suddenly the future looks bright for the Chicago Black Hawks. Their 1981-82 results were adversely affected by a series of serious injuries and they placed a decidedly unspectacular fourth in the Norris Division of the National Hockey League. But an impressive hint of what might lie ahead was provided in the Stanley Cup playoffs when, with most of their wounds healed, Hawks scored resounding upsets over Minnesota North Stars and St. Louis Blues, and took Vancouver Canucks to a fifth contest before losing out in the Campbell Conference final.

"Using injuries as an excuse can be a dangerous crutch but facts are facts. We did lose some of our best people for extended periods," said general manager Bob Pulford, who took over as coach near the end of the campaign and later relinquished that post to newcomer Orval Tessier. "We were very competitive once we were able to use something resembling our normal roster."

Knee miseries cost defencemen Keith Brown and Bob Murray half the schedule each. Forwards Darryl Sutter (arm) and Glen Sharpley (eye) were out about the same length of time. Captain Terry Ruskowski missed 20 games.

But there was encouragement in abundance.

"All those fellows took part in the playoffs," said Pulford, "indicating they'll be all right next season.

"And their absences forced us to move some of our young guys along more quickly than planned. Now, with that experience behind them, they may stick in the NHL."

Doug Crossman, Dave Feamster, and Jerry Dupont on

defence, and forwards Bill Gardner and Troy Murray are examples of Chicago's young talent.

Last season's Hawks also came up with a critical ingredient they had lacked since Stan Mikita and Bobby Hull were young — a big gunner. Sophomore pro Denis Savard set a club record with 119 points.

He was working with rugged Al Secord on his left, and their right wing from now on could very well be Tony Tanti, who just finished shooting 143 goals in two years with Oshawa juniors.

In fact, the only area where things aren't looking up for Hawks is in the nets. That spot hasn't been a worry since Tony Esposito came along in the late 1960s, but Tony O, at 38, may finally be vulnerable. His 1981-82 average was a shocking 4.52 over 52 outings and he lost 25 games. In the playoffs, Murray Bannerman did the bulk of goalkeeping.

Hawks were looking down the road at the 1982 junior draft. Their first pick was Ken Yaremchuk, a Savard-like centre and a 157-point junior last winter. He is expected to spend another term with the teenagers.

Subsequently, Pulford turned over coaching duties to the highly respected Tessier, a proven success in both junior and minor pro ranks. He had won the '82 American Hockey League title with Chicago's New Brunswick farm club.

Tom Lysiak

Unable to furnish the leadership Atlanta Flames were looking for, Tom Lysiak has found a hockey home in Chicago.

Hawks got him in a March, 1979 trade, but never put an ounce of pressure on him. Expecting less, they got more.

He's been able to produce 237 points in the 234 games he's played for the Chicago club and has finally lived up to that rich potential he once displayed.

"I was keenly aware of the fact that, as the No. 1 draft choice in Atlanta, I was supposed to be a big man," says Lysiak. "That may have been one of the reasons I was such a disappointment to the people I worked for — and myself. Here in Chicago, I haven't had that same feeling and, through relaxing, I've been a lot more effective."

Al Secord

Boston Bruins were guilty of a grave error when they traded left winger Al Secord to the Hawks in December, 1980. But Secord himself says you shouldn't blame them for it.

"I was playing pretty badly," he admits. "But there was a reason. I was confused and bitter. I was drafted, you see, for my aggressiveness, but I always felt I could score goals and make other contributions. That thinking was discouraged and I was unhappy about it."

Hawks placed Secord on a line with their slickest centre, Denis Savard, and he responded with 44 goals. Only five left wings received more support than he did in all-star voting.

Don't get the idea, though, that Secord has become a soft touch. While making the most of his new offensive opportunities, he maintains his position as one of the NHL's most intimidating scrappers. He served 303 penalty minutes last season.

Doug Wilson

The institution of matrimony gets credit for Doug Wilson's emergence as the NHL's No. 1 defenceman, a solid leader in both all-star and Norris Trophy votes.

"I'd been very sick and the ailment was diagnosed as a blood disorder called hypoglycemia," explains Wilson, 25. "It can be controlled by diet so I was lucky I'd just got married. I don't think I could have made it on a bachelor's cooking.

"Then I had to play a large portion of last season with a broken jaw wired up. Again, special foods were called for."

Wilson, one of the most mobile rearguards in the NHL, collected 85 scoring points by virtue of shrewd playmaking and a truly exceptional shot.

"On top of everything else, he's the best bodychecker we've had in Chicago since Doug Jarrett retired," said former coach Keith Magnuson.

Denis Savard

Bob Pulford, Chicago's head man, is not easily impressed. So he managed to control his enthusiasm when sophomore centre Denis Savard established two team records last season — for points (119) and assists (87).

"But he showed me something in the playoffs," Pulford conceded. "Under that kind of pressure and against stepped-up checking, he got us 18 points and never took a backward step. Now that is impressive."

Pulford had used a first-round priority to draft Savard from Montreal juniors in 1980 and the youngster, who turned 20 at midterm, generated a very satisfactory 75 points.

"Giving him Al Secord as a winger helped," Pulford noted. "Savard is not big, by any means, although he's rugged enough. But Secord can soak up a lot of physical punishment and handle a lot of the corner work. He gives Savard room to operate."

Glen Sharpley

For several bleak weeks last winter, Glen Sharpley had a notion his hockey career was over. An eye wouldn't function properly as the result of an on-ice injury, and he missed 44 games before a Toronto specialist devised a treatment which would help.

"Getting my eyesight back was a tremendous relief in itself," Sharpley said, "but there was also the matter of putting things together again as a player."

A shoulder problem and a bout with mononucleosis had bothered Sharpley earlier after he'd joined Hawks in a December, 1980, transaction.

"I just hadn't had a chance to prove anything to the Chicago people," said Sharpley, whose nine playoff points were a giant step in that direction.

Rich Preston

A torn knee cartilage requiring surgery kept winger Rich Preston out of 33 Hawk matches during the 1980-81 schedule. And when he did return, he was ineffective.

"I did a lot of thinking during the next summer and finally came to the conclusion I simply hadn't been confident that the knee was as strong as ever," he says. "I was babying it.

"There was no need to feel that way, so I started out with a new attitude last season. And I was right. I was able to do everything I'd ever done before."

Preston and captain Terry Ruskowski are athletes Hawks

reclaimed from Winnipeg Jets of the old World Hockey Association. Neither is a prolific scorer but both are excellent checkers.

Troy Murray

In his final year of amateur competition, centre Troy Murray won two major championships. First, he was an important member of Team Canada when it took the world junior title. Then, he played a pivotal role in North Dakota's victory at the U.S. college finals.

Shortly after the latter triumph, he was given a professional contract by the Chicago Black Hawks.

But general manager Bob Pulford remained skeptical.

"It'll be a good education for him to be with us during the playoffs, just to absorb the atmosphere," Pulford said. "But I can't see dropping the kid into such a tough situation."

As it happened, though, Murray played seven Stanley Cup matches and was by no means Chicago's worst man in any of them.

Darryl Sutter

Believing that every NHL club should have at least one of Alberta's Sutter brothers on the roster, Hawks drafted left winger Darryl in 1978. He spent a development year in the minors and then rapped in 40 goals as a 1980-81 NHL rookie.

An arm injury knocked Sutter, now 24, out of half of the Hawks' schedule last season, but he still sniped 23 goals in the 40 games he did play. Eventually, his damaged arm muscles required surgical repairs but he managed to return for three Stanley Cup appearances.

"The difficulty resulted from a Sutter asset, which is tremendous zest for competition," said Pulford. "Darryl insisted on playing before the arm was healed properly because he couldn't stand being on the sidelines. He worsened the situation but his motivation was good."

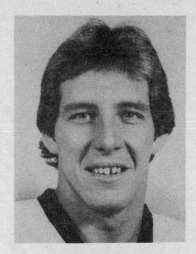

Al Secord

Denis Savard

BLACK HAWKS' 1982-83 ROSTER

1981-82 RECORD

Forwards	Ht.	Wt.	Place of Birth	Date	1981-82 Club	G	A	Pts.
Ted Bulley	6-1	197	Windsor, Ont.	March 25, 1955	Chicago	12	18	30
Bill Gardner	5-10	170	Toronto, Ont.	May 19, 1960	Chicago	8	15	23
Tim Higgins	6-10	181	Ottawa, Ont.	Feb. 7, 1958	Chicago	20	30	50
Reg Kerr	5-10	179	Oxbow, Sask.	Oct. 16, 1957	Chicago	11	28	39
Tom Lysiak	6-1	195	High Prairie, Alta.	April 22, 1953	Chicago	32	50	82
Peter Marsh	6-1	180	Halifax, N.S.	Dec. 21, 1956	Chicago	10	18	28
Grant Mulvey	6-3	200	Sudbury, Ont.	Sept. 17, 1956	Chicago	30	19	49
Rick Paterson	5-9	187	Kingston, Ont.	Feb. 10, 1958	Chicago	4	7	11
Rick Preston	5-11	185	Regina, Sask.	May 22, 1952	Chicago	15	28	43
Terry Ruskowski	5-10	178	Prince Albert, Sask.	Dec. 21, 1954	Chicago	7	30	37
Denis Savard	5-10	170	Point Gatineau, Que.	Feb. 4, 1961	Chicago	32	87	119
Al Secord	6-1	205	Sudbury, Ont.	March 3, 1958	Chicago	44	31	75
Glen Sharpley	6-0	187	Toronto, Ont.	Sept. 6, 1956	Chicago	9	7	16
Darryl Sutter	5-11	170	Viking, Alta.	Aug. 19, 1958	Chicago	23	12	35
Tony Tanti	5-9	181	Toronto, Ont.	Sept. 7, 1963	Oshawa (OMJHL)	62	64	126

Defencemen

Name			Birthplace	Birthdate	Team			
Keith Brown	6-1	192	Corner Brook, Nfld.	May 6, 1960	Chicago	4	20	24
Doug Crossman	6-2	190	Peterborough, Ont.	May 30, 1960	Chicago	12	28	40
Jerome Dupont	6-3	190	Ottawa, Ont.	Feb. 21, 1962	Chicago	0	4	4
Dave Feamster	5-11	180	Detroit, Mich.	Sept. 10, 1958	Chicago	0	2	2
Greg Fox	6-2	190	Vancouver, B.C.	Aug. 12, 1953	Chicago	2	19	21
Dave Hutchison	6-3	205	London, Ont.	May 2, 1952	Chicago	5	18	23
John Marks	6-2	203	Winnipeg, Man.	March 22, 1948	Chicago	1	0	1
Bob Murray	5-10	183	Kingston, Ont.	Nov. 26, 1954	Chicago	8	22	30
Doug Wilson	6-1	187	Ottawa, Ont.	July 5, 1957	Chicago	39	46	85

Goalies

Name			Birthplace	Birthdate	Team	GPI	GA	Avg.
Murray Bannerman	5-11	184	Fort Frances, Ont.	April 27, 1957	Chicago	29	116	4.17
Tony Esposito	5-11	185	Sault Ste. Marie, Ont.	April 23, 1943	Chicago	52	231	4.52
Bob Janecyk	6-1	180	Chicago, Ill.	May 18, 1957	New Brunswick (AHL)	50	140	2.76

WASHINGTON CAPITALS

In a Tough Spot

1981-82 Finish: Last, Patrick Division.
Strengths: Some scoring and defence, improved netminding.
Weaknesses: Need depth, more of everything.
Probable 1982-83 Finish: Fourth.

Under the old National Hockey League system, the 1981-82 Washington Capitals would have qualified for Stanley Cup play. They were 16th in the overall standings.

Caps' record over the regular schedule was superior to that of the Los Angeles Kings, who upset the Edmonton Oilers in the first round of the playoffs. But that didn't help the Washington team, which was fifth in the tough Patrick Division, while Kings claimed the No. 4 spot in the softer Smythe section.

Beginning in 1982, you see, Stanley Cup participants were the top four from each group, regardless of point totals.

"So the luck of the draw became a factor," shrugged Roger Crozier, who ran the Caps after general manager Max McNab was fired in the autumn.

"Maybe the time will come when we're in an easy spot and people are feeling sorry for L.A. In the meantime, we're stuck. And besides, it's pretty difficult to accomplish anything after the kind of start we had last season."

Caps dropped 11 of their first 14 games and that showing cost both McNab and coach Gary Green their jobs.

The successor to Green was Bryan Murray, who had been handling Washington's American League farm club at Hershey and had been named 1980-81 Coach of the Year in the minors.

"My approach is to make fairly stiff demands on the players, ask a lot of them," Murray said. "I've found that's the way to get the most out of your people."

And the Caps did improve under Murray. They were the youngest side in the entire NHL with an average age of 23.4 and they posted the 12th best defensive record.

Murray's work was largely responsible, of course, but Crozier pulled off a flurry of player moves which helped, too. Veterans like Jean Pronovost, Pierre Bouchard, Orest Kindrachuk and Bob Kelly were phased out. And Crozier dealt for defencemen Lee Norwood and Doug Hicks, rugged Randy Holt, and forward Bobby Gould.

"We've got the makings of something here, a solid beginning." Crozier noted. "And we own some excellent kids, including Scott Stevens, a junior defenceman we drafted in June."

"What we need very badly at this point is depth, numbers. As it is, we're vulnerable to injuries or slumps and it's hard to help ourselves with trades. So all we can do is build around the nucleus we've got which, as I mentioned, is excellent."

Dennis Maruk

In all but three seasons, Peewee Maruk's 1981-82 exploits would have been sufficient to win him an NHL scoring championship. However, the points he produced got him no more than fourth place behind Wayne Gretzky, Mike Bossy and Peter Stastny. He was third in goals with 60.

On the basis of that output, Maruk was chosen Washington's most valuable player and placed No. 4 among NHL centres in all-star voting.

"As a scorer, Maruk is a threat from any area at any time," said Caps' former general manager, Max McNab. "As a playmaker, he's one of the best."

Caps obtained Maruk from the Minnesota North Stars in 1978, giving up the draft pick that the stars used to claim Tom McCarthy. Since then, Maruk has played 263 Washington games and accumulated 350 points.

Mike Gartner

Most NHL players will tell you 22-year-old Mike Gartner is the fastest skater in the game today.

"He is also one of the best right wingers," says coach Bryan Murray. "He's got a lot more than tremendous speed going for him. He's very much the complete player."

Gartner was still a junior when he turned professional with

Cincinnati's World Hockey Association club in 1978. Caps took him in the NHL draft and then hired him when the Cincy operation folded. He has shot 119 goals in his first three NHL campaigns.

Team Canada has recruited Gartner for its efforts at the world championships of 1981 and 1982.

"I enjoy these trips," Gartner says, "but one of these times, I wouldn't mind being unavailable in April because we're in the Stanley Cup playoffs."

Ryan Walter

Besides Dennis Maruk, the only Washington player to receive really substantial backing at last season's all-star polls was captain Ryan Walter. He is a left wing.

Even before that, the industrious Walter had been named Caps' most popular man.

It had been the best of his four NHL campaigns, with 87 points. Then, when Caps failed to reach the playoffs, he was selected to compete for Canada at the global championships.

"You can't wipe out the terrible start we had but, if you could set it aside, we were pretty competitive in the NHL last year," says Walter. "The addition of New Jersey to our division figures to help us next time around so I'm looking forward to being in the playoffs for the first time in 1983."

Rick Green

For three consecutive years now, large Rick Green has been honored as Washington's best defenceman. He is also one of the finest in the entire NHL, but the fact won't be properly recognized until the Caps burst forth as a contending club.

Defensively, they were superior to playoff participants like Quebec Nordiques, Calgary Flames, St. Louis Blues, Chicago Black Hawks and Los Angeles Kings last season.

"And Green has to be considered one of the main reasons," says coach Bryan Murray. "He is our main man behind the blue line."

Only 26, Green has now completed six NHL campaigns.

Bobby Carpenter

Barely 18 and fresh out of a Boston area high school, Bobby Carpenter was told he might have to spend his first pro season in the minors. He'd been the first American player ever drafted in the NHL's first round — the No. 3 pick, actually — but his experience has been limited. He said he understood.

However, it was abundantly clear he belonged in the NHL, almost from day one of the Washington training camp.

Carpenter collected 32 goals and 35 assists as an NHL freshman. Only seven rookies did better statistically.

"He had to meet a lot of challenges, too — and did," said captain Ryan Walter. "Several teams assumed they could intimidate him physically but they were wrong. He didn't back away from anybody and very quickly earned universal respect."

Mike Palmateer

Can Palmy make a comeback with the 1982-83 Caps? He'll be trying.

Palmateer had been outstanding all through his first season in the Washington nets but an ailing knee limited him to 11 appearances last year.

"My information was that complete rest over a long period would correct the problem," says Palmateer, 28. "But you're right in putting a question mark beside my name."

Palmateer had been obtained from Toronto in a 1980 trade. Defenceman Robert Picard was transferred to Leafs but later moved on to Montreal in exchange for another goalkeeper, Bunny Larocque.

"Palmateer at his best would be a great plus," says Murray, "but we can't afford to be in a spot where we'd be stuck without him. We did have decent netminding last season, you know."

Dave Parro made 52 starts for Washington and Al Jensen, from the Detroit organization, turned in an 8-and-8 record.

Then, at the NHL's June congress, Caps took out further goalie insurance by dealing for Calgary's erstwhile first-stringer, Pat Riggin. He had become available when the Flames got Don Edwards from Buffalo.

Chris Valentine

"He skates like a slow motion replay," said Washington's former general manager, Max McNab, speaking of rookie winger Chris Valentine. "But take a closer look and you start seeing good things. He always turns up where the puck is or vice-versa. And he makes excellent plays for his linemates."

Valentine was the 194th junior graduate chosen in the NHL's 1981 draft, and one of the least likely candidates at Caps' training camp. And, as a matter of fact, he opened the campaign with a Washington farm club.

But in 60 NHL matches, Valentine produced 26 goals and 34 assists, good for fifth place among Washington's attackers.

Bengt Gustafsson

One of Max McNab's most important acts, as Caps' general manager, was to engage a full-time European representative. Arne Stromberg, formerly coach of Sweden's national team, has been maintaining a steady flow of fresh talent across the Atlantic to Washington.

Bengt-Ake Gustafsson has scored 69 goals in his three NHL seasons.

Defenceman Timo Blomqvist, a 1981-82 NHL freshman, is an outstanding Finnish import. His initial NHL year was interrupted by an injury but he could be important in the forthcoming campaign.

And Caps are enthusiastic about a Swedish rearguard named Peter Andersson. He was an all-star at last season's world junior championships and then moved up to be a regular with Sweden's No. 1 side at the main global tournament. He was drafted on Stromberg's say-so.

Bobby Carpenter

Dennis Maruk

CAPITALS' 1982-83 ROSTER

1981-82 RECORD

Forwards	Ht.	Wt.	Place of Birth	Date	1981-82 Club	G	A	Pts.
Bobby Carpenter	6-0	185	Beverly, Mass.	June 13, 1963	Washington	32	35	67
Glen Currie	6-1	177	Montreal, Que.	July 18, 1958	Washington	7	7	14
Gaetan Duchesne	5-11	177	Quebec City, Que.	July 11, 1962	Washington	3	21	24
Mike Gartner	6-0	180	Ottawa, Ont.	Oct. 29, 1959	Washington	35	45	80
Bobby Gould	5-11	195	Petrolia, Ont.	Sept. 2, 1957	Cal.-Wash.	21	13	34
Bengt Gustafsson	6-0	185	Karlskoga, Sweden	March 23, 1958	Washington	26	34	60
Alan Haworth	5-10	188	Drummondville, Que.	Sept. 1, 1960	Buffalo	21	18	39
Ken Houston	6-2	207	Chatham, Ont.	Sept. 15, 1953	Calgary	22	22	44
Dennis Maruk	5-8	165	Toronto, Ont.	Nov. 17, 1955	Washington	60	76	136
Torrie Robertson	5-11	185	Victoria, B.C.	Aug. 2, 1961	Washington	8	13	21
Chris Valentine	6-0	191	Belleville, Ont.	Dec. 6, 1961	Washington	30	37	67
Ryan Walter	6-0	195	New Westminster, B.C.	April 23, 1958	Washington	38	49	87

Defencemen

Name	Ht.	Wt.	Birthplace	Birthdate	Team			
Timo Blomqvist	6-0	198	Helsinki, Finland	Jan. 23, 1961	Washington	1	11	12
Rick Green	6-3	207	Belleville, Ont.	Feb. 20, 1956	Washington	3	25	28
Doug Hicks	6-0	185	Cold Lake, Alta.	May 28, 1955	Edm.-Wash.	3	21	24
Randy Holt	5-11	184	Pembroke, Ont.	Jan. 15, 1953	Cal.-Wash.	2	6	8
Paul MacKinnon	6-0	190	Brantford, Ont.	Nov. 6, 1958	Washington	2	9	11
Terry Murray	6-2	190	Shawville, Que.	July 20, 1950	Washington	3	22	25
Lee Norwood	6-0	190	Oakland, Calif.	Feb. 2, 1960	Que.-Wash.	7	10	17
Greg Theberge	5-10	187	Peterborough, Ont.	Sept. 3, 1959	Washington	5	32	37
Darren Veitch	6-0	188	Saskatoon, Sask.	April 24, 1960	Washington	9	44	53

Goalies

Name	Ht.	Wt.	Birthplace	Birthdate	Team	GPI	GA	Avg.
Al Jensen	5-10	180	Hamilton, Ont.	Nov. 27, 1958	Washington	26	81	3.81
Mike Palmateer	5-9	170	Toronto, Ont.	Jan. 13, 1954	Washington	11	47	4.83
Dave Parro	5-10	185	Saskatoon, Sask.	April 30, 1957	Washington	52	206	4.20
Pat Riggin	5-9	163	Kincardine, Ont.	May 26, 1959	Calgary	52	207	4.23

LOS ANGELES KINGS

They're Building with Youth

1981-82 Finish: Fourth in Smythe Division.
Strengths: Good scoring, youth.
Weaknesses: Still playing catch-up.
Probable 1982-83 Finish: Last in Smythe.

It was a long, long time before Los Angeles Kings took an interest in the yearly amateur draft that most National Hockey League teams use to procure young talent — and regard as absolutely essential to their well-being.

That shortsighted policy was catching up to the Kings last season when they dropped 36 points in the standings, finishing a dismal fourth in the Smythe Division standings with a worse record than 16 other NHL clubs.

''At the same time, though,'' notes general manager George Maguire, ''we got some indication we were heading in the right direction when we upset a very strong Edmonton team in the first round of the Stanley Cup playoffs.

''That victory was keyed, to a large extent, by the juniors we've been bringing into the organization. And it's about time, too.''

In the 11 drafts between 1968 and '79, Kings exercised their first pick on only one occasion. That was in 1975, when they selected Tim Young. And he was immediately dealt to the Minnesota North Stars.

''All the other times, L.A. had traded its No. 1 choice, and usually the first few, ahead of time. History shows us this is precisely the opposite of what you should do,'' says Wren Blair, Kings' director of personnel. ''Those early picks, year after year, are your lifeblood, without which you die. New York Islanders are the best possible illustration of what they mean. That team was built with the draft.''

The modus operandi began to change in 1980. Kings retained their own first-round priority and owned another, as part of the payment for Rogie Vachon's earlier flight to Detroit Red Wings.

They took defenceman Larry Murphy and right winger Jim Fox.

"Then, when we got centre Doug Smith in 1981, right there we had the basis of a strong club at some point not too far down the line," Blair states. "But it's a laborious process and we realize there may be some suffering in the meantime. We had no choice but to bite the bullet and take our lumps. We started late with this thing and there's a lot of ground to make up before we're even level with clubs we really should be competitive with right now."

Kings' owner, Dr. Jerry Buss, decreed a change of coaches last winter after they reeled to loss No. 23 in only their 41st match. Coach Parker MacDonald was made the assistant general manager, and Don Perry, who'd worked for Blair in the minors, was elevated from the American League farm club at New Haven as the replacement.

"I guess I'm an old-fashioned coach," says Perry. "I still haven't learned that stuff like defence, hard work and body contact are out of style in hockey."

Maybe they aren't. It didn't seem that way, anyhow, in Kings' playoff conquest of Edmonton's first-place Oilers.

Charlie Simmer

"One of the best developments in the 1982 playoffs," says GM George Maguire, "was the way Charlie Simmer was able to operate. It was welcome proof that he's 100 percent all right."

Simmer had emerged as the NHL's top left wing with successive 56-goal, all-star seasons, when his right leg was shattered in a March 2, 1981 game in Toronto. He didn't play again until last November and then with the damaged leg held together by a metal plate and nine screws.

"I had to start out early with spot duty and power-play shifts," Simmer said, "and the biggest thing was to develop confidence that I could depend on the leg. You've got to be able to play without even thinking about it."

Simmer worked with increasing effectiveness but in Stanley Cup competition, with 11 points in 10 games, finally resembled his old self in every way.

Steve Bozek

L.A. Kings acquired the rights to centre Steve Bozek in 1980, but had to wait while he was finishing his college career at Northern Michigan University.

"He was worth a little patience," says coach Perry. "To me, he was one of the best rookies in the NHL last season."

Although Bozek fired 33 goals, he didn't receive a single vote in the Calder Trophy election, which picks the No. 1 freshman.

"He was good in the playoffs, too, scoring four goals," Perry adds, "and that says plenty about him."

Kings' Stanley Cup leader was another newcomer, 21-year-old Daryl Evans. He got 13 points in 10 games.

Marcel Dionne

Only eight players in the entire history of the NHL ever produced more than the 1,180 points credited to Marcel Dionne. And because those men have all retired, Dionne is the leading scorer among active players.

He is only 31, too, so Gordie Howe's record of 1,850 would seem well within his reach.

The stocky Dionne is more concerned, however, about his 1981-82 results, which he terms unsatisfactory. He had his fifth 50-goal year and accumulated 117 points, but it was his poorest effort since 1978.

"Look at the standings and you'll see what I'm talking about," he says. "And then it was the same old story in the playoffs. Beating Edmonton was a wonderful high, of course, but we didn't go much further, did we?"

Dave Taylor

According to the all-star panel, Dave Taylor was Kings' best player last season. He stood fifth among all the right wings for the highest rating bestowed upon any L.A. skater.

"Taylor's point totals are spectacular, but he's the 'honest brakeman' sort of guy," says personnel boss Wren Blair. "He excels through working hard. Because of that, he's exactly the right type to work on a forward line with Marcel Dionne and Charlie Simmer."

The 210th junior drafted by the NHL in 1975, Taylor came out of Clarkson College in New York to spend one year of preparation before bursting through as a genuine NHL star. In the four years since, he has scored 166 goals and totalled 399 points.

Larry Murphy

The sophomore jinx, practically a tradition in pro sport, was no trouble at all for Larry Murphy.

His rookie season, 1980-81, had been one of unmitigated triumph. He was sixth at the all-star defence polls, second among all freshmen, and scored more points than either Bobby Orr or Denis Potvin had done in his debut year.

The second time around, Murphy collected 22 goals and 44 assists.

"Defensively, as a unit, we had a very poor year," notes Murphy, 21, "and I've got to accept my share of the blame. But I wasn't totally dissatisfied, especially when we came on quite well at the end."

Mario Lessard

In 1981, Mario Lessard was numbered among the NHL's top netminders.

A year later, he could be found down near the bottom of the statistical tables. He gave up more opposition goals in fewer matches.

"There wasn't all that much difference in my play," says Lessard, 28. "A goalie's numbers relate more to the way his whole team is playing and I think it's fair to say we had a bad year, overall. And I was only a part of it."

Both Lessard and his 24-year-old understudy, Doug Keans, are very rare commodities — players L.A. drafted out of junior hockey and developed themselves.

Jim Fox

Here's a forecast: Jim Fox will win the Lady Byng Trophy one of these years.

He fits the Lady Byng requirements perfectly — a highly effective player who operates within the boundaries prescribed in the rulebook.

In three seasons with Ottawa juniors, right winger Fox had 396 points and only 46 minutes in the slammer.

As an NHL rookie, after Kings drafted him, he collected 42 points and served only four minor penalties.

And finally, as an NHL sophomore, he reached new highs of 30 goals, 38 assists and a still slight 23 penalty minutes.

''Tough play has its advantages,'' says Fox, ''but the bottom line still is that you can't help your team while you're in the penalty box.''

Dave Lewis

There are two distinct types of defencemen in the NHL right now.

Most, like Randy Carlyle and Doug Wilson, are the keys to their teams' offences and can be judged by their point totals.

Then there are the stay-at-home rearguards who patrol their own zones and protect their goalies. They're a much rarer breed of cat, and their scarcity is one reason scores are so high today.

''That is my role, while guys like Larry Murphy carry the puck and make the plays and get the headlines,'' says Dave Lewis, who was traded to L.A. in 1980 before he could be a part of New York Islanders' Stanley Cup successes.

So complete is Lewis's preoccupation with defence, that his single goal last term was only the 27th of his entire NHL career.

Mario Lessard

Dave Taylor

KINGS' 1982-83 ROSTER

1981-82 RECORD

Forwards	Ht.	Wt.	Place of Birth	Date	1981-82 Club	G	A	Pts.
Dan Bonar	5-9	175	Brandon, Man.	Sept. 23, 1956	Los Angeles	13	23	36
Steve Bozek	5-11	186	Castlegar, B.C.	Nov. 26, 1960	Los Angeles	33	23	56
Marcel Dionne	5-8	185	Drummondville, Que.	Aug. 3, 1951	Los Angeles	50	67	117
Daryl Evans	5-8	185	Toronto, Ont.	Jan. 12, 1961	Los Angeles	2	6	8
Jim Fox	5-8	175	Coniston, Ont.	May 18, 1960	Los Angeles	30	38	68
Dean Hopkins	6-1	210	Cobourg, Ont.	June 6, 1959	Los Angeles	2	13	15
Steve Jensen	6-2	195	Minneapolis, Minn.	April 14, 1955	Los Angeles	8	19	27
John Paul Kelly	6-1	215	Edmonton, Alta.	Nov. 15, 1959	Los Angeles	12	11	23
Mike Murphy	6-0	188	Toronto, Ont.	Sept. 12, 1950	Los Angeles	5	10	15
Bernie Nicholls	6-0	185	Haliburton, Ont.	June 24, 1961	Los Angeles	14	18	32
Charlie Simmer	6-3	210	Terrace Bay,Ont.	March 20, 1954	Los Angeles	15	24	39
Doug Smith	5-11	180	Ottawa, Ont.	May 17, 1963	Los Angeles	16	14	30
Dave Taylor	6-0	195	Levack, Ont.	Dec. 4, 1955	Los Angeles	39	67	106
Greg Terrion	5-11	190	Peterborough, Ont.	May 2, 1960	Los Angeles	15	22	37

Defencemen

Rick Chartraw	6-2	205	Caracas, Venezuela	July 13, 1954	Los Angeles	2	8	10
Al Hangsleben	6-1	195	Warroad, Minn.	Feb. 22, 1953	Wash.-L.A.	3	7	10
Mark Hardy	5-11	195	Semaden, Switz.	Feb. 1, 1959	Los Angeles	6	39	45
Jerry Korab	6-3	218	Sault Ste. Marie, Ont.	Sept. 15, 1948	Los Angeles	5	13	18
Dave Lewis	6-2	205	Kindersley, Sask.	July 3, 1953	Los Angeles	1	13	14
Larry Murphy	6-1	210	Scarborough, Ont.	March 8, 1961	Los Angeles	22	44	66
Ian Turnbull	6-0	195	Montreal, Que.	Dec. 22, 1953	Tor.-L.A.	11	17	28
Jay Wells	6-1	208	Paris, Ont.	May 18, 1959	Los Angeles	1	8	9

Goalies

						GPI	GA	Avg.
Doug Keans	5-7	175	Pembroke, Ont.	Jan. 7, 1958	Los Angeles	31	103	4.30
Mario Lessard	5-9	190	East Broughton, Ont.	June 25, 1954	Los Angeles	52	213	4.36

HARTFORD WHALERS

The Kish of Fortune

1981-82 Finish: Last, Adams Division.
Strengths: Promising kids, new coach.
Weaknesses: Short of offence, defence.
Probable 1982-83 Finish: Last again.

Larry Kish couldn't have timed things more favorably. The finest of his 18 winters as a hockey coach took place at the precise time when the Hartford Whalers were in need of a man to fill that very position.

Illness prevented Larry Pleau, director of operations for Connecticut's National Hockey League franchise, from completing the 1981-82 campaign as coach, and his assistant, John Cunniff, took over on a temporary basis.

Over in Binghamton, N.Y., Kish was experiencing great success with Whalers' American League farm club. These AHL Whalers won their division championship and reached the Calder Cup finals before losing to New Brunswick Hawks.

So it was only logical that Pleau would name Kish, 40, as his successor at the bench.

"I've been handling Hartford's minor leaguers for a couple of years now," Kish says, "so I'll have a few advantages right off the bat.

"I know these kids for one thing. Bob Sullivan, to name one, got me 47 goals last season and was an AHL all-star. There are a few in that category.

"And with me, there'll be no disruption in the continuity of what this organization has been doing. I'll simply carry on with what Larry Pleau and the owner, Howard Baldwin, now have in place."

Pleau has been moving swiftly, hustling to overcome a broad array of shortcomings. He has been averaging about a deal a week, acquiring a veteran here, a youngster there, and the odd draft choice besides.

"I assigned very high priority to the solution of our

goaltending problem. I felt we couldn't make much progress until we got a solid NHL man for that job," said Pleau.

That hurdle was surmounted in the summer of 1981 when Pleau signed Greg Millen, a young netminder who'd decided not to accept a new contract with Pittsburgh Penguins.

In other transactions over the 1981-82 campaign, Pleau acquired such people as Russ Anderson, Paul Shmyr, Pierre Larouche, Garry Howatt and George Lyle.

"Ultimately, of course, the future rests with juniors," Pleau noted, "and we've got some headway to report in that area. Several of our recent draft picks have received NHL exposure and the No. 1 from '81, Ron Francis, is a highly productive regular with us now."

And Pleau picked up some good young talent in a recent trade with Philadelphia and Edmonton. The Whalers sent veteran defenceman Mark Howe to the Flyers in return for Greg Adams and a first-round draft pick. Don Nachbauer, a center-left wing with Hartford, was sent to Edmonton in return for experienced defenceman Risto Siltanen and third-round draft pick Brent Loney.

Doug Sulliman

Whalers gave up their most prolific scorer, Mike Rogers, in a 1981 deal with New York Rangers but were delighted with the athletes they received in exchange. Giant Chris Kotsopoulos is a hard-hitting defender. And 23-year-old Doug Sulliman could be one of the NHL's better young right wingers. He got 29 goals and 40 assists last season in his Hartford debut.

"I had appeared in 63 games with Rangers but I didn't really play," Sulliman says.

"I never felt management was behind me. In Hartford, they let me know right away that I was needed and wanted and believe me, that meant a lot."

Pierre Larouche

Montreal Canadiens gave centre Pierre Larouche the Christmas gift he'd been clamoring for when they shipped him to Hartford in a December 21, 1981 trade. Unhappy under coach Bob Berry, Larouche had been seeking to leave Montreal.

"All I want to do is play regularly," Larouche said, "and in Hartford, I'll get that opportunity."

"And how," said Whalers' Larry Pleau. "We feel extremely fortunate to have acquired a centre of Larouche's calibre, especially so soon after dealing Mike Rogers."

Larouche had been a 50-goal collector with Pittsburgh Penguins and later during his stay with Canadiens.

"And," Pleau added, "he's only 27 years old. He's been a big leaguer since 1974."

Blaine Stoughton

Wayne Gretzky, Mike Bossy, Dino Ciccarelli. These men are magicians around the enemy nets, able to turn the slightest opportunity into a score. Count Blaine Stoughton in that same illustrious group.

"If we were a top club, he'd be one of the NHL's greatest stars," says general manager Larry Pleau. "He's got the same uncanny touch, the same incredible instincts."

Right winger Stoughton has put in 151 goals over the three seasons since he returned to the NHL as a Whaler regular.

He had left in 1976 when Toronto Maple Leafs didn't offer him a new contract, and he moved to Cincinnati in the World Hockey Association.

Ron Francis

This was the plan: Ron Francis would return to the Sault Ste. Marie juniors after attending Whalers' 1981 training camp.

"He'd been our first draft pick but he was only 18," says Pleau. "We thought he'd need another year of junior competition before he'd be ready for the NHL.

"But he was as good as any centre we had and, before long, we realized he belonged in the NHL right away."

Francis played 59 games in his major league initiation and produced 25 goals and 43 assists. Only six freshmen scored more.

"I'll tell you what made a great difference," Francis said. "It was what I learned from Dave Keon, in the room and on the ice. Just watching him — how he positions himself, for example — was an education.''

Greg Millen

An invitation to play for Team Canada at the 1981 world championships marked an important turning point in Greg Millen's netminding career. For the first time, he received widespread recognition — which really was overdue — as one of the best young goalies in the NHL.

"I used to go home to Toronto in the summer and constantly have people asking what I did for a living or where I'd been all winter," Millen said, "even though I'd been an NHL first-stringer for a long while."

Millen had also made news in 1981 by leaving Pittsburgh Penguins and signing with Whalers as a free agent. The Hartford club got its money's worth very promptly. Millen worked in 55 games for them, relieved from time to time by Mike Veisor.

Rick Meagher

If at first you don't succeed, well, give it another whirl.

In 1977, Whalers tried to sign Boston University standout Rick Meagher for their World Hockey Association roster but were outbid by Montreal Canadiens of the NHL.

The New England organization finally got Meagher in a 1980 deal and was delighted to discover its scouts had been right all along. Given an NHL opportunity last season, Meagher scored 24 goals.

"It was a lucky break for me because I'd been stuck with Montreal's farm club, whereas Hartford had a spot for me," said Meagher, who was a triple All-American at Boston U. and the school's No. 1 athlete of the 1970s.

Chris Kotsopoulos

There's always a huge reception when the Hartford Whalers visit Toronto for an NHL game against the Leafs. Defenceman Chris Kotsopoulos can fill the Gardens with relatives and friends from the city's Greek community.

New York Rangers found this burly backstopper playing in

the International League at Toledo and brought him to their American League affiliate at New Haven in 1979. A season later, he was in the NHL with the Rangers and, a year after that, was a part of the package shipped to Hartford for Mike Rogers.

"Chris is a bruising defenceman who gets a piece of everybody who comes into his area," says general manager Larry Pleau. "He also made some very useful contributions (13 goals, 20 assists) to our offence last season and in the NHL of today, that's a very important extra dimension.

Greg Millen

Doug Sullimen

154

WHALERS' 1982-83 ROSTER

1981-82 RECORD

Forwards	Ht.	Wt.	Place of Birth	Date	1981-82 Club	G	A	Pts.
Greg Adams	6-1	190	Duncan, B.C.	March 31, 1960	Philadelphia	4	15	19
Jordy Douglas	6-0	195	Winnipeg, Man.	Jan. 20, 1958	Hartford	10	7	17
Ron Francis	5-11	175	Sault Ste. Marie, Ont.	March 1, 1963	Hartford	25	43	68
Garry Howatt	5-9	175	Grand Centre, Alta.	Sept. 26, 1952	Hartford	18	32	50
Pierre Larouche	5-11	175	Tachereau, Que.	Nov. 16, 1955	Mont.-Hart.	34	37	71
George Lyle	6-2	205	North Vancouver, B.C.	Nov. 24, 1953	Det.-Hart.	3	14	17
Rick Meagher	5-10	175	Belleville, Ont.	Nov. 4, 1953	Hartford	24	19	43
Warren Miller	5-11	180	St. Paul, Minn.	Jan. 1, 1954	Hartford	10	12	22
Ray Neufeld	6-2	215	St. Boniface, Man.	April 15, 1959	Hartford	4	3	7
Blaine Stoughton	5-11	185	Gilbert Plains, Man.	March 13, 1953	Hartford	52	39	91
Doug Sulliman	5-9	195	Glace Bay, N.S.	Aug. 29, 1959	Hartford	29	40	69

Defencemen

Russ Anderson	6-3	210	Minneapolis, Minn.	Feb. 12, 1955	Pitt.-Hart.	1	4	5
Norm Barnes	6-0	190	Toronto, Ont.	Aug. 24, 1953	Hartford	1	4	5
Marty Howe	6-1	195	Detroit, Mich.	Feb. 18, 1954	Hartford	0	4	4
Chris Kotsopoulos	6-3	215	Toronto, Ont.	Nov. 27, 1958	Hartford	13	20	33
Jack McIlhargey	6-0	190	Edmonton, Alta.	March 7, 1952	Hartford	1	5	6
Mark Renaud	6-0	185	Windsor, Ont.	Feb. 21, 1959	Hartford	1	17	18
Paul Shmyr	5-11	170	Cudworth, Sask.	Jan. 28, 1946	Hartford	1	11	12
Risto Siltanen	5-9	180	Tampere, Finland	Oct. 31, 1958	Edmonton	15	48	63
Blake Wesley	6-1	200	Red Deer, Alta.	July 10, 1959	Hartford	9	18	27

Goalies

						GPI	GA	Avg.
Greg Millen	5-9	160	Toronto, Ont.	June 25, 1957	Hartford	55	229	4.29
Mike Veisor	5-9	158	Toronto, Ont.	Aug. 25, 1952	Hartford	13	53	4.54

156

TORONTO MAPLE LEAFS

The Pickings Are Softer

1981-82 Finish: Fifth, Norris Division.
Strengths: Salming, Larocque, some good forwards.
Weaknesses: Green on defence, understaffed.
Probable 1982-83 Finish: Fourth

There was one positive development at least last summer as Toronto Maple Leafs struggled to salvage something — anything — from the wreckage of the worst year in their history.

It happened when Colorado Rockies, after being purchased by New Jersey interests, were moved to the Meadowlands rink and into the Patrick Division of the National Hockey League. Winnipeg Jets were then shifted out of the Norris Division, where they'd finished second last season, and into the Smythe section as the Rockies' replacement.

So suddenly, there were only three teams in front of the Leafs in their Norris group standings, instead of four.

"Presto, we're back in the Stanley Cup playoffs as long as we can stay ahead of the Detroit Red Wings again," said Harold Ballard, owner of the Toronto outfit. "That's such an advantage I turned down $1 million in compensation payments to switch divisions myself."

But Leafs won't be content simply to maintain their position. They hope to improve.

Look at it this way: They can't get much worse, after losing 44 of 80 games and yielding 380 goals for the NHL's worst defensive record.

"I felt we had no choice but to stick with the kids we had confidence in, no matter how much it hurt," said Mike Nykoluk, who had taken over as Leafs' coach midway through the 1980-81 schedule. "We had to throw those rookies in there and let them learn because there was just no point in losing with guys who'd never get any better."

Freshmen Jim Benning, Fred Boimistruck and Bob McGill worked regularly on defence and, as Nykoluk warned, the results were calamitous. The opposition averaged 4.75 goals a game against Toronto.

As sophomores, these young men were to be joined by another greenhorn in the bulky person of Gary Nylund.

Placing 19th in the combined 1981-82 tables gave Leafs third pick in the amateur draft, so it's clear Nylund was one of the more talented junior graduates. He's 6-foot-4 and weighs 210 pounds, and was a western all-star while playing for Portland Winter Hawks.

"I like his size and toughness," said Nykoluk, "because one of the things we've got to do is earn respect. We had the poorest home record in the league last season and that shouldn't be allowed to happen.

"We've got to play with authority in our own building and our own end of the rink.

"And the outlook isn't all bad. Benning, Boimistuck and McGill went through a very difficult ordeal but I think they learned a lot."

Elsewhere, the changeover under Nykoluk and general manager Gerry MacNamara swept out Toronto standbys like Darryl Sittler, the beloved captain, Ian Turnbull, Laurie Boschman and Wilf Paiement, along with veterans Rene Robert and Don Luce. And Dan Maloney, after retiring last summer, became Nykoluk's assistant.

"It's a pretty complete housecleaning," Nykoluk agreed, "but that was the decision, to rebuild almost from square one."

Rick Vaive

The best possible measurement of Rick Vaive's growing status with the Leafs was provided by his installation as team captain after Darryl Sittler was traded to Philadelphia.

"We felt Ricky had the character and the playing ability to take on that kind of a leadership role," said coach Mike Nykoluk, "and as it worked out, he reacted very positively to the responsibilities involved."

Vaive, 23, went on to become Toronto's first 50-goal scorer. He totalled 54 altogether, six of them game-winners, and five counted while killing penalties.

After that, Vaive went overseas to excel for Team Canada at the world championships and returned home to negotiate the second richest contract ever granted by Toronto.

Bill Derlago

The Maple Leafs haven't always received favorable reviews for their trades but nobody can find fault with a transaction they completed in February, 1980. In it, they dealt Tiger Williams and Jerry Butler to Vancouver Canucks and in exchange received Rick Vaive and Bill Derlago.

Vaive, of course, counted 54 goals last season. His regular centre was Bill Derlago, who compiled 84 points. Butler, on the other hand, hardly played at all and Williams had only 17 goals for the Canucks.

Derlago, who'd been a first-round draft pick by the Canucks, was called upon to carry an especially heavy load when centres Darryl Sittler and Laurie Boschman were hurt, and then later traded away.

"We had planned on being strong in the middle and a lot of the time Billy was about all we had there," said coach Mike Nykoluk. "We were asking a great deal of him and he came through extremely well."

Michel Larocque

"We had a terrible defensive record last season, but you mustn't blame our goalies for it," says coach Mike Nykoluk. "They were outstanding. I'd hate to think what some of the scores would have been if they hadn't played so well."

Leafs had obtained Bunny Larocque from Montreal Canadiens near the end of the 1980-81 schedule, and he appeared in 50 matches last term. Vincent Tremblay, his 22-year-old assistant, played in 40. Each posted 10 victories.

"As you know, my complaint in Montreal was that I wasn't getting enough work. I was afraid I was going to lose my touch," says Larocque. "It's for sure I got plenty to do in Toronto.

"You have to remember our kids on defence were just learning. I think they're going to be outstanding and, if I can help in that process, I'll be very happy. In the long run, it'll be better for me, too, eh?"

John Anderson

If plus-minus figures are an accurate yardstick of a player's worth, then red-headed John Anderson was one of Leafs' most valuable men last season.

Exclusive of penalty situations, the Toronto club outscored its adversaries by 14 goals while Anderson was on the ice. That plus-14 was the best on the roster.

Playing left wing with Bill Derlago and Rick Vaive most of the time, Anderson had 31 goals for his best statistics since reaching the NHL in 1977.

"I'd been concerned when I dropped off to 17 goals," says Anderson, who operates a chain of hamburger restaurants in Toronto, "so I regarded it as a kind of breakthrough when the shots started going in for me."

Jim Benning

One of the youngest men ever to play in the NHL, Jim Benning put in five months of difficult on-the-job training as a Leaf rearguard last season. He didn't celebrate his 19th birthday until April 29, after the last game.

"It's a tough way to learn but the lessons really sink in," Benning said. "And they come at you quickly. I don't think there was a shift when I didn't pick up some useful information and, by the end of it, I was beginning to feel more comfortable, a little surer of myself."

Leafs had been attracted by the 111 assists Benning compiled during his final junior term, but he had ony 24 as a Toronto rookie.

"I was trying to be a bit cautious," Benning explained. "I wanted to master the defensive part of the job before I started taking chances with the puck."

Bill Harris

"He's money in the bank," coach Mike Nykoluk says, referring to Billy Harris, "just waiting to be withdrawn when we need him."

The veteran Harris came to Leafs in a mid-season deal with the Los Angeles Kings for Ian Turnbull, but he damaged a shoulder almost immediately and was unable to play for three months.

"He's one of the really solid two-way wingers in the NHL," says Nykoluk. "He'll be a great asset with a young club like ours. He'll be a teacher."

Just 30 now, Harris was an original member of New York

Islanders but was sent to L.A. shortly before their first Stanley Cup victory in 1980. He was part of the trade for Butch Goring.

Fred Boimistruck

The most mature of Leafs' 1981-82 freshmen was defence-man Fred Boimistruck, perhaps because he had been in on two successive Memorial Cup victories with Cornwall juniors.

He ended up his first NHL campaign at 20 years of age with a very creditable plus-nine record.

"It really is a dramatic change," said Boimistruck. "In junior competition, any club you meet might have two or three top players. Relatively speaking, everybody in the NHL is at that level. There are no easy shifts. There's no chance to relax. You learn in a hurry."

Borje Salming

The 1981-82 campaign may have been the best of Borje Salming's nine in the NHL since he came over to North America from Sweden in 1973. But he received scarcely any all-star recognition.

"He didn't have the great stats and our defensive record was so bad," says coach Nykoluk. "But the Leafs have never had to depend on B.J. the way we did this time. He was on his own so much, doing it all. And he played great hockey all year, game in and game out."

Salming's health was better than it had been in several years and he made no secret of the fact he liked playing for Nykoluk. So his attitude was more positive.

"I'm enjoying myself again," he said. "It's as simple as that."

Miroslav Frycer

Not long after playing for Czechoslovakia in the 1981 world championships, right wing Miroslav Frycer escaped from behind the Iron Curtain and moved to Canada, where he signed with Quebec Nordiques.

But his hockey career was pretty much on hold, except for revealing little bursts of brilliance, until he was shipped to Toronto in exchange for Wilf Paiement. Given extra ice time by the needy Leafs, he began to display a turn of speed and an assortment of tricks that could carry him to offensive stardom in the NHL.

An obvious sidekick for him will be centre Peter Ihnacak, another defecting Czech. He left the team during the '82 global tournament last April in Helsinki, and became Leaf property when claimed on the second round of the amateur entry draft in June. A future Frycer-Ihnacak combination is precisely what the Leafs have in mind.

Rocky Saganiuk

MAPLE LEAFS' 1982-83 ROSTER

1981-82 RECORD

Forwards	Ht.	Wt.	Place of Birth	Date	1981-82 Club	G	A	Pts.
John Anderson	5-11	190	Toronto, Ont.	March 28, 1956	Toronto	31	26	57
Normand Aubin	6-0	185	Montreal, Que.	July 26, 1960	Toronto	14	12	26
Bill Derlago	5-10	194	Birtle, Man.	Aug. 25, 1958	Toronto	34	50	84
Miroslav Frycer	6-0	198	Ostrava, CSSR	Sept. 27, 1959	Que.-Tor.	24	21	45
Stewart Gavin	5-11	185	Ottawa, Ont.	March 15, 1960	Toronto	5	6	11
Billy Harris	6-2	195	Toronto, Ont.	Jan. 29, 1952	L.A.-Tor.	3	3	6
Terry Martin	5-11	175	Barrie, Ont.	Oct. 25, 1955	Toronto	25	24	49
Walt Poddubny	6-1	203	Thunder Bay, Ont.	Feb. 14, 1960	Ed.-Tor.	3	4	7
Rocky Saganiuk	5-8	185	Myrnam, Alta.	Dec. 15, 1957	Toronto	17	16	33
Rick Vaive	6-0	180	Ottawa, Ont.	May 14, 1959	Toronto	54	35	89

Defencemen

Name	Ht.	Wt.	Birthplace	Birthdate	Team			
Jim Benning	6-0	185	Edmonton, Alta.	April 29, 1963	Toronto	7	24	31
Fred Boimistruck	5-11	191	Sudbury, Ont.	Jan. 14, 1962	Toronto	2	11	13
Trevor Johansen	5-9	200	Thunder Bay, Ont.	March 30, 1957	L.A.-Tor.	4	10	14
Jim Korn	6-3	210	Hopkins, Minn.	July 28, 1957	Det.-Tor.	2	10	12
Bob Manno	6-0	185	Niagara Falls, Ont.	Oct. 31, 1956	Toronto	9	41	50
Bob McGill	6-0	202	Edmonton, Alta.	April 27, 1962	Toronto	1	10	11
Barry Melrose	6-1	205	Kelvington, Sask.	Dec. 21, 1956	Toronto	1	5	6
Gary Nylund	6-4	210	Surrey, B.C.	Oct. 28, 1963	Portland (WHL)	7	59	66
Borje Salming	6-1	185	Kiruna, Sweden	April 17, 1951	Toronto	12	44	56

Goalies

Name	Ht.	Wt.	Birthplace	Birthdate	Team	GPI	GA	Avg.
Michel Larocque	5-10	185	Hull, Que.	April 6, 1952	Toronto	50	207	4.69
Bob Parent	5-9	175	Windsor, Ont.	Feb. 19, 1958	Cincinnati (CHL)	62	241	4.08
Vincent Tremblay	6-1	180	Quebec City, Que.	Oct. 21, 1959	Toronto	40	155	4.57

DETROIT RED WINGS

Well, It's a Beginning

1981-82 Finish: Trailed Norris, 20th in NHL.
Strengths: Defence okay, improving youth.
Weaknesses: Lack scoring, goalkeeping a question.
Probable 1982-83 Finish: Not much better.

Restaurant tycoon Mike Ilitch purchased Detroit Red Wings last summer because he believes "this is the best franchise in the National Hockey League."

The sale ended half a century in which the Norris family had operated Motown's hockey club, and Bruce Norris emphasized he wasn't getting out because Wings could no longer be profitable but because they had become a headache he no longer needed. He spends most of his time in Florida, whereas Ilitch runs his vast food chain from a Detroit base.

"This team is a sleeping giant," Ilitch declared, "just waiting for somebody to do something with it. As bad as things have been, three wins have always resulted in a sellout. All the fans need is a tiny bit of encouragement.

"And there's nowhere to go but up after making the playoffs once in 12 years."

There was plenty, of course, for Ilitch and his new staff — general manager Jim Devellano and coach Nick Polano — to do. But if you could peek behind Wings' miserable 1981-82 record, featuring 47 defeats and only 270 goals scored, the faint outlines of a decent nucleus could be detected.

The defence, for example, was more than adequate and there was a pair of young netminders capable of working effectively behind that solid corps.

Reed Larsson, Jim Schoenfeld, when he's well, Willie Huber, newcomer Colin Campbell, and Greg Smith aren't Norris Trophy candidates, but they're highly efficient rearguards by anybody's standards. And Larry Trader was coming along as one of junior hockey's better defensive prospects.

Last season's Detroit management felt Greg Stefan and Corrado Micalef were 21-year-olds who would provide solid goalkeeping after their apprenticeship as first-year pros.

Also available was 33-year-old Gilles Gilbert, hampered last season by a chronic bad back but still a dependable NHL netminder of his good days.

So the real problem was attack. Only two NHL teams were weaker last year.

"We'd drafted Claude Loiselle in 1981 but left him with the juniors in Windsor, where he got 36 goals and 73 assists. He's going to be an asset," said Devellano, formerly chief scout for the champion New York Islanders.

"And we got lucky in the '82 draft, obtaining the excellent young centre we needed so badly. At 6-foot-1 and 175 pounds, Murray Craven is just a growing boy and had 81 points in 72 games at Medicine Hat.

"Listen, we were pretty bad last season and I may be crazy for saying this, but I think the makings are there. We don't have any depth at all so injuries can kill us, but we do have talent."

Polano, Devellano's choice as coach, had spent a winter on Buffalo's staff after an extensive career in the minors.

Mark Kirton

In Mark Kirton's own opinion, he's a victim of typecasting. He's been tabbed as strictly a defensive player and he'd like to pad the role.

"There's nothing wrong with being a good checker," he says, "but I happen to have a lot of confidence in my scoring ability, too. I think I can be an all-around player if I'm given the chance."

But the 1981-82 Wings saved Kirton for defensive situations and tough faceoffs, and let other centres handle the attack.

Under the circumstances, it was remarkable ex-Leaf Kirton was able to amass 14 goals and 28 assists.

Mike Blaisdell

Wings rushed Mike Blaisdell into their NHL lineup after claiming him in the first round of the 1980 junior draft. But he wasn't ready and ended up completing the year with the American League farm team at Glens Falls, N.Y.

"I felt disappointment at the time but I now realize it was exactly what I needed," Blaisdell says. "I had scored 71 goals in my final junior year but I still had to learn how to check. And I required some maturity which I developed in the minors."

With his education complete at age 22, Blaisdell returned to the Wings last season and contributed a very useful 23 goals and 32 assists.

Mark Osborne

A 20-year-old rookie, Mark Osborne, led all Detroit attackers last season with 26 goals and 41 assists.

"It's very satisfying," Osborne said, "especially because my only thought at training camp in 1981 was just to make the Detroit team. To me, that was a reasonable objective, just to get into the NHL."

Wings had drafted Osborne, a Torontonian, in 1980 but let him spend another term with Niagara Falls juniors. However, he did do well when called up to Adirondack Red Wings in the American League playoffs.

Osborne wasn't even included when Wings listed a 1981-82 roster in advance, "but he was pretty well our best left winger right from the outset," according to coach Wayne Maxner. "He's exactly what you look for, a guy who does a solid defensive job and gets his share of points, too."

Osborne, a swift skater, is one of the largest NHL forwards as well, and uses his stride to cover a lot of ground.

Danny Gare

Wings look forward to vast improvement in Danny Gare, the feisty right winger they obtained in a trade with Buffalo Sabres last season. Gare feels their confidence is justified.

"On a personal level, the deal represented a very difficult

adjustment,'' says Gare, 27, who had been Sabres' captain and one of their most popular players. "On top of that, I ran into some health problems, too.''

Gare had produced two 50-goal years for Buffalo and was acknowledged as Sabres' inspirational leader. Those were the two main reasons why Wings wanted him and gave up Dale McCourt, Mike Foligno and Brent Peterson in exchange for Gare, Jim Schoenfeld and Derek Smith.

In 37 Detroit matches after arriving, and in spite of a bout with pneumonia, Gare was able to generate 13 goals and 10 assists. That was well below his normal average.

John Ogrodnick

When John Ogrodnick counted 35 goals as a 1980-81 NHL rookie with Detroit, Wings knew they had the big bomber they needed on left wing.

Last season, they made another discovery: without a play-making centre like the departed Dale McCourt, Ogrodnick is not quite as effective.

He slumped after McCourt was traded to Buffalo and wound up with only 28 scores.

But Ogrodnick is just 23 and Wings are making impressive improvements at mid-ice, so a major comeback would seem almost inevitable.

Reed Larson

Players born and developed in the U.S. have ceased to be a novelty in the NHL. Towards the end of the 1981-82 schedule, there were 45 of them.

One of the first, an object of curiosity when he broke in, was Detroit defenceman Reed Larson.

Now 26, Larson joined Wings in 1976 after finishing up at the University of Minnesota and has been a standout regular ever since.

Larson is highly respected around the NHL for his low, powerful, accurate shot, and it resulted last term in 21 goals and 39 assists. He is consistently among his team's offensive leaders.

Greg Smith

Wings were strongly criticized last season when they gave up their first-round 1982 draft choice to Minnesota North Stars for two players.

The brickbats increased in number and intensity when Stars used that pick to claim talented Brian Bellows.

But the trade was not totally foolhardy, from a Detroit point of view. Bellows would have been extremely useful, of course, but at the time the Wings desperately needed assistance on defence. Greg Smith, whom they obtained from Minnesota, represented just that.

Smith is a steady and vastly experienced rearguard of 27.

Willie Huber

When general manager Max McNab was assembling Canada's defence for the 1982 world championships, he issued an urgent invitation to Detroit's Willie Huber.

As it turned out, an injury prevented Huber from accepting. But the compliment stood.

"Huber is a deceptive athlete," McNab said. "He is so big he looks a bit awkward. But if you watch closely, you'll find out he gets the job done.

"He covers a tremendous amount of territory with that huge reach of his. I mean it's a long way around when he extends his body and puts out that stick. He can get up the ice very quickly, too. And he handles the puck very competently."

Huber is, in fact, the NHL's largest individual at 6-foot-5 and 230 pounds.

Greg Smith

Willie Huber

RED WINGS' 1982-83 ROSTER

1981-82 RECORD

Forwards	Ht.	Wt.	Place of Birth	Date	1981-82 Club	G	A	Pts.
Mike Blaisdell	6-1	196	Moose Jaw, Sask.	Jan. 18, 1961	Detroit	23	32	55
Jody Gage	5-11	182	Toronto, Ont.	Nov. 29, 1959	Detroit	9	9	18
Danny Gare	5-9	175	Nelson, B.C.	May 14, 1954	Buff.-Det.	20	24	44
Mark Kirton	5-10	175	Regina, Sask.	Feb. 3, 1958	Detroit	14	28	42
Claude Loiselle	5-11	170	Ottawa, Ont.	May 29, 1963	Windsor (OMJHL)	36	73	109
Walt McKechnie	6-2	200	London, Ont.	June 19, 1947	Detroit	18	37	55
Don Murdoch	5-11	180	Cranbrook, B.C.	Oct. 25, 1956	Detroit	9	13	22
Ted Nolan	6-0	185	Sault Ste. Marie, Ont.	April 7, 1958	Detroit	4	13	17
John Ogrodnick	6-0	190	Ottawa, Ont.	June 20, 1959	Detroit	28	26	54
Mark Osborne	6-1	185	Toronto, Ont.	Aug. 13, 1961	Detroit	26	41	67
Tom Rowe	6-0	190	Lynn, Mass.	May 26, 1956	Hart.-Wash.-Det.	5	1	6
Derek Smith	5-11	177	Quebec City, Que.	July 31, 1954	Buff.-Det.	9	13	22
Eric Vail	6-2	210	Timmins, Ont.	Sept. 16, 1953	Cal.-Det.	14	15	29
Paul Woods	5-10	170	Hespeler, Ont.	April 12, 1955	Detroit	10	17	27

Defencemen

John Barrett	6-1	210	Ottawa, Ont.	July 1, 1958	Detroit	1	12	13
Colin Campbell	5-9	160	London, Ont.	Jan. 28, 1953	Vancouver	0	8	8
Willie Huber	6-5	228	Straaskirchen, W.G.	Jan. 15, 1958	Detroit	15	30	45
Reed Larson	6-0	188	Minneapolis, Minn.	July 30, 1956	Detroit	21	39	60
Jim Schoenfeld	6-2	210	Galt. Ont.	Sept. 4, 1952	Buff.-Det.	8	11	19
Greg Smith	6-0	195	Ponoka, Alta.	July 8, 1955	Detroit	10	22	32

Goalies

						GPI	GA	Avg.
Gilles Gilbert	6-1	175	St. Esprit, Que.	March 31, 1949	Detroit	27	105	4.26
Larry Lozinski	5-11	175	Hudson Bay, Sask.	March 11, 1958	Adirondack (AHL)	53	172	3.34
Corrado Micalef	5-8	172	Sherbrooke, Que.	April 20, 1961	Detroit	18	63	4.67
Greg Stefan	5-11	173	Oshawa, Ont.	Feb. 11, 1961	Adirondack (AHL)	27	89	3.68

NEW JERSEY DEVILS

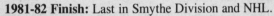

Some Right Moves at Last

1981-82 Finish: Last in Smythe Division and NHL.
Strengths: Hard to detect one.
Weaknesses: Take your pick.
Probable 1982-83 Finish: You guessed it.

A flop in Kansas City and a dud in Denver, the National Hockey League's most troubled franchise has now taken up residence in the Meadowlands sports complex on what used to be New Jersey swampland across from lower Manhattan.

Colorado Rockies — last in the Smythe Division, last in the combined NHL standings, and last in attendance — were purchased by John McMullen, whose record as owner of the Houston Astros in baseball's National League has created feelings of hope among hockey people.

"It's not just that McMullen has solved one of our most urgent problems," says NHL president John Ziegler. "His history in sport shows he'll do whatever is necessary to develop a contending team."

Ziegler's people repaid McMullen with a few favors in return — or did they?

He was given permission to move his club from apathetic Denver to an area where all sporting enterprises have been monstrous successes, like the New York Giants in football, the Cosmos in soccer, and horse racing at the Meadowlands track.

That was good. But the Jerseyites, named Devils, will have to compete in the very strong Patrick Division. And that means the primary objective, qualifying for the Stanley Cup playoffs, is even further away than before.

"But it also means we'll have better attractions coming into our building," McMullen rationalizes. "And while we seem to be in a difficult position right now, it may not be long before other people envy us for being in this group. Sports tend to move in cycles like that, you know."

Apart from such generalizations, there really isn't much to

be optimistic about as Rockies set out on their inaugural year in New Jersey.

One excellent summer manoeuvre did provide an important foothold on the future, though.

Earlier trades had undermined the Rockies' position in the vital amateur drafts of 1982 and '83, but that grave problem was corrected when defenceman Rob Ramage was dealt to St. Louis Blues. The payment consisted of Blues' first-round choices those same two summers.

The '82 pick was used to grab Rocky Trottier, an 18-year-old clone of his talented brother, Islander centre Bryan Trottier. He's a sturdy player who'd have been in greater demand if injuries hadn't shortened his 1981-82 campaign with the juniors in Billings, Montana.

Max McNab, formerly Washington Capitals' general manager, is vice-president in charge of hockey operations, Colorado GM Billy MacMillan resumes coaching duties, and Marshall Johnston, Rockies' coach, was named assistant.

Glenn Resch

Chico Resch received the Bill Masterton Trophy last season as the NHL player exhibiting exceptional "perseverance, sportsmanship and dedication."

Those words applied, all right, and you could have added heroism, because Resch played 61 games in goal behind the leaky Colorado defence. Some felt it was the greatest achievement of his career, obtaining 16 victories and 11 ties with that aggregation.

"I don't know if he ever played better hockey," said coach Marshall Johnston. "That's why it's so nice to see him get that recognition."

"I didn't do much more than all the other guys who went through this season," said Resch. "But as a goalie, I was in a position where it might have looked as though I had a tougher row to hoe."

Don Lever

At one time, left winger Don Lever was part of what was to be a glorious future for Vancouver Canucks. He was the first junior they drafted in 1972.

However, the Vancouver fans never appreciated Lever's laborious, unspectacular approach to the game, and he eventually was traded to Atlanta (later Calgary) Flames for Ivan Boldirev and Darcy Rota.

Then he was sent to Colorado Rockies last season, with Bob MacMillan, for Lanny McDonald.

Lever, 30, was his usual effective self in Denver, collecting 22 goals and 28 assists in 59 games.

Brent Ashton

It was a highly complicated three-way transaction which moved left winger Brent Ashton to Colorado Rockies before the 1981-82 schedule opened.

Vancouver Canucks had made tentative arrangements to sign two Czechoslovakian veterans, Ivan Hlinka and Jiri Bubla. But Rockies and Winnipeg Jets had prior claims in a special draft of Czech imports. The Jets took Hlinka and the Rockies claimed Bubla. Then they commenced negotiations with Canucks.

Here was the eventual solution: Bubla and Hlinka went to Vancouver; Jets got Lucien DeBlois from the Rockies; the highly rated Ashton wound up in Denver.

Ashton's record shows steady improvement — five goals as a rookie, then 18, and finally 22 last season.

Steve Tambellini

Owner of a surname that is prominent in Canadian hockey history is centre Steve Tambellini.

The last team to win a world championship for Canada was from Trail, B.C., in 1961, and its swift, clever centre was Adie Tambellini. Son Steve is just as fast and has gone his famous father one better by reaching the NHL.

Adie Tambellini was one of the first Canadians to play in Europe, and it was while he was living in Austria that Steve learned to skate and did his first stickhandling.

He became a professional in Islanders' organization but was part of the 1981 trade that also moved Chico Resch to Colorado and Mike McEwen to Long Island.

Bob MacMillan

Bobby Mac has been a hockey professional since 1972 and East Rutherford, N.J., is the eighth town in which he has been employed.

The career began at St. Paul in the World Hockey Association and then he moved to New York, Providence, St. Louis, Atlanta, Calgary, Denver, and now the Meadowlands.

The Calgary club dealt MacMillan and Don Lever to Colorado last season for Lanny McDonald.

MacMillan got Rockies a very tidy 18 goals and 32 assists in 57 games but is still striving to reconquer his 1978-79 heights — 37 goals, 71 assists, and the Lady Byng Trophy. He is the brother of general manager Bill MacMillan.

Tapio Levo

A great many hockey scouts are convinced defenceman Tapio Levo will turn out to be one of the best European players ever imported to the NHL. They felt that way in 1981 when the Rockies signed him and they have seen nothing to sway their opinions.

The Colorado club spent a lot of money to acquire Levo. It was even helpful to hire two other Finns, Jukka Porvari and Veli-Pekka Ketola, mostly to keep Levo company when he immigrated.

But injuries intervened and Levo, 26, missed more than half the Colorado schedule.

Once he did return, he lived up to all expectations and in 34 matches posted nine goals and 13 assists.

Dwight Foster

No NHL player has stranger, or stronger, motivation than Dwight Foster. He is driven, in a way, by his own feelings of self-esteem.

Foster is the player the Rockies received from Boston Bruins when they traded their first-round draft pick for the year in which superstar Brian Bellows would be eligible.

''They've been criticized for having made a stupid deal,''

says Foster, "but one of the things that always comes through is that the player they got in return, me, is a big zero.

"Maybe it was a poor trade. It's not for me to say, but I'm anxious to show that they at least got a decent hockey player out of it."

Foster's 1981-82 statistics don't offer such proof, but the fact remains he was a No. 1 pick himself in 1977 and, at 25, is just leaving an injury jinx behind.

Joe Cirella

Rob Ramage had to be sacrificed last summer in a trade that was absolutely vital to the future of the New Jersey franchise.

"One of the reasons we were able to do it," said GM Bill MacMillan, "was our confidence in Joe Cirella as a defenceman."

Colorado Rockies were the fifth to choose in the NHL's 1981 amateur draft, and their decision was to take Cirella, a defenceman with Oshawa, Ont. juniors.

"He was only 18 so we considered letting him put in another year of junior competition," said MacMillan, "but then we decided he could help us in the NHL, while learning.

"As it happened, he made such excellent progress, while playing 65 games for us, that we could afford to give up Ramage."

Don Lever

**Chico Resch,
Masterton Trophy winner**

DEVILS' 1982-83 ROSTER

1981-82 RECORD

Forwards	Ht.	Wt.	Place of Birth	Date	1981-82 Club	G	A	Pts.
Brent Ashton	6-1	210	Saskatoon, Sask.	May 18, 1960	Colorado	24	36	60
Aaron Broten	5-10	175	Roseau, Minn.	Nov. 4, 1960	Colorado	15	24	39
Dave Cameron	6-0	185	Charlottetown, P.E.I.	July 29, 1958	Colorado	11	12	23
Dwight Foster	5-10	190	Toronto, Ont.	April 2, 1957	Colorado	12	19	31
Paul Gagne	5-10	178	Iroquois Falls, Ont.	Feb. 6, 1962	Colorado	10	12	22
Veli-Pekka Ketola	6-3	220	Pori, Finland	March 28, 1948	Colorado	9	5	14
Don Lever	5-11	185	South Porcupine, Ont.	Nov. 14, 1952	Cal.-Col.	30	39	69
Bob MacMillan	5-11	185	Charlottetown, P.E.I.	Sept. 3, 1952	Cal.-Col.	22	39	61
Merlin Malinowski	6-0	190	North Battleford, Sask.	Sept. 25, 1958	Colorado	13	28	41
Kevin Maxwell	5-9	165	Edmonton, Alta.	March 30, 1960	Minn.-Col.	6	9	15
Bob Miller	5-11	185	Medford, Mass.	Sept. 28, 1956	Colorado	11	20	31
Steve Tambellini	6-0	190	Trail, B.C.	May 14, 1958	Colorado	29	30	59
Rocky Trottier	5-11	185	Val Marie, Sask.	1964	Billings (WHL)	13	21	34
Stan Weir	6-1	170	Ponoka, Alta.	March 7, 1952	Edm.-Col.	5	16	21
John Wensink	6-0	200	Cornwall, Ont.	April 1, 1953	Colorado	5	3	8

Defencemen

Joe Cirella	6-2	193	Hamilton, Ont.	May 9, 1963	Colorado	7	12	19
Mike Kitchen	5-10	178	Newmarket, Ont.	Feb. 1, 1956	Colorado	1	8	9
Tapio Levo	6-2	200	Pori, Finland	Sept. 24, 1955	Colorado	9	13	22
Bob Lorimer	6-1	190	Toronto, Ont.	Aug. 25, 1953	Colorado	5	15	20
Joe Micheletti	6-0	185	International Falls, Minn.	Oct. 24, 1954	St. L.-Col.	5	17	22
Joel Quenneville	6-0	188	Windsor, Ont.	Sept. 15, 1958	Colorado	5	10	15

Goalies

						GPI	GA	Avg.
Phil Myre	6-1	185	Ste. Anne de Bellevue, Que.	Nov. 1, 1948	Colorado	24	112	5.35
Glenn Resch	5-9	165	Moose Jaw, Sask.	July 10, 1948	Colorado	61	230	4.03

Ric Seiling, Buffalo Sabres

Rick Green, Washington Capitals

Ray Bourque, Boston Bruins

Barry Beck, New York Rangers

**Rick Walmsley, Montreal Canadiens,
Jennings Trophy co-winner**

**Denis Heron, Montreal Canadiens,
Jennings Trophy co-winner**

PART THREE

FACTS AND FIGURES

FINAL STANDINGS, 1981-82

CAMPBELL CONFERENCE

NORRIS DIVISION

	GP	W	L	T	GF	GA	Pts.
Minnesota	80	37	23	20	346	288	94
Winnipeg	80	33	33	14	319	332	80
St. Louis	80	32	40	8	315	349	72
Chicago	80	30	38	12	332	363	72
Toronto	80	20	44	16	298	380	56
Detroit	80	21	47	12	270	351	54

SMYTHE DIVISION

	GP	W	L	T	GF	GA	Pts.
Edmonton	80	48	17	15	417	295	111
Vancouver	80	30	33	17	290	286	77
Calgary	80	29	34	17	334	345	75
Los Angeles	80	24	41	15	314	369	63
Colorado	80	18	49	13	241	362	49

WALES CONFERENCE

ADAMS DIVISION

	GP	W	L	T	GF	GA	Pts.
Montreal	80	46	17	17	360	223	109
Boston	80	43	27	10	323	285	96
Buffalo	80	39	26	15	307	273	93
Quebec	80	33	31	16	356	345	82
Hartford	80	21	41	18	264	351	60

PATRICK DIVISION

	GP	W	L	T	GF	GA	Pts.
Islanders	80	54	16	10	385	250	118
Rangers	80	39	27	14	316	306	92
Philadelphia	80	38	31	11	325	313	87
Pittsburgh	80	31	36	13	310	337	75
Washington	80	26	41	13	319	338	65

COMBINED STANDINGS

		W	L	T	F	A	Pts.
1.	Islanders	54	16	10	385	250	118
2.	Edmonton	48	17	15	417	295	111
3.	Montreal	46	17	17	360	223	109
4.	Boston	43	27	10	323	285	96
5.	Minnesota	37	23	20	346	288	94
6.	Buffalo	39	26	15	307	273	93
7.	Rangers	39	27	14	316	306	92
8.	Philadelphia	38	31	11	325	313	87
9.	Quebec	33	31	16	356	345	82
10.	Winnipeg	33	33	14	319	332	80
11.	Vancouver	30	33	17	290	286	77
12.	Pittsburgh	31	36	13	310	337	75
13.	Calgary	29	34	17	334	345	75
14.	St. Louis	32	40	8	315	349	72
15.	Chicago	30	38	12	332	363	72
16.	Washington	26	41	13	319	338	65
17.	Los Angeles	24	41	15	314	369	63
18.	Hartford	21	41	18	264	351	60
19.	Toronto	20	44	16	298	380	56
20.	Detroit	21	47	12	270	351	54
21.	Colorado	18	49	13	241	362	49

HOME AND AWAY

	AT HOME					ON THE ROAD			
	W	L	T	Pts.		W	L	T	Pts.
NYI	33	3	4	70	Mtl.	21	11	8	50
Edm.	31	5	4	66	NYI	21	13	6	48
Mtl.	25	6	9	59	NYR	20	12	8	48
Phi.	25	10	5	55	Edm.	17	12	11	45
Buf.	23	8	9	55	Bos.	19	15	6	44
Min.	21	7	12	54	Min.	16	16	8	40
Bos.	24	12	4	52	Buf.	16	18	6	38
Van.	20	8	12	52	Wpg.	15	20	5	35
Que.	24	13	3	51	Phi.	13	21	6	32
Pit.	21	11	8	50	Que.	9	18	13	31
Cal.	20	11	9	49	Cal.	9	23	8	26
St.L.	22	14	4	48	Chi.	10	25	5	25
Chi.	20	13	7	47	Pit.	10	25	5	25
Wpg.	18	13	9	45	Van.	10	25	5	25
NYR	19	15	6	44	Was.	10	25	5	25
L.A.	19	15	6	44	St.L.	10	26	4	24
Was.	16	16	8	40	Har.	8	24	8	24
Det.	15	19	6	36	Tor.	8	24	8	24
Har.	13	17	10	36	L.A.	5	26	9	19
Col.	14	21	5	33	Det.	6	28	6	18
Tor.	12	20	8	32	Col.	4	28	8	16

INDIVIDUAL SCORING

BOSTON BRUINS

		GP	G	A	Pts.	PM
Rick Middleton	Boston	75	51	43	94	12
Barry Pederson	Boston	80	44	48	92	53
Peter McNab	Boston	80	36	40	76	19
Ray Bourque	Boston	65	17	49	66	51
Brad Park	Boston	75	14	42	56	82
Terry O'Reilly	Boston	70	22	30	52	213
Steve Kasper	Boston	73	20	31	51	72
Keith Crowder	Boston	71	23	21	44	101
Wayne Cashman	Boston	64	12	31	43	59
Tom Fergus	Boston	61	15	24	39	12
Mike O'Connell	Boston	80	5	34	39	75
Don Marcotte	Boston	69	13	22	35	14
Norm Leveille	Boston	65	14	19	33	49
Bruce Crowder	Boston	63	16	11	27	31
Stan Jonathan	Boston	67	6	17	23	57
Mike Gillis	Boston	53	9	8	17	54
Mike Milbury	Boston	51	2	10	12	71
Brad McCrimmon	Boston	78	1	8	9	83
Randy Hillier	Boston	25	0	8	8	29
Larry Melnyk	Boston	48	0	8	8	84
M. Krushelnyski	Boston	17	3	3	6	2
Marco Baron	Boston	44	0	2	2	35
Craig MacTavish	Boston	2	0	1	1	0
Rogie Vachon	Boston	38	0	1	1	0
Dave Barr	Boston	2	0	0	0	0
Doug Morrison	Boston	3	0	0	0	0
Dick Redmond	Boston	17	0	0	0	4

BUFFALO SABRES

		GP	G	A	Pts.	PM
Mike Foligno	Detroit	26	13	13	26	28
	Buffalo	56	20	31	51	149
	Total	82	33	44	77	177
Gil Perreault	Buffalo	62	31	42	73	40
Dale McCourt	Detroit	26	13	14	27	6
	Buffalo	52	20	22	42	12
	Total	78	33	36	69	18

J. Van Boxmeer	Buffalo	69	14	54	68	62
Yvon Lambert	Buffalo	77	25	39	64	38
Jean F. Sauve	Buffalo	69	19	36	55	46
Tony McKegney	Buffalo	73	23	29	52	41
Craig Ramsay	Buffalo	80	16	35	51	8
Lindy Ruff	Buffalo	79	16	32	48	194
Ric Seiling	Buffalo	57	22	25	47	58
Alan Haworth	Buffalo	57	21	18	39	30
Andre Savard	Buffalo	62	18	20	38	24
Mike Ramsey	Buffalo	80	7	23	30	56
Richie Dunn	Buffalo	72	7	19	26	73
Steve Patrick	Buffalo	41	8	8	16	64
Larry Playfair	Buffalo	77	6	10	16	258
Brent Peterson	Detroit	15	1	0	1	6
	Buffalo	46	9	5	14	43
	Total	61	10	5	15	49
Bill Hajt	Buffalo	65	2	9	11	44
Bob Mongrain	Buffalo	24	6	4	10	6
Gilles Hamel	Buffalo	16	2	7	9	2
Bob Hess	Buffalo	33	0	8	8	14
Ron Fischer	Buffalo	15	0	7	7	6
R. Cunneyworth	Buffalo	20	2	4	6	47
Don Edwards	Buffalo	62	0	2	2	2
Haanu Virta	Buffalo	3	0	1	1	4
Sean McKenna	Buffalo	3	0	1	1	2
Jim Walsh	Buffalo	4	0	1	1	4
Jeff Eatough	Buffalo	1	0	0	0	0
Kai Suikkanen	Buffalo	1	0	0	0	0
Val James	Buffalo	7	0	0	0	16
Mike Moller	Buffalo	9	0	0	0	0
Paul Harrison	Pittsburgh	13	0	0	0	0
	Buffalo	6	0	0	0	2
	Total	19	0	0	0	2

CALGARY FLAMES

		GP	G	A	Pts.	PM
Mel Bridgman	Philadelphia	9	7	5	12	47
	Calgary	63	26	49	75	94
	Total	72	33	54	87	141
Lanny McDonald	Colorado	16	6	9	15	20
	Calgary	55	34	33	67	37
	Total	71	40	42	82	57

Guy Chouinard	Calgary	64	23	57	80	12
P. Rautakallio	Calgary	80	17	51	68	40
Jim Peplinski	Calgary	74	30	37	67	115
Kevin Lavalee	Calgary	75	32	29	61	30
Paul Reinhart	Calgary	62	13	48	61	17
Willi Plett	Calgary	78	21	36	57	288
Kent Nilsson	Calgary	41	26	29	55	8
Ken Houston	Calgary	70	22	22	44	91
Jamie Hislop	Calgary	80	16	25	41	35
Phil Russell	Calgary	71	4	25	29	110
Gary McAdam	Calgary	46	12	15	27	18
Denis Cyr	Calgary	45	12	10	22	13
Dan Labraaten	Calgary	43	10	12	22	6
Bob Murdoch	Calgary	73	3	17	20	76
Steve Konroyd	Calgary	63	3	14	17	78
Bill Clement	Calgary	69	4	12	16	28
C. Bourgeois	Calgary	54	2	13	15	112
Pat Riggin	Calgary	52	0	5	5	4
Dave Hindmarch	Calgary	9	3	0	3	0
Pat Ribble	Washington	12	1	2	3	14
	Calgary	3	0	0	0	2
	Total	15	1	2	3	16
Ed Beers	Calgary	5	1	1	2	21
Mike Dwyer	Calgary	5	0	2	2	0
Gord Wappel	Calgary	11	1	0	1	6
Carl Mokosak	Calgary	1	0	1	1	0
Rejean Lemelin	Calgary	34	0	1	1	0
Randy Turnbull	Calgary	1	0	0	0	2
Bruce Eakin	Calgary	1	0	0	0	0
Bobby Lalonde	Calgary	1	0	0	0	0
Allan MacInnis	Calgary	2	0	0	0	0
Tim Hunter	Calgary	2	0	0	0	9

CHICAGO BLACK HAWKS

		GP	G	A	Pts.	PM
Denis Savard	Chicago	80	32	87	119	82
Doug Wilson	Chicago	76	39	46	85	54
Tom Lysiak	Chicago	71	32	50	82	84
Al Secord	Chicago	80	44	31	75	303
Tim Higgins	Chicago	74	20	30	50	85
Grant Mulvey	Chicago	73	30	19	49	141

Rich Preston	Chicago	75	15	28	43	30
Doug Crossman	Chicago	70	12	28	40	24
Reg Kerr	Chicago	59	11	28	39	39
T. Ruskowski	Chicago	60	7	30	37	120
Darryl Sutter	Chicago	40	23	12	35	31
Ted Bulley	Chicago	59	12	18	30	120
Bob Murray	Chicago	45	8	22	30	48
Peter Marsh	Chicago	57	10	18	28	47
Keith Brown	Chicago	33	4	20	24	26
Bill Gardner	Chicago	69	8	15	23	20
Dave Hutchison	Chicago	66	5	18	23	246
Greg Fox	Chicago	79	2	19	21	137
Glen Sharpley	Chicago	36	9	7	16	11
Rick Paterson	Chicago	48	4	7	11	8
Jerry Dupont	Chicago	34	0	4	4	51
Steve Ludzik	Chicago	8	2	1	3	2
Flo Robidoux	Chicago	4	1	2	3	0
Miles Zaharko	Chicago	15	1	2	3	18
Dave Feamster	Chicago	29	0	2	2	29
Tony Esposito	Chicago	52	0	2	2	0
John Marks	Chicago	13	1	0	1	7
M. Bannerman	Chicago	29	0	1	1	0
Troy Murray	Chicago	1	0	0	0	0
Tony Tanti	Chicago	2	0	0	0	0
Steve Larmer	Chicago	3	0	0	0	0

COLORADO ROCKIES

		GP	G	A	Pts.	PM
Don Lever	Calgary	23	8	11	19	6
	Colorado	59	22	28	50	20
	Total	82	30	39	69	26
Bob MacMillan	Calgary	23	4	7	11	14
	Colorado	57	18	32	50	27
	Total	80	22	39	61	41
Brent Ashton	Colorado	80	24	36	60	26
S. Tambellini	Colorado	79	29	30	59	14
Rob Ramage	Colorado	80	13	29	42	201
M. Malinowski	Colorado	69	13	28	41	32
Aaron Broten	Colorado	58	15	24	39	6
Dwight Foster	Colorado	70	12	19	31	41
Bob Miller	Colorado	56	11	20	31	27

Dave Cameron	Colorado	66	11	12	23	103
Paul Gagne	Colorado	59	10	12	22	17
Tapio Levo	Colorado	34	9	13	22	14
J. Micheletti	St. Louis	20	3	11	14	28
	Colorado	21	2	6	8	4
	Total	41	5	17	22	32
Stan Weir	Edmonton	51	3	13	16	13
	Colorado	10	2	3	5	10
	Total	61	5	16	21	23
Bob Lorimer	Colorado	79	5	15	20	68
Joe Cirella	Colorado	65	7	12	19	52
Kevin Maxwell	Minnesota	12	1	4	5	8
	Colorado	34	5	5	10	44
	Total	46	6	9	15	52
J. Quenneville	Colorado	64	5	10	15	55
Veli Ketola	Colorado	44	9	5	14	4
Graeme Nicolson	Colorado	44	2	7	9	51
Mike Kitchen	Colorado	63	1	8	9	60
John Wensink	Colorado	57	5	3	8	152
Jukka Porvari	Colorado	31	2	6	8	0
Yvon Vautour	Colorado	14	1	2	3	18
Paul Miller	Colorado	3	0	3	3	0
Jeff Larmer	Colorado	8	1	1	2	8
Phil Myre	Colorado	24	0	2	2	0
Glenn Resch	Colorado	61	0	2	2	8
Ed Cooper	Colorado	2	1	0	1	0
Rich Chernomaz	Colorado	2	0	0	0	0
P. Gustavsson	Colorado	2	0	0	0	0
Chris Kellgren	Colorado	5	0	0	0	0
Randy Pierce	Colorado	5	0	0	0	4
John Hughes	Colorado	8	0	0	0	13
Jim Dobson	Minnesota	6	0	0	0	4
	Colorado	3	0	0	0	2
	Total	9	0	0	0	6

DETROIT RED WINGS

		GP	G	A	Pts.	PM
Mark Osborne	Detroit	80	26	41	67	61
Reed Larson	Detroit	80	21	39	60	112
Mike Blaisdell	Detroit	80	23	32	55	48
Walt McKechnie	Detroit	74	18	37	55	35
John Ogrodnick	Detroit	80	28	26	54	28

Willie Huber	Detroit	74	15	30	45	98
Danny Gare	Buffalo	22	7	14	21	25
	Detroit	37	13	10	23	74
	Total	59	20	24	44	99
Mark Kirton	Detroit	74	14	28	42	62
V. Nedomansky	Detroit	68	12	28	40	22
Greg Smith	Detroit	69	10	22	32	79
Eric Vail	Calgary	6	4	1	5	0
	Detroit	52	10	14	24	35
	Total	58	14	15	29	35
Paul Woods	Detroit	75	10	17	27	48
Derek Smith	Buffalo	12	3	1	4	2
	Detroit	49	6	14	20	10
	Total	61	9	15	24	12
Don Murdoch	Detroit	49	9	13	22	23
Jim Schoenfeld	Buffalo	13	3	2	5	30
	Detroit	39	5	9	14	69
	Total	52	8	11	19	99
Jody Gage	Detroit	31	9	9	18	2
Ted Nolan	Detroit	41	4	13	17	45
John Barrett	Detroit	69	1	12	13	93
Mark Lofthouse	Detroit	12	3	4	7	13
Greg Joly	Detroit	37	1	5	6	30
Brad Smith	Detroit	33	2	0	2	80
Claude Loiselle	Detroit	4	1	0	1	2
Claude Legris	Detroit	1	0	1	1	0
Rejean Cloutier	Detroit	2	0	1	1	2
Joe Paterson	Detroit	3	0	0	0	0
Corrado Micalef	Detroit	18	0	0	0	9
Gilles Gilbert	Detroit	27	0	0	0	2
Bob Sauve	Buffalo	14	0	0	0	2
	Detroit	41	0	0	0	0
	Total	55	0	0	0	2

EDMONTON OILERS

		GP	G	A	Pts.	PM
Wayne Gretzky	Edmonton	80	92	120	212	26
Glenn Anderson	Edmonton	80	38	67	105	71
Paul Coffey	Edmonton	80	29	60	89	106
Mark Messier	Edmonton	78	50	38	88	119
Jari Kurri	Edmonton	71	32	54	86	32

Name	Team	GP	G	A	Pts.	PM
Dave Lumley	Edmonton	66	32	42	74	96
Risto Siltanen	Edmonton	63	15	48	63	24
Matti Hagman	Edmonton	72	21	38	59	18
Pat Hughes	Edmonton	68	24	22	46	99
Kevin Lowe	Edmonton	80	9	31	40	63
Dave Hunter	Edmonton	63	16	22	38	63
Laurie Boschman	Toronto	54	9	19	28	150
	Edmonton	11	2	3	5	37
	Total	65	11	22	33	187
Lee Fogolin	Edmonton	80	4	25	29	154
Brett Callighen	Edmonton	46	8	19	27	28
Dave Semenko	Edmonton	59	12	12	24	194
Garry Lariviere	Edmonton	62	1	21	22	41
Garry Unger	Edmonton	46	7	13	20	69
Charlie Huddy	Edmonton	41	4	11	15	48
Tom Roulston	Edmonton	35	11	3	14	22
Mike Forbes	Edmonton	16	1	7	8	26
Grant Fuhr	Edmonton	48	0	6	6	6
Ken Berry	Edmonton	15	2	3	5	9
Marc Habscheid	Edmonton	7	1	3	4	2
Lance Nethery	NY Rangers	5	0	0	0	0
	Edmonton	3	0	2	2	2
	Total	8	0	2	2	2
C. Brackenbury	Edmonton	14	0	2	2	12
Andy Moog	Edmonton	8	0	1	1	2
Todd Strueby	Edmonton	3	0	0	0	0
Don Jackson	Edmonton	8	0	0	0	18
Ron Low	Edmonton	29	0	0	0	12

HARTFORD WHALERS

Name	Team	GP	G	A	Pts.	PM
Blaine Stoughton	Hartford	80	52	39	91	57
Pierre Larouche	Montreal	22	9	12	21	0
	Hartford	45	25	25	50	12
	Total	67	34	37	71	12
Doug Sulliman	Hartford	77	29	40	69	39
Ron Francis	Hartford	59	25	43	68	51
Mark Howe	Hartford	76	8	45	53	18
Garry Howatt	Hartford	80	18	32	50	242
Rick Meagher	Hartford	65	24	19	43	51
C. Kotsopoulos	Hartford	68	13	20	33	147
Blake Wesley	Hartford	78	9	18	27	123

Don Nachbaur	Hartford	77	5	21	26	117
Warren Miller	Hartford	74	10	12	22	68
Dave Keon	Hartford	78	8	11	19	6
Mark Renaud	Hartford	48	1	17	18	39
Jordy Douglas	Hartford	30	10	7	17	44
George Lyle	Detroit	11	1	2	3	4
	Hartford	14	2	12	14	9
	Total	25	3	14	17	13
D. Bourbonnais	Hartford	24	3	9	12	11
Paul Shmyr	Hartford	66	1	11	12	134
Ray Neufeld	Hartford	19	4	3	7	4
Mickey Volcan	Hartford	26	1	5	6	29
Jack McIlhargey	Hartford	50	1	5	6	60
Norm Barnes	Hartford	20	1	4	5	19
Don Gillen	Hartford	34	1	4	5	22
Russ Anderson	Pittsburgh	31	0	1	1	98
	Hartford	25	1	3	4	85
	Total	56	1	4	5	183
Greg Millen	Hartford	55	0	5	5	2
Marty Howe	Hartford	13	0	4	4	2
Stuart Smith	Hartford	17	0	3	3	15
Randy MacGregor	Hartford	2	1	1	2	2
Paul MacDermid	Hartford	3	1	0	1	2
Gilles Lupien	Hartford	1	0	1	1	2
Mike Fidler	Hartford	2	0	1	1	0
Dan Fridgen	Hartford	2	0	1	1	0
Je. Brownschidle	Hartford	3	0	1	1	2
Mike Veisor	Hartford	13	0	1	1	0
Mike McDougal	Hartford	3	0	0	0	0
Dave McDonald	Hartford	3	0	0	0	0
Glenn Merkosky	Hartford	7	0	0	0	2
Michel Galarneau	Hartford	10	0	0	0	4

LOS ANGELES KINGS

		GP	G	A	Pts.	PM
Marcel Dionne	Los Angeles	78	50	67	117	50
Dave Taylor	Los Angeles	78	39	67	106	130
Jim Fox	Los Angeles	77	30	38	68	23
Larry Murphy	Los Angeles	79	22	44	66	95
Steve Bozek	Los Angeles	71	33	23	56	68
Mark Hardy	Los Angeles	77	6	39	45	130
Charlie Simmer	Los Angeles	50	15	24	39	42

Greg Terrion	Los Angeles	61	15	22	37	23
Dan Bonar	Los Angeles	79	13	23	36	111
Bernie Nicholls	Los Angeles	22	14	18	32	27
Doug Smith	Los Angeles	80	16	14	30	64
Ian Turnbull	Toronto	12	0	2	2	8
	Los Angeles	42	11	15	26	81
	Total	54	11	17	28	89
Steve Jensen	Los Angeles	45	8	19	27	19
John Kelly	Los Angeles	70	12	11	23	100
Jerry Korab	Los Angeles	50	5	13	18	91
Mike Murphy	Los Angeles	28	5	10	15	20
Dean Hopkins	Los Angeles	41	2	13	15	102
Paul Mulvey	Pittsburgh	27	1	7	8	76
	Los Angeles	11	0	7	7	50
	Total	38	1	14	15	126
Dave Lewis	Los Angeles	64	1	13	14	75
A. Hangsleben	Washington	17	1	1	2	19
	Los Angeles	18	2	6	8	65
	Total	35	3	7	10	84
Rick Chartraw	Los Angeles	33	2	8	10	56
Jay Wells	Los Angeles	60	1	8	9	145
Daryl Evans	Los Angeles	14	2	6	8	2
Rick Martin	Los Angeles	3	1	3	4	2
Scott Gruhl	Los Angeles	7	2	1	3	2
Al Sims	Los Angeles	8	1	1	2	16
Warren Holmes	Los Angeles	3	0	2	2	0
Rob Palmer	Los Angeles	5	0	2	2	0
Mario Lessard	Los Angeles	52	0	2	2	6
Glenn Goldup	Los Angeles	2	0	0	0	2
Bobby Sheehan	Los Angeles	4	0	0	0	2
Dave Morrison	Los Angeles	4	0	0	0	0

MINNESOTA NORTH STARS

		GP	G	A	Pts.	PM
Bobby Smith	Minnesota	80	43	71	114	84
Dino Ciccarelli	Minnesota	76	55	52	107	138
Neal Broten	Minnesota	73	38	59	97	42
Steve Payne	Minnesota	74	33	44	77	76
Craig Hartsburg	Minnesota	76	17	60	77	115
Al MacAdam	Minnesota	79	18	43	61	37
Steve Christoff	Minnesota	69	26	30	56	14
Brad Palmer	Minnesota	72	22	23	45	18

Tom McCarthy	Minnesota	40	12	30	42	36
Tim Young	Minnesota	49	10	31	41	67
Gordie Roberts	Minnesota	79	4	30	34	119
Brad Maxwell	Minnesota	51	10	21	31	96
Mark Johnson	Pittsburgh	46	10	11	21	30
	Minnesota	10	2	2	4	10
	Total	56	12	13	25	40
Mike Eaves	Minnesota	25	11	10	21	0
K. E. Andersson	Minnesota	70	9	12	21	18
A. Hakansson	Minnesota	72	12	4	16	29
Fred Barrett	Minnesota	69	1	15	16	89
Curt Giles	Minnesota	74	3	12	15	87
Jack Carlson	Minnesota	57	8	4	12	103
Bill Nyrop	Minnesota	42	4	8	12	35
Ken Solheim	Minnesota	29	4	5	9	4
Gary Sargent	Minnesota	15	0	5	5	18
Murray Brumwell	Minnesota	21	0	3	3	18
Dan Poulin	Minnesota	3	1	1	2	2
Ron Meighan	Minnesota	7	1	1	2	2
Gilles Meloche	Minnesota	51	0	1	1	6
Warren Young	Minnesota	1	0	0	0	0
Udo Kiessling	Minnesota	1	0	0	0	2
Archie Henderson	Minnesota	1	0	0	0	0
Peter Hayek	Minnesota	1	0	0	0	0
Roger Melin	Minnesota	2	0	0	0	0
Mike Antonovich	Minnesota	2	0	0	0	0
Dave Richter	Minnesota	3	0	0	0	11
Don Friest	Minnesota	10	0	0	0	31
Don Beaupre	Minnesota	29	0	0	0	19

MONTREAL CANADIENS

		GP	G	A	Pts.	PM
Keith Acton	Montreal	78	36	52	88	88
Guy Lafleur	Montreal	66	27	57	84	24
Mark Napier	Montreal	80	40	41	81	14
Mario Tremblay	Montreal	80	33	40	73	66
Pierre Mondou	Montreal	73	35	33	68	57
Larry Robinson	Montreal	71	12	47	59	41
Steve Shutt	Montreal	57	31	24	55	40
Doug Jarvis	Montreal	80	20	28	48	20
Bob Gainey	Montreal	79	21	24	45	24
Rejean Houle	Montreal	51	11	32	43	34
Rod Langway	Montreal	66	5	34	39	116

		GP	G	A	Pts.	PM
D. Wickenheiser	Montreal	56	12	23	35	43
D. Risebrough	Montreal	59	15	18	33	116
Brian Engblom	Montreal	76	4	29	33	76
Mark Hunter	Montreal	71	18	11	29	143
Robert Picard	Montreal	62	2	26	28	106
Gaston Gingras	Montreal	34	6	18	24	28
Craig Laughlin	Montreal	36	12	11	23	33
Chris Nilan	Montreal	49	7	4	11	204
Gilbert Delorme	Montreal	60	3	8	11	55
Rick Walmsley	Montreal	38	0	2	2	4
Jeff Brubaker	Montreal	3	0	1	1	32
Dave Orleski	Montreal	1	0	0	0	0
Bill Kitchen	Montreal	1	0	0	0	7
Rich Sevigny	Montreal	19	0	0	0	10
Denis Herron	Montreal	27	0	0	0	4

NEW YORK ISLANDERS

		GP	G	A	Pts.	PM
Mike Bossy	Islanders	80	64	83	147	22
Bryan Trottier	Islanders	80	50	79	129	88
John Tonelli	Islanders	80	35	58	93	57
Clark Gillies	Islanders	79	38	39	77	75
Denis Potvin	Islanders	60	24	37	61	83
Bob Bourne	Islanders	76	27	26	53	77
Duane Sutter	Islanders	77	18	35	53	100
Mike McEwen	Islanders	73	10	39	49	50
Bob Nystrom	Islanders	74	22	25	47	103
Brent Sutter	Islanders	43	21	22	43	114
Stefan Persson	Islanders	70	6	37	43	99
Anders Kallur	Islanders	58	18	22	40	18
Wayne Merrick	Islanders	68	12	27	39	20
Tomas Jonsson	Islanders	70	9	25	34	51
Butch Goring	Islanders	67	15	17	32	10
Billy Carroll	Islanders	72	9	20	29	32
Dave Langevin	Islanders	73	1	20	21	82
Ken Morrow	Islanders	75	1	18	19	56
Hector Marini	Islanders	30	4	9	13	53
Gord Lane	Islanders	51	0	13	13	98
Greg Gilbert	Islanders	1	1	0	1	0
Bill Smith	Islanders	46	0	1	1	24
Neil Hawryliw	Islanders	1	0	0	0	0
Paul Boutilier	Islanders	1	0	0	0	0
R. Melanson	Islanders	36	0	0	0	14

NEW YORK RANGERS

		GP	G	A	Pts.	PM
Mike Rogers	Rangers	80	38	65	103	43
Ron Duguay	Rangers	72	40	36	76	82
Mark Pavelich	Rangers	79	33	43	76	67
Ed Johnstone	Rangers	68	30	28	58	57
Don Maloney	Rangers	54	22	36	58	73
R. Ruotsalainen	Rangers	78	18	38	56	27
Dave Maloney	Rangers	64	13	36	49	105
Robbie Ftorek	Quebec	19	1	8	9	4
	Rangers	30	8	25	33	24
	Total	49	9	33	42	28
Barry Beck	Rangers	60	9	29	38	111
Dave Silk	Rangers	64	15	20	35	39
Mikko Leinonen	Rangers	53	11	19	30	18
Mike Allison	Rangers	48	7	15	22	74
Tom Laidlaw	Rangers	79	3	18	21	104
Steve Vickers	Rangers	34	9	11	20	13
Andre Dore	Rangers	56	4	16	20	64
Nick Fotiu	Rangers	70	8	10	18	151
R. McClanahan	Hartford	17	0	3	3	11
	Rangers	22	5	9	14	10
	Total	39	5	12	17	21
Ron Greschner	Rangers	29	5	11	16	16
Dean Talafous	Rangers	29	6	7	13	8
Carol Vadnais	Rangers	50	5	6	11	45
Ed Hospodar	Rangers	41	3	8	11	152
Peter Wallin	Rangers	40	2	9	11	12
Tom Younghans	Minnesota	3	1	0	1	0
	Rangers	47	3	5	8	17
	Total	50	4	5	9	17
Tim Bothwell	Rangers	13	0	3	3	10
Steve Weeks	Rangers	49	0	3	3	0
Mark Morrison	Rangers	9	1	1	2	0
Mike Backman	Rangers	3	0	2	2	4
Anders Hedberg	Rangers	4	0	1	1	0
John Davidson	Rangers	1	0	0	0	2
Ed Mio	Rangers	25	0	0	0	4

PHILADELPHIA FLYERS

		GP	G	A	Pts.	PM
Ken Linseman	Philadelphia	79	24	68	92	275
Brian Propp	Philadelphia	80	44	47	91	117
Bill Barber	Philadelphia	80	45	44	89	85
Ron Flockhart	Philadelphia	72	33	39	72	44
Darryl Sittler	Toronto	38	18	20	38	24
	Philadelphia	35	14	18	32	50
	Total	73	32	38	70	74
Bobby Clarke	Philadelphia	62	17	46	63	154
Ray Allison	Philadelphia	51	17	37	54	104
Tim Kerr	Philadelphia	61	21	30	51	138
Reggie Leach	Philadelphia	66	26	21	47	18
Ilkka Sinisalo	Philadelphia	66	15	22	37	22
Behn Wilson	Philadelphia	59	13	23	36	135
Paul Holmgren	Philadelphia	41	9	22	31	183
Bob Hoffmeyer	Philadelphia	57	7	20	27	142
Brad Marsh	Calgary	17	0	1	1	10
	Philadelphia	66	2	22	24	106
	Total	83	2	23	25	116
Al Hill	Philadelphia	41	6	13	19	58
Greg Adams	Philadelphia	33	4	15	19	105
Glen Cochrane	Philadelphia	63	6	12	18	329
Mark Botell	Philadelphia	32	4	10	14	31
Tom Gorence	Philadelphia	66	5	8	13	8
Jimmy Watson	Philadelphia	76	3	9	12	99
Fred Arthur	Philadelphia	74	1	7	8	47
Bob Dailey	Philadelphia	12	1	5	6	22
Frank Bathe	Philadelphia	28	1	3	4	68
Steve Smith	Philadelphia	8	0	1	1	0
Lindsay Carson	Philadelphia	18	0	1	1	32
Rick St. Croix	Philadelphia	29	0	1	1	2
Pete Peeters	Philadelphia	44	0	1	1	19
Dave Michayluk	Philadelphia	1	0	0	0	0
Thomas Eriksson	Philadelphia	1	0	0	0	4
Gordie Williams	Philadelphia	1	0	0	0	2
Mark Taylor	Philadelphia	2	0	0	0	0
Gary Morrison	Philadelphia	7	0	0	0	2
Reid Bailey	Philadelphia	10	0	0	0	23

PITTSBURGH PENGUINS

		GP	G	A	Pts.	PM
Rick Kehoe	Pittsburgh	71	33	52	85	8
Randy Carlyle	Pittsburgh	73	11	64	75	131
Pat Boutette	Pittsburgh	80	23	51	74	230
Paul Gardner	Pittsburgh	59	36	33	69	28
Mike Bullard	Pittsburgh	75	37	27	64	91
George Ferguson	Pittsburgh	71	22	31	53	45
Rick MacLeish	Hartford	34	6	16	22	16
	Pittsburgh	40	13	12	25	28
	Total	74	19	28	47	44
Paul Baxter	Pittsburgh	76	9	34	43	407
Greg Malone	Pittsburgh	78	15	24	39	125
Pat Price	Pittsburgh	77	7	31	38	322
Peter Lee	Pittsburgh	74	18	16	34	98
Doug Shedden	Pittsburgh	38	10	15	25	12
Gregg Sheppard	Pittsburgh	58	11	10	21	35
Ron Stackhouse	Pittsburgh	76	2	19	21	102
Rod Schutt	Pittsburgh	35	8	12	20	42
A. St. Laurent	Los Angeles	16	2	4	6	28
	Pittsburgh	18	8	5	13	4
	Total	34	10	9	19	32
Bobby Simpson	Pittsburgh	26	9	9	18	4
Steve Gatzos	Pittsburgh	16	6	8	14	14
Pat Graham	Pittsburgh	42	6	8	14	55
Mario Faubert	Pittsburgh	14	4	8	12	14
Greg Hotham	Toronto	3	0	0	0	0
	Pittsburgh	25	4	6	10	16
	Total	28	4	6	10	16
Jim Hamilton	Pittsburgh	11	5	3	8	2
Marc Chorney	Pittsburgh	60	1	6	7	63
K. McClelland	Pittsburgh	10	1	4	5	4
Randy Boyd	Pittsburgh	23	0	2	2	49
Michel Dion	Pittsburgh	62	0	1	1	4
David Hannan	Pittsburgh	1	0	0	0	0
Bennett Wolf	Pittsburgh	1	0	0	0	2
Tony Feltrin	Pittsburgh	4	0	0	0	4
Gary Edwards	Pittsburgh	6	0	0	0	2
Gary Rissling	Pittsburgh	16	0	0	0	55

QUEBEC NORDIQUES

		GP	G	A	Pts.	PM
Peter Stastny	Quebec	80	46	93	139	91
Real Cloutier	Quebec	67	37	60	97	34
Marian Stastny	Quebec	74	35	54	89	27
Michel Goulet	Quebec	80	42	42	84	48
Anton Stastny	Quebec	68	26	46	72	16
Dale Hunter	Quebec	80	22	50	72	272
Wilf Paiement	Toronto	69	18	40	58	203
	Quebec	8	7	6	13	18
	Total	77	25	46	71	221
Marc Tardif	Quebec	75	39	31	70	55
Mario Marois	Quebec	71	11	32	43	161
Jacques Richard	Quebec	59	15	26	41	77
Dave Pichette	Quebec	67	7	30	37	152
Alain Cote	Quebec	79	15	16	31	82
Pat Hickey	Toronto	1	0	0	0	0
	Rangers	53	15	14	29	32
	Quebec	7	0	1	1	4
	Total	61	15	15	30	36
Pierre Lacroix	Quebec	68	4	23	27	74
Pierre Aubry	Quebec	62	10	13	23	27
Norm Rochefort	Quebec	72	4	14	18	115
Andre Dupont	Quebec	60	4	12	16	100
Jere Gillis	Rangers	26	3	9	12	16
	Quebec	12	2	1	3	0
	Total	38	5	10	15	16
Wally Weir	Quebec	62	3	5	8	173
Basil McRae	Quebec	20	4	3	7	69
Jean Hamel	Quebec	40	1	6	7	32
G. Therrien	Quebec	14	0	7	7	6
Dale Hoganson	Quebec	30	0	6	6	16
Dan Bouchard	Quebec	60	0	3	3	36
Richard David	Quebec	5	1	1	2	4
Terry Johnson	Quebec	6	0	1	1	5
Michel Plasse	Quebec	8	0	1	1	0
John Garrett	Hartford	16	0	1	1	2
	Quebec	12	0	0	0	0
	Total	28	0	1	1	2
Chris Tanguay	Quebec	2	0	0	0	0
Michel Bolduc	Quebec	3	0	0	0	0
Louis Sleigher	Quebec	8	0	0	0	0

ST. LOUIS BLUES

		GP	G	A	Pts.	PM
Bernie Federko	St. Louis	74	30	62	92	70
Blake Dunlop	St. Louis	77	25	53	78	32
Brian Sutter	St. Louis	74	39	36	75	239
J. Pettersson	St. Louis	77	38	31	69	28
Perry Turnbull	St. Louis	79	33	26	59	161
Joe Mullen	St. Louis	45	25	34	59	4
Mike Zuke	St. Louis	76	13	40	53	41
Wayne Babych	St. Louis	51	19	25	44	51
J. Brownschidle	St. Louis	80	5	33	38	26
Mike Crombeen	St. Louis	71	19	8	27	32
Larry Patey	St. Louis	70	14	12	26	97
Guy Lapointe	Montreal	47	1	19	20	72
	St. Louis	8	0	6	6	4
	Total	55	1	25	26	76
Rick Lapointe	St. Louis	71	2	20	22	127
Rick Wilson	St. Louis	48	3	18	21	24
Blair Chapman	St. Louis	18	6	11	17	8
Ed Kea	St. Louis	78	2	14	16	62
Kari Eloranta	Calgary	19	0	5	5	14
	St. Louis	12	1	7	8	6
	Total	31	1	12	13	20
Bill Baker	Colorado	14	0	3	3	17
	St. Louis	35	3	5	8	50
	Total	49	3	8	11	67
Jim Pavese	St. Louis	42	2	9	11	101
Ralph Klassen	St. Louis	45	3	7	10	6
Bill Stewart	St. Louis	22	0	5	5	25
Mark Reeds	St. Louis	9	1	3	4	0
Perry Anderson	St. Louis	5	1	2	3	0
A. Vigneault	St. Louis	14	1	2	3	43
Richie Hansen	St. Louis	2	0	2	2	0
Mike Liut	St. Louis	64	0	2	2	2
Alain Lemieux	St. Louis	3	0	1	1	0
Bob Crawford	St. Louis	3	0	1	1	0
Gary Edwards	St. Louis	10	0	1	1	0
Gerry Hart	St. Louis	35	0	1	1	100
Scott Campbell	St. Louis	3	0	0	0	52
Neil Labatte	St. Louis	4	0	0	0	6
Glen Hanlon	Vancouver	28	0	0	0	22
	St. Louis	2	0	0	0	0
	Total	30	0	0	0	22

TORONTO MAPLE LEAFS

		GP	G	A	Pts.	PM
Rick Vaive	Toronto	77	54	35	89	157
Bill Derlago	Toronto	75	34	50	84	42
John Anderson	Toronto	69	31	26	57	30
Borje Salming	Toronto	69	12	44	56	170
Bob Manno	Toronto	72	9	41	50	67
Terry Martin	Toronto	72	25	24	49	39
Miroslav Frycer	Quebec	49	20	17	37	47
	Toronto	10	4	6	10	31
	Total	59	24	23	47	78
Rene Robert	Toronto	55	13	24	37	37
Rocky Saganiuk	Toronto	65	17	16	33	49
Jim Benning	Toronto	74	7	24	31	46
Normand Aubin	Toronto	43	14	12	26	22
Dan Maloney	Toronto	44	8	7	15	71
Trevor Johansen	Los Angeles	46	3	7	10	69
	Toronto	13	1	3	4	4
	Total	59	4	10	14	73
F. Boimistruck	Toronto	57	2	11	13	32
Jim Korn	Detroit	59	1	7	8	104
	Toronto	11	1	3	4	44
	Total	70	2	10	12	148
Stewart Gavin	Toronto	38	5	6	11	29
Robert McGill	Toronto	68	1	10	11	263
Don Luce	Toronto	39	4	4	8	32
Ron Zanussi	Toronto	43	0	8	8	14
Walt Poddubny	Edmonton	4	0	0	0	0
	Toronto	11	3	4	7	8
	Total	15	3	4	7	8
Billy Harris	Los Angeles	16	1	3	4	6
	Toronto	20	2	0	2	4
	Total	36	3	3	6	10
Barry Melrose	Toronto	64	1	5	6	186
Fred Perlini	Toronto	7	2	3	5	0
Paul Marshall	Toronto	10	2	2	4	2
Gary Yaremchuk	Toronto	18	0	3	3	10
Michel Larocque	Toronto	50	0	3	3	2
Ernie Godden	Toronto	5	1	1	2	6
Bruce Boudreau	Toronto	12	0	2	2	6
John Gibson	Los Angeles	6	0	0	0	18
	Toronto	27	0	2	2	67
	Total	33	0	2	2	85

		GP	G	A	Pts.	PM
Vince Tremblay	Toronto	40	0	2	2	2
D. McCutcheon	Toronto	1	0	0	0	2
Paul Higgins	Toronto	3	0	0	0	17
Craig Muni	Toronto	3	0	0	0	2

VANCOUVER CANUCKS

		GP	G	A	Pts.	PM
Thomas Gradin	Vancouver	76	37	49	86	32
Stan Smyl	Vancouver	80	34	44	78	144
Ivan Boldirev	Vancouver	78	33	40	73	45
Curt Fraser	Vancouver	79	28	39	67	175
Ivan Hlinka	Vancouver	72	23	37	60	16
Tony Currie	St. Louis	48	18	22	40	17
	Vancouver	12	5	3	8	2
	Total	60	23	25	48	19
Lars Molin	Vancouver	72	15	31	46	10
Kevin McCarthy	Vancouver	71	6	39	45	84
Darcy Rota	Vancouver	51	20	20	40	139
Dave Williams	Vancouver	77	17	21	38	341
Blair MacDonald	Vancouver	59	18	15	33	20
Jim Nill	St. Louis	61	9	12	21	127
	Vancouver	8	1	2	3	5
	Total	69	10	14	24	132
Lars Lindgren	Vancouver	75	5	16	21	74
Per-Olov Brasar	Vancouver	53	6	12	18	6
Gary Lupul	Vancouver	41	10	7	17	26
Ron Delorme	Vancouver	59	9	8	17	177
Doug Halward	Vancouver	37	4	13	17	40
Harold Snepsts	Vancouver	68	3	14	17	153
Rick Lanz	Vancouver	39	3	11	14	48
Marc Crawford	Vancouver	40	4	8	12	29
Neil Belland	Vancouver	28	3	6	9	16
Anders Eldebrink	Vancouver	38	1	8	9	21
Colin Campbell	Vancouver	47	0	8	8	131
Jerry Butler	Vancouver	25	3	1	4	15
Moe Lemay	Vancouver	5	1	2	3	0
Jiri Bubla	Vancouver	23	1	1	2	16
Richard Brodeur	Vancouver	52	0	2	2	0
Joe McDonnell	Vancouver	7	0	1	1	12
Gerry Minor	Vancouver	13	0	1	1	6
A. Schliebener	Vancouver	22	0	1	1	10
Garth Butcher	Vancouver	5	0	0	0	9

WASHINGTON CAPITALS

		GP	G	A	Pts.	PM
Dennis Maruk	Washington	80	60	76	136	126
Ryan Walter	Washington	78	38	49	87	142
Mike Gartner	Washington	80	35	45	80	121
Bobby Carpenter	Washington	80	32	35	67	69
Chris Valentine	Washington	60	30	37	67	92
B. Gustafsson	Washington	70	26	34	60	40
Darren Veitch	Washington	67	9	44	53	54
Greg Theberge	Washington	57	5	32	37	49
Bobby Gould	Calgary	16	3	0	3	4
	Washington	60	18	13	31	69
	Total	76	21	13	34	73
Rick Green	Washington	65	3	25	28	93
Terry Murray	Washington	74	3	22	25	60
Doug Hicks	Edmonton	49	3	20	23	55
	Washington	12	0	1	1	11
	Total	61	3	21	24	66
Gaetan Duchesne	Washington	74	9	14	23	46
T. Robertson	Washington	54	8	13	21	204
Lee Norwood	Quebec	2	0	0	0	2
	Washington	26	7	10	17	115
	Total	28	7	10	17	117
Tim Tookey	Washington	28	8	8	16	35
Glen Currie	Washington	43	7	7	14	14
Wes Jarvis	Washington	26	1	12	13	18
L. Franceschetti	Washington	30	2	10	12	23
Timo Blomqvist	Washington	44	1	11	12	62
Paul MacKinnon	Washington	39	2	9	11	35
Randy Holt	Calgary	8	0	0	0	9
	Washington	53	2	6	8	250
	Total	61	2	6	8	259
Tom Rowe	Hartford	21	4	0	4	36
	Washington	6	1	1	2	18
	Total	27	5	1	6	54
Jim McTaggart	Washington	19	2	4	6	20
Tony Cassolato	Washington	12	1	4	5	4
Roland Stoltz	Washington	14	2	2	4	14
Bob Kelly	Washington	16	0	4	4	12
Richard Bidner	Washington	12	2	1	3	7
Jean Pronovost	Washington	10	1	2	3	4
Howard Walker	Washington	16	0	2	2	26

		GP	G	A	Pts.	PM
Al Jensen	Washington	26	0	2	2	6
Mike Siltala	Washington	3	1	0	1	2
O. Kindrachuk	Washington	4	1	0	1	2
Mike Palmateer	Washington	11	0	1	1	6
Dave Parro	Washington	52	0	1	1	4
Eric Calder	Washington	1	0	0	0	0
Pierre Bouchard	Washington	1	0	0	0	10
Errol Rausse	Washington	2	0	0	0	0
Harvie Pocza	Washington	2	0	0	0	2
Tony Camazzola	Washington	3	0	0	0	4
Jim McGeough	Washington	4	0	0	0	0
Jay Johnston	Washington	6	0	0	0	4

WINNIPEG JETS

		GP	G	A	Pts.	PM
Dale Hawerchuk	Winnipeg	80	45	58	103	47
Morris Lukowich	Winnipeg	77	43	49	92	102
Dave Christian	Winnipeg	80	25	51	76	28
David Babych	Winnipeg	79	19	49	68	92
Paul MacLean	Winnipeg	74	36	25	61	106
Willy Lindstrom	Winnipeg	74	32	27	59	33
Lucien De Blois	Winnipeg	65	25	27	52	87
Thomas Steen	Winnipeg	73	15	29	44	42
Bengt Lundholm	Winnipeg	66	14	30	44	10
Normand Dupont	Winnipeg	62	13	25	38	22
Doug Smail	Winnipeg	72	17	18	35	55
Larry Hopkins	Winnipeg	41	10	15	25	22
Tim Watters	Winnipeg	69	2	22	24	97
Tim Trimper	Winnipeg	74	8	8	16	100
Ron Wilson	Winnipeg	39	3	13	16	49
Don Spring	Winnipeg	78	0	16	16	21
Craig Levie	Winnipeg	40	4	9	13	48
Moe Mantha	Winnipeg	25	0	12	12	28
Bryan Maxwell	Winnipeg	45	1	9	10	110
Scott Arniel	Winnipeg	17	1	8	9	14
Serge Savard	Winnipeg	47	2	5	7	26
Jimmy Mann	Winnipeg	37	3	2	5	79
Ed Staniowski	Winnipeg	45	0	5	5	4
Barry Legge	Winnipeg	38	1	2	3	57
Barry Long	Winnipeg	5	0	2	2	4
Doug Soetaert	Winnipeg	39	0	2	2	14
Dan Geoffrion	Winnipeg	1	0	0	0	5
Murray Eaves	Winnipeg	2	0	0	0	0

GOALTENDERS' RECORDS

LEGEND: **GPI** − games played in; **Min.** − minutes played; **GA** − goals against; **EN** − empty net goals; **SO** − shutouts; **Avg.** − average goals against per 60-minute unit; **W** − wins; **L** − losses; **T** − ties. Won-lost-tied record based on goaltender on duty when winning or tying goal scored.

Goaltenders	Team	GPI	Min.	GA	EN	SO	Avg.	W	L	T
Mark Holden	Montreal	1	20	0	0	0	0.00	0	0	0
Denis Herron	Montreal	27	1547	68	0	3	2.64	12	6	8
Rick Walmsley	Montreal	38	2206	101	0	2	2.75	23	7	7
Richard Sevigny	Montreal	19	1027	53	1	0	3.10	11	4	2
Herron/Sevigny	Montreal					1				
Montreal	Total	80	4800	223		6	2.79	46	17	17
(Herron & Sevigny shared shutout against Colorado, Nov. 11, 1981)										
Bill Smith	NY Islanders	46	2685	133	0	0	2.97	32	9	4
Roland Melanson	NY Islanders	36	2115	114	3	0	3.23	22	7	6
NY Islanders	Total	80	4820	250		0	3.13	54	16	10
Jacques Cloutier	Buffalo	7	311	13	1	0	2.51	5	1	0
Bob Sauve	Buffalo	14	760	35	1	0	2.76	6	1	5
Don Edwards	Buffalo	62	3500	205	3	0	3.51	26	23	9
Paul Harrison	Buffalo	6	229	14	1	0	3.67	2	1	1
Buffalo	Total	80	4800	273		0	3.41	39	26	15
Mike Moffat	Boston	2	120	6	0	0	3.00	2	0	0
Marco Baron	Boston	44	2515	144	3	1	3.44	22	16	4
Rogie Vachon	Boston	38	2165	132	0	1	3.66	19	11	6
Boston	Total	80	4800	285		2	3.56	43	27	10
Rick Heinz	Vancouver	3	180	9	0	1	3.00	2	1	0
Richard Brodeur	Vancouver	52	3010	168	2	2	3.35	20	18	12
Glen Hanlon	Vancouver	28	1610	106	1	1	3.95	8	14	5
Vancouver	Total	80	4800	286		4	3.58	30	33	17
L. Middlebrook	Minnesota	3	140	7	0	0	3.00	0	0	2
Gilles Meloche	Minnesota	51	3026	175	2	1	3.47	26	15	9
Don Beaupre	Minnesota	29	1634	101	3	0	3.71	11	8	9
Minnesota	Total	80	4800	288		1	3.60	37	23	20
Grant Fuhr	Edmonton	48	2847	157	2	0	3.31	28	5	14
Ron Low	Edmonton	29	1554	100	2	0	3.86	17	7	1
Andy Moog	Edmonton	8	399	32	2	0	4.81	3	5	0
Edmonton	Total	80	4800	295		0	3.69	48	17	15

John Davidson	NY Rangers	1	60	1	0	0	1.00	1	0	0
J. Vanbiesbrouck	NY Rangers	1	60	1	0	0	1.00	1	0	0
Ed Mio	NY Rangers	25	1500	89	0	0	3.56	13	6	5
Steve Weeks	NY Rangers	49	2852	179	3	1	3.77	23	16	9
Steve Baker	NY Rangers	6	328	33	0	0	6.04	1	5	0
NY Rangers	Total	80	4800	306		1	3.83	39	27	14
Pete Peeters	Philadelphia	44	2591	160	3	0	3.71	23	18	3
Rick St. Croix	Philadelphia	29	1729	112	3	0	3.89	13	9	6
Pelle Lindbergh	Philadelphia	8	480	35	0	0	4.38	2	4	2
Philadelphia	Total	80	4800	313		0	3.91	38	31	11
Ed Staniowski	Winnipeg	45	2643	174	2	1	3.95	20	19	6
Doug Soetaert	Winnipeg	39	2157	155	1	2	4.31	13	14	8
Winnipeg	Total	80	4800	332		3	4.15	33	33	14
Gary Edwards	Pittsburgh	6	360	22	0	1	3.67	3	2	1
Michel Dion	Pittsburgh	62	3580	226	8	0	3.79	25	24	12
Nick Ricci	Pittsburgh	3	160	14	2	0	5.25	0	3	0
Paul Harrison	Pittsburgh	13	700	64	1	0	5.49	3	7	0
Pittsburgh	Total	80	4800	337		1	4.21	31	36	13
Al Jensen	Washington	26	1274	81	0	0	3.81	8	8	4
Dave Parro	Washington	52	2942	206	4	1	4.20	16	26	7
Mike Palmateer	Washington	11	584	47	0	0	4.83	2	7	2
Washington	Total	80	4800	338		1	4.23	26	41	13
Dan Bouchard	Quebec	60	3572	230	2	1	3.86	27	22	11
John Garrett	Quebec	12	720	62	0	0	5.17	4	5	3
Michel Plasse	Quebec	8	388	35	1	0	5.41	2	3	1
Clint Malarchuk	Quebec	2	120	14	0	0	7.00	0	1	1
Quebec	Total	80	4800	344		1	4.30	33	31	16
Pat Riggin	Calgary	52	2934	207	1	2	4.23	19	19	11
Rejean Lemelin	Calgary	34	1866	135	2	0	4.34	10	15	6
Calgary	Total	80	4800	345		2	4.31	29	34	17
Paul Skidmore	St. Louis	2	120	6	0	0	3.00	1	1	0
Mike Liut	St. Louis	64	3691	250	3	2	4.06	28	28	7
Rick Heinz	St. Louis	9	433	35	2	0	4.85	2	5	0
Gary Edwards	St. Louis	10	480	45	0	0	5.63	1	5	1
Glen Hanlon	St. Louis	2	76	8	0	0	6.32	0	1	0
St. Louis	Total	80	4800	349		2	4.36	32	40	8
Claude Legris	Detroit	1	28	0	0	0	0.00	0	0	1
Bob Sauve	Detroit	41	2365	165	5	0	4.19	11	25	4
Gilles Gilbert	Detroit	27	1478	105	2	0	4.26	6	10	6
Corrado Micalef	Detroit	18	809	63	1	0	4.67	4	10	1
Greg Stefan	Detroit	2	120	10	0	0	5.00	0	2	0
Detroit	Total	80	4800	351		0	4.39	21	47	12

John Garrett	Hartford	16	898	63	1	0	4.21	5	6	4
Greg Millen	Hartford	55	3201	229	5	0	4.29	11	30	12
Mike Veisor	Hartford	13	701	53	0	0	4.54	5	5	2
Hartford	Total	80	4800	351		0	4.39	21	48	18
R. Laferriere	Colorado	1	20	1	0	0	3.00	0	0	0
Glenn Resch	Colorado	61	3424	230	5	0	4.03	16	31	11
Phil Myre	Colorado	2	1256	112	1	0	5.35	2	17	2
Steve Janaszak	Colorado	2	100	13	0	0	7.80	0	1	0
Colorado	Total	80	4800	362		0	4.53	18	49	13
M. Bannerman	Chicago	29	1671	116	2	1	4.17	11	12	4
Tony Esposito	Chicago	52	3069	231	8	1	4.52	19	25	8
W. Skorodenski	Chicago	1	60	5	1	0	5.00	0	1	0
Chicago	Total	80	4800	363		2	4.54	30	38	12
Mike Blake	Los Angeles	2	51	2	0	0	2.35	0	0	0
Doug Keans	Los Angeles	31	1436	103	5	0	4.30	8	10	7
Mario Lessard	Los Angeles	52	2933	213	3	2	4.36	13	28	8
Jim Rutherford	Los Angeles	7	380	43	0	0	6.79	3	3	0
Los Angeles	Total	80	4800	369		2	4.61	24	41	15
Vince Tremblay	Toronto	40	2033	153	3	1	4.52	10	18	8
Michel Larocque	Toronto	50	2647	207	4	0	4.69	10	24	8
Bob Parent	Toronto	2	120	13	0	0	6.50	0	2	0
Toronto	Total	80	4800	380		1	4.75	20	44	16

TEAM PENALTIES

	GP	Min.	Avg.
Philadelphia	80	2493	31.2
Pittsburgh	80	2210	27.6
Washington	80	1922	24.0
Toronto	80	1888	23.6
Vancouver	80	1840	23.0
Chicago	80	1775	22.2
Quebec	80	1757	22.0
Los Angeles	80	1730	21.6
St. Louis	80	1580	19.8
Hartford	80	1493	18.7
Edmonton	80	1473	18.4
Montreal	80	1463	18.3
Buffalo	80	1422	17.8
NY Rangers	80	1402	17.5
Minnesota	80	1358	17.0
Calgary	80	1331	16.6
NY Islanders	80	1328	16.6
Winnipeg	80	1314	16.4
Boston	80	1266	15.8
Detroit	80	1250	15.6
Colorado	80	1138	14.2
Total	840	33,433	39.8

THE STANLEY CUP

Awarded annually to the team winning the National Hockey League's final playoff round, matching the champions of the Clarence Campbell and Prince of Wales Conferences.

1981-82 — New York Islanders	1949-50 — Detroit Red Wings
1980-81 — New York Islanders	1948-49 — Toronto Maple Leafs
1979-80 — New York Islanders	1947-48 — Toronto Maple Leafs
1978-79 — Montreal Canadiens	1946-47 — Toronto Maple Leafs
1977-78 — Montreal Canadiens	1945-46 — Montreal Canadiens
1976-77 — Montreal Canadiens	1944-45 — Toronto Maple Leafs
1975-76 — Montreal Canadiens	1943-44 — Montreal Canadiens
1974-75 — Philadelphia Flyers	1942-43 — Detroit Red Wings
1973-74 — Philadelphia Flyers	1941-42 — Toronto Maple Leafs
1972-73 — Montreal Canadiens	1940-41 — Boston Bruins
1971-72 — Boston Bruins	1939-40 — New York Rangers
1970-71 — Montreal Canadiens	1938-39 — Boston Bruins
1969-70 — Boston Bruins	1937-38 — Chicago Black Hawks
1968-69 — Montreal Canadiens	1936-37 — Detroit Red Wings
1967-68 — Montreal Canadiens	1935-36 — Detroit Red Wings
1966-67 — Toronto Maple Leafs	1934-35 — Montreal Maroons
1965-66 — Montreal Canadiens	1933-34 — Chicago Black Hawks
1964-65 — Montreal Canadiens	1932-33 — New York Rangers
1963-64 — Toronto Maple Leafs	1931-32 — Toronto Maple Leafs
1962-63 — Toronto Maple Leafs	1930-31 — Montreal Canadiens
1961-62 — Toronto Maple Leafs	1929-30 — Montreal Canadiens
1960-61 — Chicago Black Hawks	1928-29 — Boston Bruins
1959-60 — Montreal Canadiens	1927-28 — New York Rangers
1958-59 — Montreal Canadiens	1926-27 — Ottawa Senators
1957-58 — Montreal Canadiens	1925-26 — Montreal Maroons
1956-57 — Montreal Canadiens	1924-25 — Victoria Cougars
1955-56 — Montreal Canadiens	1923-24 — Montreal Canadiens
1954-55 — Detroit Red Wings	1922-23 — Ottawa Senators
1953-54 — Detroit Red Wings	1921-22 — Toronto St. Pats
1952-53 — Montreal Canadiens	1920-21 — Ottawa Senators
1951-52 — Detroit Red Wings	1919-20 — Ottawa Senators
1950-51 — Toronto Maple Leafs	1918-19 — No decision

NOTE: In the spring of 1919, the Montreal Canadiens went west to play Seattle for the Stanley Cup. After five games, with the playoff tied at two victories apiece and one draw, the series was cancelled because of a flu epidemic.

1917-18 — Toronto Arenas	1906-07 — Montreal Wanderers
1916-17 — Seattle Metropolitans	(March)
1915-16 — Montreal Canadiens	1906-07 — Kenora Thistles
1914-15 — Vancouver	(January)
Millionaires	1905-06 — Montreal Wanderers
1913-14 — Toronto Blueshirts	1904-05 — Ottawa Silver Seven
1911-12 — Quebec Bulldogs	1903-04 — Ottawa Silver Seven
1910-11 — Ottawa Senators	1902-03 — Ottawa Silver Seven
1909-10 — Montreal Wanderers	1901-02 — Montreal A.A.A.
1908-09 — Ottawa Senators	1900-01 — Winnipeg Victorias
1907-08 — Montreal Wanderers	1899-1900 — Montreal Shamrocks

STANLEY CUP PLAYOFFS, 1982

FINAL ROUND

Vancouver 5 at Islanders 6; Vancouver 4 at Islanders 6; Islanders 3 at Vancouver 0; Islanders 3 at Vancouver 1. Islanders win best-of-7 series, 4-0.

WALES CONFERENCE

Final
Quebec 1 at Islanders 4; Quebec 2 at Islanders 5; Islanders 5 at Quebec 4 (overtime goal by Merrick); Islanders 4 at Quebec 2. Islanders win best-of-7 series, 4-0.

Patrick Division Final
Rangers 5 at Islanders 4; Rangers 2 at Islanders 7; Islanders 4 at Rangers 3 (overtime goal by Trottier); Islanders 5 at Rangers 3; Rangers 4 at Islanders 2; Islanders 5 at Rangers 3. Islanders win best-of-7 series, 4-2.

Semi-finals
Pittsburgh 1 at Islanders 8; Pittsburgh 2 at Islanders 7; Islanders 1 at Pittsburgh 2; Islanders 2 at Pittsburgh 5; Pittsburgh 3 at Islanders 4. Islanders win best-of-5 series, 3-2.

Philadelphia 4 at Rangers 1; Philadelphia 3 at Rangers 7; Rangers 4 at Philadelphia 3; Rangers 7 at Philadelphia 5. Rangers win best-of-5 series, 3-1.

Adams Division Final
Quebec 3 at Boston 4; Quebec 4 at Boston 8; Boston 2 at Quebec 3 (overtime goal by Paiement); Boston 2 at Quebec 7; Quebec 4 at Boston 3; Boston 6 at Quebec 5 (overtime goal by McNab); Quebec 2 at Boston 1. Quebec wins best-of-7 series, 4-3.

Semi-finals
Quebec 1 at Montreal 5; Quebec 3 at Montreal 2; Montreal 1 at Quebec 2; Montreal 6 at Quebec 2; Quebec 3 at Montreal 2. Quebec wins best-of-5 series, 3-2.

Buffalo 1 at Boston 3; Buffalo 3 at Boston 7; Boston 2 at Buffalo 5; Boston 5 at Buffalo 2. Boston wins best-of-5 series, 3-1.

CAMPBELL CONFERENCE

Final
Vancouver 2 at Chicago 1 (overtime goal by Nill); Vancouver 1 at Chicago 4; Chicago 3 at Vancouver 4; Vancouver 6 at Chicago 2. Vancouver wins best-of-7 series, 4-1.

Smythe Division Final
Los Angeles 2 at Vancouver 3; Los Angeles 3 at Vancouver 2 (overtime goal by Bozek); Vancouver 4 at Los Angeles 3 (overtime goal by Campbell); Vancouver 5 at Los Angeles 4; Los Angeles 2 at Vancouver 5. Vancouver wins best-of-7 series, 4-1.

Semi-finals

Los Angeles 10 at Edmonton 8; Los Angeles 2 at Edmonton 3; Edmonton 5 at Los Angeles 6; Edmonton 3 at Los Angeles 2; Los Angeles 7 at Edmonton 4. Los Angeles wins best-of-5 series, 3-2.

Calgary 3 at Vancouver 5; Calgary 1 at Vancouver 2; Vancouver 3 at Calgary 1. Vancouver wins best-of-5 series, 3-0.

Norris Division Final

Chicago 5 at St. Louis 4; Chicago 1 at St. Louis 3; St. Louis 5 at Chicago 6; St. Louis 6 at Chicago 7; Chicago 2 at St. Louis 3 (overtime goal by Federko); St. Louis 0 at Chicago 2. Chicago wins best-of-7 series, 4-2.

Semi-finals

St. Louis 4 at Winnipeg 3; St. Louis 2 at Winnipeg 5; Winnipeg 3 at St. Louis 6; Winnipeg 2 at St. Louis 8. St. Louis wins best-of-5 series, 3-1.

Chicago 3 at Minnesota 2; Chicago 5 at Minnesota 3; Minnesota 7 at Chicago 1; Minnesota 2 at Chicago 5. Chicago wins best-of-5 series, 3-1.

Playoff scorers	GP	G	A	Pts.	PM
Bryan Trottier, New York Islanders	19	6	23	29	40
Mike Bossy, New York Islanders	19	17	10	27	0
Denis Potvin, New York Islanders	19	5	16	21	30
Thomas Gradin, Vancouver	17	9	10	19	10
Denis Savard, Chicago	15	11	7	18	52
Stan Smyl, Vancouver	17	9	9	18	25
Joe Mullen, St. Louis	10	7	11	18	4
Barry Pederson, Boston	11	7	11	18	2
Peter Stastny, Quebec	12	7	11	18	10
Bernie Federko, St. Louis	10	3	15	18	10
Marian Stastny, Quebec	16	3	14	17	5
Bob Bourne, New York Islanders	19	9	7	16	36
John Tonelli, New York Islanders	19	6	10	16	18

Rick Middleton, Boston	11	6	9	15	0
Tom Lysiak, Chicago	15	6	9	15	18
Stefan Persson, New York Islanders	19	1	14	15	9
Anton Stastny, Quebec	16	5	10	15	10
Peter McNab, Boston	11	6	8	14	6
Clark Gillies, New York Islanders	19	8	6	14	34
Brian Sutter, St. Louis	10	8	6	14	49
Doug Wilson, Chicago	15	3	10	13	32
Daryl Evans, Los Angeles	10	5	8	13	12
Michel Goulet, Quebec	16	8	5	13	6
Wayne Gretzky, Edmonton	5	5	7	12	8
Wayne Merrick, New York Islanders	19	6	6	12	6
Real Cloutier, Quebec	16	7	5	12	10
Wilf Paiement, Quebec	14	6	6	12	28

HART MEMORIAL TROPHY

Given annually to the National Hockey League player voted most valuable to his team.

1981-82 — Wayne Gretzky, Edmonton
1980-81 — Wayne Gretzky, Edmonton
1979-80 — Wayne Gretzky, Edmonton
1978-79 — Bryan Trottier, N.Y. Islanders
1977-78 — Guy Lafleur, Montreal
1976-77 — Guy Lafleur, Montreal
1975-76 — Bobby Clarke, Philadelphia
1974-75 — Bobby Clarke, Philadelphia
1973-74 — Phil Esposito, Boston
1972-73 — Bobby Clarke, Philadelphia
1971-72 — Bobby Orr, Boston
1970-71 — Bobby Orr, Boston
1969-70 — Bobby Orr, Boston
1968-69 — Phil Esposito, Boston
1967-68 — Stan Mikita, Chicago
1966-67 — Stan Mikita, Chicago
1965-66 — Bobby Hull, Chicago
1964-65 — Bobby Hull, Chicago
1963-64 — Jean Beliveau, Montreal

1962-63 — Gordie Howe, Detroit
1961-62 — Jacques Plante, Montreal
1960-61 — Bernie Geoffrion, Montreal
1959-60 — Gordie Howe, Detroit
1958-59 — Andy Bathgate, New York Rangers
1957-58 — Gordie Howe, Detroit
1956-57 — Gordie Howe, Detroit
1955-56 — Jean Beliveau, Montreal
1954-55 — Ted Kennedy, Toronto
1953-54 — Al Rollins, Chicago
1952-53 — Gordie Howe, Detroit
1951-52 — Gordie Howe, Detroit
1950-51 — Milt Schmidt, Boston
1949-50 — Chuck Rayner, New York Rangers
1948-49 — Sid Abel, Detroit
1947-48 — ''Buddy'' O'Connor, N.Y. Rangers
1946-47 — Maurice Richard, Montreal
1945-46 — Max Bentley, Chicago
1944-45 — Elmer Lach, Montreal
1943-44 — ''Babe'' Pratt, Toronto
1942-43 — Bill Cowley, Boston
1941-42 — Tommy Anderson, N.Y. Americans
1940-41 — Bill Cowley, Boston
1939-40 — Ebbie Goodfellow, Detroit
1938-39 — ''Toe'' Blake, Montreal
1937-38 — Eddie Shore, Boston
1936-37 — ''Babe'' Siebert, Montreal
1935-36 — Eddie Shore, Boston
1934-35 — Eddie Shore, Boston
1933-34 — Aurel Joliat, Montreal
1932-33 — Eddie Shore, Boston
1931-32 — Howie Morenz, Montreal
1930-31 — Howie Morenz, Montreal
1929-30 — Nels Stewart, Montreal
1928-29 — Roy Worters, N.Y. Americans
1927-28 — Howie Morenz, Montreal
1926-27 — Herb Gardiner, Montreal
1925-26 — Nels Stewart, Montreal
1924-25 — Billy Burch, Hamilton
1923-24 — Frank Nighbor, Ottawa

ART ROSS TROPHY

Awarded annually to the player who leads the National Hockey League in points scored.

		GP	G	A	Pts.
1981-82	Wayne Gretzky, Edmonton	80	92	120	212
1980-81	Wayne Gretzky, Edmonton	80	55	109	164
1979-80	Marcel Dionne, Los Angeles	80	53	84	137
1978-79	Bryan Trottier, N.Y. Islanders	76	47	87	134
1977-78	Guy Lafleur, Montreal	78	60	72	132
1976-77	Guy Lafleur, Montreal	80	56	80	136
1975-76	Guy Lafleur, Montreal	80	56	69	125
1974-75	Bobby Orr, Boston	80	46	89	135
1973-74	Phil Esposito, Boston	78	68	77	145
1972-73	Phil Esposito, Boston	78	55	75	130
1971-72	Phil Esposito, Boston	76	66	67	133
1970-71	Phil Esposito, Boston	78	76	76	152
1969-70	Bobby Orr, Boston	76	33	87	120
1968-69	Phil Esposito, Boston	74	49	77	126
1967-68	Stan Mikita, Chicago	72	40	47	87
1966-67	Stan Mikita, Chicago	70	35	62	97
1965-66	Bobby Hull, Chicago	65	54	43	97
1964-65	Stan Mikita, Chicago	70	28	59	87
1963-64	Stan Mikita, Chicago	70	39	50	89
1962-63	Gordie Howe, Detroit	70	38	48	86
1961-62	Bobby Hull, Chicago	70	50	34	84
1960-61	Bernie Geoffrion, Montreal	64	50	45	95
1959-60	Bobby Hull, Chicago	70	39	42	81
1958-59	Dickie Moore, Montreal	70	41	55	96
1957-58	Dickie Moore, Montreal	70	36	48	84
1956-57	Gordie Howe, Detroit	70	44	45	89
1955-56	Jean Beliveau, Montreal	70	47	41	88
1954-55	Bernie Geoffrion, Montreal	70	38	37	75
1953-54	Gordie Howe, Detroit	70	33	48	81
1952-53	Gordie Howe, Detroit	70	49	46	95
1951-52	Gordie Howe, Detroit	70	47	39	86
1950-51	Gordie Howe, Detroit	70	43	43	86
1949-50	Ted Lindsay, Detroit	69	23	55	78
1948-49	Roy Conacher, Chicago	60	26	42	68
1947-48	Elmer Lach, Montreal	60	30	31	61
1946-47	Max Bentley, Chicago	60	29	43	72
1945-46	Max Bentley, Chicago	47	31	30	61

1944-45	Elmer Lach, Montreal	50	26	54	80
1943-44	Herbie Cain, Boston	48	36	46	82
1942-43	Doug Bentley, Chicago	50	33	40	73
1941-42	Bryan Hextall, N.Y. Rangers	48	24	32	56
1940-41	Bill Cowley, Boston	46	17	45	62
1939-40	Milt Schmidt, Boston	48	22	30	52
1938-39	Toe Blake, Mtl. Canadiens	48	24	23	47
1937-38	Gordie Drillon, Toronto	48	26	26	52
1936-37	Dave Schriner, N.Y. Americans	48	21	25	46
1935-36	Dave Schriner, N.Y. Americans	48	19	26	45
1934-35	Charlie Conacher, Toronto	48	36	21	57
1933-34	Charlie Conacher, Toronto	42	32	20	52
1932-33	Bill Cook, N.Y. Rangers	48	28	22	50
1931-32	Harvey Jackson, Toronto	48	28	25	53
1930-31	Howie Morenz, Mtl. Canadiens	39	28	23	51
1929-30	Cooney Weiland, Boston	44	43	30	73
1928-29	Ace Bailey, Toronto	44	22	10	32
1927-28	Howie Morenz, Mtl. Canadiens	43	33	18	51
1926-27	Bill Cook, N.Y. Rangers	44	33	4	37
1925-26	Nels Stewart, Montreal Maroons	36	34	8	42
1924-25	Babe Dye, Toronto	29	38	6	44
1923-24	Cy Denneny, Ottawa	21	22	1	23
1922-23	Babe Dye, Toronto	22	26	11	37
1921-22	Punch Broadbent, Ottawa	24	32	14	46
1920-21	Newsy Lalonde, Mtl. Canadiens	24	33	8	41
1919-20	Joe Malone, Quebec	24	39	6	45
1918-19	Newsy Lalonde, Mtl. Canadiens	17	23	9	32
1917-18	Joe Malone, Mtl. Canadiens	20	44	x	44

x Number of assists not recorded.

LADY BYNG TROPHY

Awarded annually to the National Hockey League player showing the best combination of excellence and sportsmanship.

1981-82 — Rick Middleton, Boston
1980-81 — Rick Kehoe, Pittsburgh
1979-80 — Wayne Gretzky, Edmonton
1978-79 — Bob MacMillan, Atlanta
1977-78 — Butch Goring, L.A. Kings
1976-77 — Marcel Dionne, L.A. Kings

1975-76 — Jean Ratelle, N.Y. Rangers-Boston
1974-75 — Marcel Dionne, Detroit
1973-74 — Johnny Bucyk, Boston
1972-73 — Gilbert Perreault, Buffalo
1971-72 — Jean Ratelle, New York Rangers
1970-71 — Johnny Bucyk, Boston
1969-70 — Phil Goyette, St. Louis
1968-69 — Alex Delvecchio, Detroit
1967-68 — Stan Mikita, Chicago
1966-67 — Stan Mikita, Chicago
1965-66 — Alex Delvecchio, Detroit
1964-65 — Bobby Hull, Chicago
1963-64 — Ken Wharram, Chicago
1962-63 — Dave Keon, Toronto
1961-62 — Dave Keon, Toronto
1960-61 — Red Kelly, Toronto
1959-60 — Don McKenney, Boston
1958-59 — Alex Delvecchio, Detroit
1957-58 — Camille Henry, New York Rangers
1956-57 — Andy Hebenton, New York Rangers
1955-56 — Earl Reibel, Detroit
1954-55 — Sid Smith, Toronto
1953-54 — Red Kelly, Detroit
1952-53 — Red Kelly, Detroit
1951-52 — Sid Smith, Toronto
1950-51 — Red Kelly, Detroit
1949-50 — Edgar Laprade, New York Rangers
1948-49 — Bill Quackenbush, Detroit
1947-48 — "Buddy" O'Connor, N.Y. Rangers
1946-47 — Bobby Bauer, Boston
1945-46 — "Toe" Blake, Montreal
1944-45 — Billy Mosienko, Chicago
1943-44 — Clint Smith, Chicago
1942-43 — Max Bentley, Chicago
1941-42 — Syl Apps, Toronto
1940-41 — Bobby Bauer, Boston
1939-40 — Bobby Bauer, Boston
1938-39 — Clint Smith, N.Y. Rangers
1937-38 — Gordon Drillon, Toronto

216

1936-37 — Marty Barry, Detroit
1935-36 — "Doc" Rommes, Chicago
1934-35 — Frank Boucher, N.Y. Rangers
1933-34 — Frank Boucher, N.Y. Rangers
1932-33 — Frank Boucher, N.Y. Rangers
1931-32 — Joe Primeau, Toronto
1930-31 — Frank Boucher, N.Y. Rangers
1929-30 — Frank Boucher, N.Y. Rangers
1928-29 — Frank Boucher, N.Y. Rangers
1927-28 — Frank Boucher, N.Y. Rangers
1926-27 — Billy Burch, N.Y. Americans
1925-26 — Frank Nighbor, Ottawa
1924-25 — Frank Nighbor, Ottawa

WILLIAM JENNINGS TROPHY

Awarded annually to the goalie or goalies playing at least 25 games for the team giving up the fewest goals. Prior to 1982, these were the guidelines for the Vezina Trophy.

1981-82 — Rick Walmsley, Denis Herron, Montreal
1980-81 — Richard Sevigny, Denis Herron, Michel Larocque, Montreal
1979-80 — Don Edwards, Bob Sauve, Buffalo
1978-79 — Ken Dryden, Michel Larocque, Montreal
1977-78 — Ken Dryden, Michel Larocque, Montreal
1976-77 — Ken Dryden, Michel Larocque, Montreal
1975-76 — Ken Dryden, Montreal
1974-75 — Bernie Parent, Philadelphia
1973-74 — Bernie Parent, Philadelphia, Tony Esposito, Chicago (tied)
1972-73 — Ken Dryden, Montreal
1971-72 — Tony Esposito, Gary Smith, Chicago
1970-71 — Ed Giacomin, Gilles Villemure, New York Rangers
1969-70 — Tony Esposito, Chicago
1968-69 — Glenn Hall, Jacques Plante, St. Louis
1967-68 — Gump Worsley, Rogatien Vachon, Montreal
1966-67 — Glenn Hall, Denis DeJordy, Chicago
1965-66 — Gump Worsley, Charlie Hodge, Montreal

1964-65 — Terry Sawchuk, Johnny Bower, Toronto
1963-64 — Charlie Hodge, Montreal
1962-63 — Glenn Hall, Chicago
1961-62 — Jacques Plante, Montreal
1960-61 — Johnny Bower, Toronto
1959-60 — Jacques Plante, Montreal
1958-59 — Jacques Plante, Montreal
1957-58 — Jacques Plante, Montreal
1956-57 — Jacques Plante, Montreal
1955-56 — Jacques Plante, Montreal
1954-55 — Terry Sawchuk, Detroit
1953-54 — Harry Lumley, Toronto
1952-53 — Terry Sawchuk, Detroit
1951-52 — Terry Sawchuk, Detroit
1950-51 — Al Rollins, Toronto
1949-50 — Bill Durnan, Montreal
1948-49 — Bill Durnan, Montreal
1947-48 — W. "Turk" Broda, Toronto
1946-47 — Bill Durnan, Montreal
1945-46 — Bill Durnan, Montreal
1944-45 — Bill Durnan, Montreal
1943-44 — Bill Durnan, Montreal
1942-43 — Johnny Mowers, Detroit
1941-42 — Frank Brimsek, Boston
1940-41 — W. "Turk" Broda, Toronto
1939-40 — Dave Kerr, New York Rangers
1938-39 — Frank Brimsek, Boston
1937-38 — C. "Tiny" Thompson, Boston
1936-37 — Normie Smith, Detroit
1935-36 — C. "Tiny" Thompson, Boston
1934-35 — Lorne Chabot, Chicago
1933-34 — Charlie Gardiner, Chicago
1932-33 — C. "Tiny" Thompson, Boston
1931-32 — Charlie Gardiner, Chicago
1930-31 — Roy Worters, New York Americans
1929-30 — C. "Tiny" Thompson, Boston
1928-29 — Geo. Hainsworth, Montreal
1927-28 — Geo. Hainsworth, Montreal
1926-27 — Geo. Hainsworth, Montreal

VEZINA TROPHY

Awarded annually, by a vote among National Hockey League general managers, to the most outstanding goaltender.

1982 — Bill Smith, N.Y. Islanders

CALDER TROPHY

Awarded annually to the player adjudged most outstanding in his first National Hockey League season, providing he hasn't played more than 25 games in any previous season, or six or more in any two previous seasons.

1982 — Dale Hawerchuk, Winnipeg
1981 — Peter Stastny, Quebec
1980 — Ray Bourque, Boston
1979 — Bobby Smith, Minnesota
1978 — Mike Bossy, N.Y. Islanders
1977 — Willi Plett, Atlanta
1976 — Bryan Trottier, N.Y. Islanders
1975 — Eric Vail, Atlanta
1974 — Denis Potvin, N.Y. Islanders
1973 — Steve Vickers, N.Y. Rangers
1972 — Ken Dryden, M. Canadiens
1971 — Gilbert Perreault, Buffalo
1970 — Tony Esposito, Chicago
1969 — Danny Grant, Minnesota
1968 — Derek Sanderson, Boston
1967 — Bobby Orr, Boston
1966 — Brit Selby, Toronto
1965 — Roger Crozier, Detroit
1964 — Jacques Laperrière, M. Canadiens
1963 — Kent Douglas, Toronto
1962 — Bobby Rousseau, M. Canadiens
1961 — Dave Keon, Toronto
1960 — Bill Hay, Chicago
1959 — Ralph Backstrom, M. Canadiens

1958 — Frank Mahovlich, Toronto
1957 — Larry Regan, Boston
1956 — Glenn Hall, Detroit
1955 — Ed Litzenberger, Chicago
1954 — Camille Henry, N.Y. Rangers
1953 — Lorne Worsley, N.Y. Rangers
1952 — Bernie Geoffrion, M. Canadiens
1951 — Terry Sawchuk, Detroit
1950 — Jack Gelineau, Boston
1949 — Pentti Lund, N.Y. Rangers
1948 — Jim McFadden, Detroit
1947 — Howie Meeker, Toronto
1946 — Edgar Laprade, N.Y. Rangers
1945 — Frank McCool, Toronto
1944 — Gus Bodnar, Toronto
1943 — Gaye Stewart, Toronto
1942 — Grant Warwick, N.Y. Rangers
1941 — Johnny Quilty, M. Canadiens
1940 — Kilby MacDonald, N.Y. Rangers
1939 — Frank Brimsek, Boston
1938 — Cully Dahlstrom, Chicago
1937 — Syl Apps, Toronto
1936 — Mike Karakas, Chicago
1935 — Dave Schriner, N.Y. Americans
1934 — Russ Blinko, Mtl. Maroons
1933 — Carl Voss, Detroit

BILL MASTERTON TROPHY

An annual award, under the trusteeship of the Professional
Hockey Writers' Association, to the National Hockey League
player who best exemplifies the qualities of perseverance,
sportsmanship and dedication to hockey.

1981-82 — Glenn Resch, Colorado
1980-81 — Blake Dunlop, St. Louis
1979-80 — Al MacAdam, Minnesota
1978-79 — Serge Savard, Montreal

1977-78 — Butch Goring, Los Angeles
1976-77 — Ed Westfall, New York Islanders
1975-76 — Rod Gilbert, New York Rangers
1974-75 — Don Luce, Buffalo
1973-74 — Henri Richard, Montreal
1972-73 — Lowell McDonald, Pittsburgh
1971-72 — Bobby Clarke, Philadelphia
1970-71 — Jean Ratelle, New York Rangers
1969-70 — Pit Martin, Chicago
1968-69 — Ted Hampson, Oakland
1967-68 — Claude Provost, Montreal

JAMES NORRIS MEMORIAL TROPHY

Awarded annually to the National Hockey League defenceman
demonstrating the greatest all-around ability at that position.

1981-82 — Doug Wilson, Chicago
1980-81 — Randy Carlyle, Pittsburgh
1979-80 — Larry Robinson, Canadiens
1978-79 — Denis Potvin, N.Y. Islanders
1977-78 — Denis Potvin, N.Y. Islanders
1976-77 — Larry Robinson, Canadiens
1975-76 — Denis Potvin, N.Y. Islanders
1974-75 — Bobby Orr, Boston
1973-74 — Bobby Orr, Boston
1972-73 — Bobby Orr, Boston
1971-72 — Bobby Orr, Boston
1970-71 — Bobby Orr, Boston
1969-70 — Bobby Orr, Boston
1968-69 — Bobby Orr, Boston
1967-68 — Bobby Orr, Boston
1966-67 — Harry Howell, New York
1965-66 — Jacques Laperrière, Canadiens
1964-65 — Pierre Pilote, Chicago
1963-64 — Pierre Pilote, Chicago
1962-63 — Pierre Pilote, Chicago

1961-62 — Doug Harvey, Rangers
1960-61 — Doug Harvey, Canadiens
1959-60 — Doug Harvey, Canadiens
1958-59 — Tom Johnson, Canadiens
1957-58 — Doug Harvey, Canadiens
1956-57 — Doug Harvey, Canadiens
1955-56 — Doug Harvey, Canadiens
1954-55 — Doug Harvey, Canadiens
1953-54 — Red Kelly, Detroit

JACK ADAMS AWARD

An annual award, presented by the National Hockey League
Broadcasters' Association, to the NHL coach adjudged to have
contributed the most to his team's success.

1981-82 — Tom Watt, Winnipeg
1980-81 — Red Berenson, St. Louis
1979-80 — Pat Quinn, Philadelphia
1978-79 — Al Arbour, N.Y. Islanders
1977-78 — Bobby Kromm, Detroit
1976-77 — Scotty Bowman, Montreal
1975-76 — Don Cherry, Boston
1974-75 — Bob Pulford, Los Angeles
1973-74 — Fred Shero, Philadelphia

FRANK J. SELKE TROPHY

Awarded annually to the forward line player in the National
Hockey League showing the greatest defensive proficiency.

1981-82 — Steve Kasper, Boston
1980-81 — Bob Gainey, Montreal
1979-80 — Bob Gainey, Montreal
1978-79 — Bob Gainey, Montreal
1977-78 — Bob Gainey, Montreal

CONN SMYTHE TROPHY

Awarded to the player adjudged most valuable to his team
in the entire Stanley Cup tournament.

1981-82 — Mike Bossy, N.Y. Islanders
1980-81 — Butch Goring, N.Y. Islanders
1979-80 — Bryan Trottier, N.Y. Islanders
1978-79 — Bryan Trottier, N.Y. Islanders
1978-79 — Bob Gainey, Montreal
1977-78 — Larry Robinson, Montreal
1976-77 — Guy Lafleur, Montreal
1975-76 — Reggie Leach, Philadelphia
1974-75 — Bernie Parent, Philadelphia
1973-74 — Bernie Parent, Philadelphia
1972-73 — Yvan Cournoyer, Montreal
1971-72 — Bobby Orr, Boston
1970-71 — Ken Dryden, Montreal
1969-70 — Bobby Orr, Boston
1968-69 — Serge Savard, Montreal
1967-68 — Glenn Hall, St. Louis
1966-67 — Dave Keon, Toronto
1965-66 — Roger Crozier, Detroit
1964-65 — Jean Beliveau, Montreal

THE THOUSAND POINT CLUB

	Yrs.	GP	G	A	Pts.
Gordie Howe	29	1767	801	1049	1850
Phil Esposito	18	1282	717	873	1590
Stan Mikita	22	1394	541	926	1467
John Bucyk	23	1540	556	813	1369
Alex Delvecchio	24	1549	456	825	1281
Jean Ratelle	21	1281	491	776	1267
Norm Ullman	20	1410	490	739	1229
Jean Beliveau	20	1125	507	712	1219
Marcel Dionne	11	857	488	692	1180
Bobby Hull	16	1063	610	560	1170
Frank Mahovlich	18	1181	533	570	1103

Guy Lafleur	11	794	459	636	1095
Bobby Clarke	13	991	318	747	1065
Henri Richard	20	1256	358	688	1046
Rod Gilbert	18	1065	406	615	1021
Gil Perreault	12	871	391	610	1001

CANADA CUP, 1981

Round-Robin Results

Sept. 1: U.S. **3** Sweden **1**;   Soviet Union **1** Czechoslovakia **1**;
Canada **9** Finland **0**

Sept. 3: Czechoslovakia **7** Finland **1**;   Soviet Union **6**
Sweden **3**;   Canada **8** U.S. **3**

Sept. 5: Sweden **5** Finland **0**;   Soviet Union **4** U.S. **1**;
Canada **4** Czechoslovakia **4**

Sept. 7: Canada **4** Sweden **3**;   U.S. **6** Czechoslovakia **2**;
Soviet Union **6** Finland **1**

Sept. 9: Finland **4** U.S. **4**;   Czechoslovakia **7** Sweden **1**;
Canada **7** Soviet Union **3**

Sept. 11 (semi-finals): Soviet Union **4** Czechoslovakia **1**;
Canada **4** U.S. **1**

Sept. 13 (final): Soviet Union **8** Canada **1**

Scoring Leaders

	GP	G	A	Pts.
Wayne Gretzky, Canada	7	5	7	12
Mike Bossy, Canada	7	8	3	11
Bryan Trottier, Canada	7	3	8	11
Guy Lafleur, Canada	7	2	9	11
Alexei Kasatonov, S.U.	7	1	10	11
Gilbert Perreault, Canada	3	3	6	9
Sergei Makarov, S.U.	7	3	6	9
Sergei Shepelev, S.U.	7	6	2	8
Vladimir Krutov, S.U.	7	4	4	8
Vacheslav Fetisov, S.U.	7	1	7	8
Clark Gillies, Canada	7	2	5	7
Denis Potvin, Canada	7	2	5	7

NHL ALL-STARS SINCE 1931

1981-82
Goal: Bill Smith, Islanders; Defence: Doug Wilson, Chicago, and Ray Bourque, Boston; Centre: Wayne Gretzky, Edmonton; Left wing: Mark Messier, Edmonton; Right wing: Mike Bossy, Islanders.

1980-81
Goal: Mike Liut, St. Louis; Defence: Denis Potvin, Islanders, and Randy Carlyle, Pittsburgh; Centre: Wayne Gretzky, Edmonton; Left wing: Charlie Simmer, Los Angeles; Right wing: Mike Bossy, Islanders.

1979-80
Goal: Tony Esposito, Chicago; Defence: Larry Robinson, Montreal, and Ray Bourque, Boston; Centre: Marcel Dionne, Los Angeles; Left wing: Charlie Simmer, Los Angeles; Right wing: Guy Lafleur, Montreal.

1978-79
Goal: Ken Dryden, Montreal; Defence: Denis Potvin, Islanders, and Larry Robinson, Montreal; Centre: Bryan Trottier, Islanders; Left wing: Clark Gillies, Islanders; Right wing: Guy Lafleur, Montreal.

1977-78
Goal: Ken Dryden, Montreal; Defence: Denis Potvin, Islanders, and Brad Park, Boston; Centre: Bryan Trottier, Islanders; Left wing: Clark Gillies, Islanders; Right wing: Guy Lafleur, Montreal.

1976-77
Goal: Ken Dryden, Montreal; Defence: Larry Robinson, Montreal, and Borje Salming, Toronto; Centre: Marcel Dionne, Los Angeles; Left wing: Steve Shutt, Montreal; Right wing: Guy Lafleur, Montreal.

1975-76
Goal: Ken Dryden, Montreal; Defence: Denis Potvin, Islanders, and Brad Park, Boston; Centre: Bobby Clarke, Philadelphia; Left wing: Bill Barber, Philadelphia; Right wing: Guy Lafleur, Montreal.

1974-75
Goal: Bernie Parent, Philadelphia; Defence: Bobby Orr, Boston, and Denis Potvin, Islanders; Centre: Bobby Clarke, Philadelphia; Left wing: Richard Martin, Buffalo; Right wing: Guy Lafleur, Montreal.

1973-74
Goal: Bernie Parent, Philadelphia; Defence: Bobby Orr, Boston, and Brad Park, Rangers; Centre: Phil Esposito, Boston; Left wing: Richard Martin, Buffalo; Right wing: Ken Hodge, Boston.

1972-73
Goal: Ken Dryden, Montreal; Defence: Bobby Orr, Boston, and Guy Lapointe, Montreal; Centre: Phil Esposito, Boston; Left wing: Frank Mahovlich, Montreal; Right wing: Mickey Redmond, Detroit.

1971-72
Goal: Tony Esposito, Chicago; Defence: Bobby Orr, Boston, and Brad Park, Rangers; Centre: Phil Esposito, Boston; Left wing: Bobby Hull, Chicago; Right wing: Rod Gilbert, Rangers.

1970-71
Goal: Ed Giacomin, Rangers; Defence: Bobby Orr, Boston, and J.C. Tremblay, Montreal; Centre: Phil Esposito, Boston; Left wing: John Bucyk, Boston; Right wing: Ken Hodge, Boston.

1969-70
Goal: Tony Esposito, Chicago; Defence: Bobby Orr, Boston, and Brad Park, Rangers; Centre: Phil Esposito, Boston; Left wing: Bobby Hull, Chicago; Right wing: Gordie Howe, Detroit.

1968-69
Goal: Glenn Hall, St. Louis; Defence: Bobby Orr, Boston, and Tim Horton, Toronto; Centre: Phil Esposito, Boston; Left wing: Bobby Hull, Chicago; Right wing: Gordie Howe, Detroit.

1967-68
Goal: Gump Worsley, Montreal; Defence: Bobby Orr, Boston, and Tim Horton, Toronto; Centre: Stan Mikita, Chicago; Left wing: Bobby Hull, Chicago; Right wing: Gordie Howe, Detroit.

1966-67

Goal: Ed Giacomin, Rangers; Defence: Pierre Pilote, Chicago, and Harry Howell, Rangers; Centre: Stan Mikita, Chicago; Left wing: Bobby Hull, Chicago; Right wing: Ken Wharram, Chicago.

1965-66

Goal: Glenn Hall, Chicago; Defence: Jacques Laperrière, Montreal, and Pierre Pilote, Chicago; Centre: Stan Mikita, Chicago; Left wing: Bobby Hull, Chicago; Right wing: Gordie Howe, Detroit.

1964-65

Goal: Roger Crozier, Detroit; Defence: Pierre Pilote, Chicago, and Jacques Laperrière, Montreal; Centre: Norm Ullman, Detroit; Left wing: Bobby Hull, Chicago; Right wing: Claude Provost, Montreal.

1963-64

Goal: Glenn Hall, Chicago; Defence: Pierre Pilote, Chicago, and Tim Horton, Toronto; Centre: Stan Mikita, Chicago; Left wing: Bobby Hull, Chicago; Right wing: Ken Wharram, Chicago.

1962-63

Goal: Glenn Hall, Chicago; Defence: Pierre Pilote, Chicago, and Carl Brewer, Toronto; Centre: Stan Mikita, Chicago; Left wing: Frank Mahovlich, Toronto; Right wing: Gordie Howe, Detroit.

1961-62

Goal: Jacques Plante, Montreal; Defence: Doug Harvey, Rangers, and Guy Talbot, Montreal; Centre: Stan Mikita, Chicago; Left wing: Bobby Hull, Chicago; Right wing: Andy Bathgate, Rangers.

1960-61

Goal: Johnny Bower, Toronto; Defence: Doug Harvey, Montreal, and Marcel Pronovost, Detroit; Centre: Jean Beliveau, Montreal; Left wing: Frank Mahovlich, Toronto; Right wing: Bernie Geoffrion, Montreal.

1959-60
Goal: Glenn Hall, Chicago; Defence: Doug Harvey, Montreal, and Marcel Pronovost, Detroit; Centre: Jean Beliveau, Montreal; Left wing: Bobby Hull, Chicago; Right wing: Gordie Howe, Detroit.

1958-59
Goal: Jacques Plante, Montreal; Defence: Tom Johnson, Montreal, and Bill Gadsby, Rangers; Centre: Jean Beliveau, Montreal; Left wing: Dickie Moore, Montreal; Right wing: Andy Bathgate, Rangers.

1957-58
Goal: Glenn Hall, Chicago; Defence: Doug Harvey, Montreal, and Bill Gadsby, Rangers; Centre: Henri Richard, Montreal; Left wing: Dickie Moore, Montreal; Right wing: Gordie Howe, Detroit.

1956-57
Goal: Glenn Hall, Detroit; Defence: Doug Harvey, Montreal, and Red Kelly, Detroit; Centre: Jean Beliveau, Montreal; Left wing: Ted Lindsay, Detroit; Right wing: Gordie Howe, Detroit.

1955-56
Goal: Jacques Plante, Montreal; Defence: Doug Harvey, Montreal, and Bill Gadsby, Rangers; Centre: Jean Beliveau, Montreal; Left wing: Ted Lindsay, Detroit; Right wing: Maurice Richard, Montreal.

1954-55
Goal: Harry Lumley, Toronto; Defence: Doug Harvey, Montreal, and Red Kelly, Detroit; Centre: Jean Beliveau, Montreal; Left wing: Sid Smith, Toronto; Right wing: Maurice Richard, Montreal.

1953-54
Goal: Harry Lumley, Toronto; Defence: Red Kelly, Detroit, and Doug Harvey, Montreal; Centre: Ken Mosdell, Montreal; Left wing: Ted Lindsay, Detroit; Right wing: Gordie Howe, Detroit.

1952-53
Goal: Terry Sawchuk, Detroit; Defence: Red Kelly, Detroit, and Doug Harvey, Montreal; Centre: Fleming Mackell, Boston; Left wing: Ted Lindsay, Detroit; Right wing: Gordie Howe, Detroit.

1951-52
Goal: Terry Sawchuk, Detroit; Defence: Red Kelly, Detroit, and Doug Harvey, Montreal; Centre: Elmer Lach, Montreal; Left wing: Ted Lindsay, Detroit; Right wing: Gordie Howe, Detroit.

1950-51
Goal: Terry Sawchuk, Detroit; Defence: Red Kelly, Detroit, and Bill Quackenbush, Boston; Centre: Milt Schmidt, Boston; Left wing: Ted Lindsay, Detroit; Right wing: Gordie Howe, Detroit.

1949-50
Goal: Bill Durnan, Montreal; Defence: Gus Mortson, Toronto, and Ken Reardon, Montreal; Centre: Sid Abel, Detroit; Left wing: Ted Lindsay, Detroit; Right wing: Maurice Richard, Montreal.

1948-49
Goal: Bill Durnan, Montreal; Defence: Bill Quackenbush, Detroit, and Jack Stewart, Detroit; Centre: Sid Abel, Detroit; Left wing: Roy Conacher, Chicago; Right wing: Maurice Richard, Montreal.

1947-48
Goal: Turk Broda, Toronto; Defence: Bill Quackenbush, Detroit, and Jack Stewart, Detroit; Centre: Elmer Lach, Montreal; Left wing: Ted Lindsay, Detroit; Right wing: Maurice Richard, Montreal.

1946-47
Goal: Bill Durnan, Montreal; Defence: Ken Reardon, Montreal, and Emile Bouchard, Montreal; Centre: Milt Schmidt, Boston; Left wing: Doug Bentley, Chicago; Right wing: Maurice Richard, Montreal.

1945-46
Goal: Bill Durnan, Montreal; Defence: Johnny Crawford, Boston, and Emile Bouchard, Montreal; Centre: Max Bentley, Chicago; Left wing: Gaye Stewart, Toronto; Right wing: Maurice Richard, Montreal.

1944-45
Goal: Bill Durnan, Montreal; Defence: Emile Bouchard, Montreal, and Flash Hollett, Detroit; Centre: Elmer Lach, Montreal; Left wing: Toe Blake, Montreal; Right wing: Maurice Richard, Montreal.

1943-44
Goal: Bill Durnan, Montreal; Defence: Earl Seibert, Chicago, and Babe Pratt, Toronto; Centre: Bill Cowley, Boston; Left wing: Doug Bentley, Chicago; Right wing: Lorne Carr, Toronto.

1942-43
Goal: Johnny Mowers, Detroit; Defence: Earl Seibert, Chicago, and Jack Stewart, Detroit; Centre: Bill Cowley, Boston; Left wing: Doug Bentley, Chicago; Right wing: Lorne Carr, Toronto.

1941-42
Goal: Frank Brimsek, Boston; Defence: Earl Seibert, Chicago, and Tommy Anderson, Americans; Centre: Syl Apps, Toronto; Left wing: Lynn Patrick, Rangers; Right wing: Bryan Hextall, Rangers.

1940-41
Goal: Turk Broda, Toronto; Defence: Dit Clapper, Boston, and Wally Stanowski, Toronto; Centre: Bill Cowley, Boston; Left wing: Dave Schriner, Toronto; Right wing: Bryan Hextall, Rangers.

1939-40
Goal: Dave Kerr, Rangers; Defence: Dit Clapper, Boston, and Ebbie Goodfellow, Detroit; Centre: Milt Schmidt, Boston; Left wing: Toe Blake, Montreal; Right wing: Bryan Hextall, Rangers.

1938-39
Goal: Frank Brimsek, Boston; Defence: Eddie Shore, Boston, and Dit Clapper, Boston; Centre: Syl Apps, Toronto; Left wing: Toe Blake, Montreal; Right wing: Gordie Drillon, Toronto.

1937-38
Goal: Tiny Thompson, Boston; Defence: Eddie Shore, Boston, and Babe Siebert, Mtl. Canadiens; Centre: Bill Cowley, Boston; Left wing: Paul Thompson, Chicago; Right wing: Cecil Dillon, Rangers and Gordie Drillon, Toronto (tied).

1936-37
Goal: Norm Smith, Detroit; Defence: Babe Siebert, Mtl. Canadiens, and Ebbie Goodfellow, Detroit; Centre: Marty Barry, Detroit; Left wing: Harvey Jackson, Toronto; Right wing: Larry Aurie, Detroit.

1935-36
Goal: Tiny Thompson, Boston; Defence: Eddie Shore, Boston, and Babe Siebert, Boston; Centre: Hooley Smith, Mtl. Maroons; Left wing: Dave Schriner, Americans; Right wing: Charlie Conacher, Toronto.

1934-35
Goal: Lorne Chabot, Chicago; Defence: Eddie Shore, Boston, and Earl Seibert, Rangers; Centre: Frank Boucher, Rangers; Left wing: Harvey Jackson, Toronto; Right wing: Charlie Conacher, Toronto.

1933-34
Goal: Charlie Gardiner, Chicago; Defence: King Clancy, Toronto, and Lionel Conacher, Chicago; Centre: Frank Boucher, Rangers; Left wing: Harvey Jackson, Toronto; Right wing: Charlie Conacher, Toronto.

1932-33
Goal: John Ross Roach, Detroit; Defence: Eddie Shore, Boston, and Ching Johnson, Rangers; Centre: Frank Boucher, Rangers; Left wing: Baldy Northcott, Mtl. Maroons; Right wing: Bill Cook, Rangers.

1931-32
Goal: Charlie Gardiner, Chicago; Defence: Eddie Shore, Boston, and Ching Johnson, Rangers; Centre: Howie Morenz, Mtl. Canadiens; Left wing: Harvey Jackson, Toronto; Right wing: Bill Cook, Rangers.

1930-31
Goal: Charlie Gardiner, Chicago; Defence: King Clancy,
Toronto, and Eddie Shore, Boston; Centre: Howie Morenz,
Mtl. Canadiens; Left wing: Aurel Joliat, Mtl. Canadiens;
Right wing: Bill Cook, Rangers.

NATIONAL HOCKEY LEAGUE ADMINISTRATION

Headquarters: 920 Sun Life Building, Montreal, Quebec,
Canada H3B 2W2. Phone: 514-871-9220
U.S. Office: 1221 Avenue of the Americas, New York,
N.Y. 10020. Phone: 212-398-1100
Toronto Office: Suite 202, One Greensboro Drive, Rexdale,
Ont., Canada M9W 1C8. Phone: 416-245-2926

President: John A. Ziegler, Jr.
Chairman, Board of Governors: William W. Wirtz
Honorary Chairman: Clarence S. Campbell
Executive Vice-President: Brian O'Neill
Vice-President, Officiating: Ian (Scotty) Morrison
Director of Central Registry: Don Ellis
Director of Media Relations: Michael Griffin
Public Relations Director: Rodger Gottlieb
Director of Security: Frank Torpey
Curator, Hockey Hall of Fame: Maurice "Lefty" Reid,
Hockey Hall of Fame, Exhibition Place, Toronto, Ontario,
Canada M6K 3O3

BOSTON BRUINS
Office: 150 Causeway St., Boston, Mass. 02114
Arena: Boston Garden (14,673)
President and Governor: Paul Mooney
General Manager: Harry Sinden
Assistant General Manager: Tom Johnson
Coach: Gerry Cheevers
Assistant Coaches: Gary Doak, Jean Ratelle
Director of Scouting: Gary Darling
Director of Public Relations: Nate Greenberg

BUFFALO SABRES
Office: Memorial Auditorium, Buffalo, N.Y. 14202
Arena: Memorial Auditorium (16,433)
President and Chairman: Seymour Knox III
Vice-President: Northrup R. Knox
General Manager and Head Coach: Scotty Bowman
Assistant Coaches: Jim Roberts, Red Berenson
Director of Public Relations: Paul Wieland
Director of Scouting: Bucky Kane

CALGARY FLAMES
Office: P.O. Box 1540, Station M, Calgary, Alta. T2P 3B9
Arena: The Corral (6,492)
General Manager and Governor: Cliff Fletcher
Assistant General Manager: David Poile
Coach: Bob Johnson
Assistant Coach: Bob Murdoch
Director of Player Development: Al MacNeil
Chief Scout: Gerry Blair
Scouting Co-ordinator: Ian McKenzie
Director of Public Relations: Al Coates

CHICAGO BLACK HAWKS
Office: 1800 West Madison St., Chicago, Ill. 60612
Arena: Chicago Stadium (17,263)
Chairman: Arthur W. Wirtz
President: William W. Wirtz
Vice-Presidents: Tommy Ivan, Michael Wirtz
General Manager: Bob Pulford
Assistant General Manager: Jack Davison
Coach: Orval Tessier

DETROIT RED WINGS
Office: 600 Civic Center Drive, Detroit, Mich. 48226
Arena: Joe Louis Sports Arena (19,275)
President: Mike Ilitch
General Manager: Jim Devellano
Coach: Nick Polano

EDMONTON OILERS
Office: Northlands Coliseum, Edmonton, Alta. T5B 4M9
Arena: Northlands Coliseum (15,246)
Owner and Governor: Peter Pocklington
President, General Manager, Coach: Glen Sather
Assistant Coaches: Ted Green, John Muckler
Assistant General Manager: Bruce MacGregor
Chief Scout: Barry Fraser
Director of Public Relations: Bill Tuele

HARTFORD WHALERS
Office: One Civic Center Plaza, Hartford, Conn. 06103
Arena: Hartford Coliseum (14,510)
Managing General Partner: Howard Baldwin
General Manager: Larry Pleau
Coach: Larry Kish
Director of Player Development: Gordie Howe
Director of Scouting: Bill Dineen
Director of Public Relations: Bob Casey
Statistician: Frank Polnaszek

LOS ANGELES KINGS
Office: 3900 West Manchester Blvd., Inglewood, Calif. 90306
Arena: The Forum (16,005)
Chairman of the Board: Dr. Jerry Buss
General Manager: George Maguire
Assistant General Manager: Parker MacDonald
Director of Player Personnel: Wren Blair
Chief Scout: Ted O'Connor
Coach: Don Perry
Assistant Coach: Brad Selwood

MINNESOTA NORTH STARS
Office: 7901 Cedar Ave. S., Bloomington, Minn. 55420
Arena: Met Center (15,184)
Chairman: George Gund III
Vice-Chairman: Gordon Gund
General Manager: Lou Nanne
Assistant General Manager: John Mariucci

Coach: Glen Sonmor
Assistant Coach: Murray Oliver
Chief Scout: Harry Howell
Information Director: Dick Dillman

MONTREAL CANADIENS
Office: 2313 Ste. Catharine St. W., Montreal, Que. H3H 1N2
Arena: The Forum (18,350)
President: Morgan McCammon
Managing Director: Irving Grundman
Senior Vice-President: Jean Beliveau
Vice-President, Hockey: Toe Blake
Special Ambassador: Maurice Richard
Director of Recruitment: Ron Caron
Chief Scout: Doug Robinson
Director of Development: Claude Ruel
Coach: Bob Berry
Special Assignments: Jacques Laperrière
Director of Publicity: Claude Mouton

NEW JERSEY DEVILS
Office: Brendan Byrne Arena, Box 504,
         East Rutherford, N.J. 07073
Arena: Brendan Byrne Arena (19,130)
Chairman of the Board: John McMullen
Vice-President, Hockey Operations: Max McNab
General Manager, Head Coach: Bill MacMillan
Assistant Coach: Marshall Johnston
Director of Player Development: Bert Marshall
Eastern Scout: Frank Mario
Western Scout: Rudy Filion

NEW YORK ISLANDERS
Office: Nassau Veterans' Coliseum, Uniondale, N.Y. 11553
Arena: Nassau Coliseum (15,000)
Chairman: John Pickett
President, General Manager: Bill Torrey
Coach: Al Arbour
Assistant Coach: Lorne Henning
Chief Scout: Gerry Ehman

NEW YORK RANGERS
Office: 4 Pennsylvania Plaza, New York, N.Y. 10001
Arena: Madison Square Garden (17,500)
Garden President: David (Sonny) Werblin
Chairman: Michael Burke
Director of Hockey Operations: Craig Patrick
Head Coach: Herb Brooks
Assistant Coaches: Walt Tkaczuk, Wayne Thomas
Chief Scout: Danny Summers
Public Relations Director: John Halligan

PHILADELPHIA FLYERS
Office: The Spectrum, Pattison Place, Philadelphia, Pa. 19148
Arena: The Spectrum (17,077)
Executive Chairman: Edward Snider
Board Chairman: Joseph Scott
Vice-President, General Manager: Keith Allen
Coach, Assistant General Manager: Bob McCammon
Assistant Coach: Bernie Parent
Director of Scouting: John Brogan
Personnel Director: Marcel Pelletier
Press Relations Director: Joe Kadlec

PITTSBURGH PENGUINS
Office: Civic Arena, Pittsburgh, Pa. 15219
Arena: Civic Arena (16,033)
Executive Chairman: Edward J. DeBartolo, Sr.
Board Chairman, President: Vincent J. Bartimo
General Manager: Baz Bastien
Coach: Ed Johnston
Assistant Coach: Mike Corrigan
Director of Personnel: Ken Schinkel
Director of Media Relations: Terry Schiffauer

QUEBEC NORDIQUES
Office: 5555 3rd Ave. W., Charlesbourg, Que. G1H 6R1
Arena: The Coliseum (15,300)
President: Marcel Aubut
General Manager: Maurice Filion

Assistant General Manager: Martin Maddin
Coach: Michel Bergeron
Assistant Coach: Charles Thiffault
Director of Player Development: Gilles Leger
Chief Scout: George Armstrong
Public Relations Director: Michel Parizeau

ST. LOUIS BLUES
Office: 5700 Oakland Ave., St. Louis, Mo. 63110
Arena: The Checkerdome (17,967)
President, General Manager, Coach: Emile Francis
Assistant Coach: Barclay Plager
Assistant to the President: Dennis Ball
Chief Scout: Lou Passador
Director of College Scouting: Art Beeglund
Director of Player Personnel: Steve Brklacich
Director of Public Relations: Susie Mathieu

TORONTO MAPLE LEAFS
Office: 60 Carlton St., Toronto, Ont. M5B 1L1
Arena: Maple Leaf Gardens (16,300)
President: Harold E. Ballard
Chairman of the Board: Paul MacNamara
Vice-President: Francis (King) Clancy
General Manager: Gerry MacNamara
Coach: Mike Nykoluk
Assistant Coach: Dan Maloney
Executive Assistant: Gord Stellick
Publicity Director: Stan Obodiac

VANCOUVER CANUCKS
Office: 100 North Renfrew St., Vancouver, B.C. V5K 3N7
Arena: Pacific Coliseum (15,613)
Chairman: Frank A. Griffiths
President: William Hughes
Vice-President: Jake Milford
General Manager: Harry Neale
Coach: Roger Neilson
Assistant Coach: Ron Smith

Director of Player Personnel: Larry Popein
Chief Scout: Jack McDonald
Public Relations Director: Norm Jewison

WASHINGTON CAPITALS
Office: Capital Center, Landover, Md. 20786
Arena: Capital Center (18,130)
President: Abe Pollin
Director: Peter O'Malley
General Manager: Roger Crozier
Coach: Bryan Murray
Director of Player Recruitment: Jack Button

WINNIPEG JETS
Office: 15 - 1430 Maroons Rd., Winnipeg, Man. R3G 0L5
Arena: Winnipeg Arena (15,250)
Chairman of the Board: Bob Graham
President: Michael Gobuty
General Manager: John Ferguson
Coach: Tom Watt
Assistant Coach: Bill Sutherland
Director of Player Personnel: Mike Doran
Chief Scout: Les Binkley
Director of Information: Ken Fenson

PART FOUR

HOCKEY'S HALL OF FAME

It was a proud moment in September when Yvan Cournoyer was officially installed in the Hockey Hall of Fame.

His credentials, to be sure, were more than adequate, for he had been one of the truly memorable right wingers in the National Hockey League all through his 16 seasons with Montreal Canadiens. Among his noteworthy achievements were 428 goals and 863 points in only 968 games, plus four nominations to the second all-star team.

But the tribute which surely means the most, and for which the Roadrunner must be envied by thousands of hockey players, is to be found on the nameplates adorning the Stanley Cup.

Cournoyer's name appears there ten times. In his 16 seasons with Montreal, on ten occasions the Canadiens won this most cherished of all hockey trophies, symbolizing the championship of the world's major professional league.

Always elusive and dangerous with his extraordinary speed, Cournoyer played especially well in Stanley Cup competition. On 15 occasions, he furnished the decisive goal in Montreal playoff victories. He counted 64 goals and 63 assists in 147 post-season matches.

The other ex-players added to the Hall roster this year were Rod Gilbert and Norm Ullman, together with Emile Francis in the builders' category for executives.

Ullman stands eighth among all point-getters in the NHL, down through the years. In two decades divided between Detroit Red Wings and Toronto Maple Leafs, he totalled 1,219 points on 490 goals and 739 assists. He was the all-star centre in 1965.

Gilbert, the 1972 all-star at right wing, spent 18 years with New York Rangers and surpassed 1,000 points, too, with 406 goals and 615 assists.

As general manager and coach, Emile (The Cat) Francis

assembled the superb New York club that lost to Boston Bruins in the 1972 Stanley Cup final. His greatest achievements, however, were to occur later when he was the individual chiefly responsible for preserving the St. Louis franchise when it was on the verge of bankruptcy and extinction.

Before locating new owners, Francis was actually drawing on his own bank account to keep the team afloat. Fresh money came in, only on the condition Francis would function as both president and general manager — and now he has assumed the coaching duties, as well.

PLAYERS ELECTED TO THE HALL OF FAME

Abel, Sidney Gerald
Adams, John James
Apps, Charles Joseph Sylvanus
Armstrong, George
Bailey, Irvine "Ace"
Bain, Donald
Baker, Hobart
Barry, Martin
Bathgate, Andrew
Beliveau, Jean
Benedict, Clinton
Bentley, Douglas
Bentley, Maxwell
Blake, Hector "Toe"
Boon, Richard R. "Dickie"
Bouchard, Emile Joseph "Butch"
Boucher, Frank
Boucher, George "Buck"
Bower, John
Bowie, Russell
Brimsek, Francis
Broadbent, Harry L. "Punch"
Broda, Walter Edward "Turk"
Bucyk, John
Burch, Billy
Cameron, Harold Hugh
Clancy, Francis Michael "King"
Clapper, Aubrey "Dit"
Cleghorn, Sprague
Colville, Neil MacNeil
Conacher, Charles W.

Connell, Alex
Cook, William Osser
Coulter, Arthur Edmund
Cournoyer, Yvan
Cowley, William Mailes
Crawford, Samuel "Rusty"
Darragh, John Proctor
Davidson, Allan M. "Scotty"
Day, Clarence Henry "Hap"
Delvecchio, Alex
Denneny, Cyril "Cy"
Drillon, Gordon Arthur
Drinkwater, Charles Graham
Dunderdale, Thomas
Durnan, William Ronald
Dutton, Mervyn A. "Red"
Dye, Cecil Henry "Babe"
Farrell, Arthur F.
Foyston, Frank
Frederickson, Frank
Gadsby, William Alexander
Gardiner, Charles Robert
Gardiner, Herbert Martin "Herb"
Gardner, James Henry
Geoffrion, Bernard "Boom Boom"
Gerard, Eddie
Gilmour, Hamilton Livingstone "Billy"
Goheen, Frank X. "Moose"
Goodfellow, Ebenezer R. "Ebbie"
Grant, Michael "Mike"
Green, Wilfred "Shorty"

240

Griffis, Silas Seth "Si"
Hainsworth, George
Hall, Glenn Henry
Hall, Joseph Henry
Harvey, Douglas Norman
Hay, George
Hern, William Milton "Riley"
Hextall, Bryan
Holmes, Harry "Hap"
Hooper, Charles Thomas "Tom"
Horner, George "Red"
Horton, Miles Gilbert "Tim"
Howe, Gordon
Howe, Sydney Harris
Howell, Henry Vernon "Harry"
Hutton, John Bower
Hyland, Harry M.
Irvin, James Dickenson "Dick"
Jackson, Harvey "Busher"
Johnson, Ernest "Moose"
Johnson, Ivan "Ching"
Johnson, Thomas Christian
Joliat, Aurel
Keats, Gordon "Duke"
Kelly, Leonard Patrick "Red"
Kennedy, Theodore "Teeder"
Lach, Elmer James
Lalonde, Edouard "Newsy"
Laviolette, Jean Baptiste "Jack"
Lehman, Hugh
LeSueur, Percy
Lindsay, Robert Blake Theodore "Te
Lumley, Harry
MacKay, Duncan "Mickey"
Mahovlich, Frank
Malone, Joe
Mantha, Sylvio
Marshall, John "Jack"
Maxwell, Fred G.
McGee, Frank
McGimsie, William George
McNamara, George
Moore, Richard Winston
Moran, Patrick Joseph
Morenz, Howie
Mosienko, William "Billy"
Nighbor, Frank
Noble, Edward Reginald "Reg"

Oliver, Harry
Orr, Robert G. "Bobby"
Patrick, Lester
Patrick, Lynn
Phillips, Tommy
Pilote, Joseph Albert Pierre
Pitre, Didier "Pit"
Plante, Jacques
Pratt, Walter "Babe"
Primeau, A. Joseph
Pronovost, Marcel
Pulford, Harvey
Quackenbush, Hubert George "Bill"
Rankin, Frank
Rayner, Claude Earl "Chuck"
Reardon, Kenneth Joseph
Richard, Henri
Richard, Maurice "Rocket"
Richardson, George Taylor
Roberts, Gordon
Ross, Arthur Howie
Russel, Blair
Russell, Ernest
Ruttan, J.D. "Jack"
Sawchuk, Terrance "Terry"
Scanlan, Fred
Schmidt, Milton Conrad
Schriner, David "Sweeney"
Seibert, Earl Walter
Seibert, Oliver Levi
Shore, Edward W. "Eddie"
Siebert, Albert C. "Babe"
Simpson, "Bullet Joe"
Smith, Alfred E.
Smith, Reginald "Hooley"
Smith, Thomas
Stanley, Allan
Stanley, Russell "Barney"
Stewart, John "Black Jack"
Stewart, Nelson "Nels"
Stuart, Bruce
Stuart, Hod
Taylor, Frederick "Cyclone"
Thompson, Cecil R. "Tiny"
Trihey, Col. Harry J.
Ullman, Norman
Vezina, Georges
Walker, John Phillip

Walsh, Martin "Marty"
Watson, Harry E.
Weiland, Ralph "Cooney"
Westwick, Harry

Whitcroft, Fred
Wilson, Gordon Allan
Worsley, Lorne "Gump"
Worters, Roy

BUILDERS
Adams, Charles
Adams, Weston W.
Ahearne, John F.
Ahearne, Thomas
Allan, Sir Montagne
Ballard, Harold
Bickell, J.P.
Brown, George V.
Brown, Walter A.
Buckland, Frank
Butterfield, Jack
Calder, Frank
Campbell, Angus D.
Campbell, Clarence
Cattarinich, Jack
Dandurand, Joseph "Leo"
Dilio, Francis Paul
Dudley, George S.
Dunn, James A.
Francis, Emile
Gibson, Dr. John L.
Gorman, Thomas "Tommy"
Hay, Charles
Hendy, James C.
Hewitt, Foster
Hewitt, William Abraham
Hume, Fred J.
Ivan, Thomas N.
Jennings, William M.
Juckes, Gordon

Kilpatrick, Gen. John Reed
Leader, George Alfred
LeBel, Robert
Lockhart, Thomas F.
Loicq, Paul
McLaughlin, Major Frederic
Molson, Hon. Harland de Montarville
Nelson, Francis
Norris, Bruce A.
Norris, Sr., James
Norris, James Dougan
Northey, William M.
O'Brien, John Ambrose
Patrick, Frank
Picard, Allan W.
Pollock, Sam
Raymond, Sen. Donat
Robertson, John Ross
Robinson, Claude
Ross, Philip
Selke, Frank J.
Smith, Frank
Smythe, Conn
Stanley of Preston, Lord
Sutherland, Capt. James
Tarasov, Anatoli V.
Turner, Lloyd
Tutt, W. Thayer
Voss, Carl
Waghorne, Fred C.
Wirtz, Arthur M.

REFEREES
Ashley, John
Chadwick, William
Elliot, Chaucer
Hewitson, Robert W.

Ion, Mickey
Rodden, Michael J.
Smeaton, Cooper J.
Storey, Roy "Red"
Udvari, Frank

**Wayne Gretzky, Edmonton Oilers, winner of the
Hart Memorial Trophy and Art Ross Trophy**